Dalits and Practices of Untouchability

Dalits and Practices of Untouchability

Sadanand Paswan

ADHYAYAN
ADHYAYAN PUBLISHERS & DISTRIBUTORS
NEW DELHI (INDIA)

Published by
ADHYAYAN PUBLISHERS & DISTRIBUTORS
4378/4B, 105, J.M.D. House, Murari Lal Street
Ansari Road Darya Ganj, New Delhi - 110002
Ph.: 011-23263018, 011-23277156, Fax: 011-23280028
Email: adhyayanpublishers@yahoo.com

Dalits and Practices of Untouchability

Edition 2011
ISBN 978-81-8435-238-2

Printed in India

Published by Harish Chandra Yadav for Adhyayan Publishers & Distributors. Laser Typeseting at A.V. Rao and Printed at Tarun Offset Printers, Delhi

Preface

The word "Dalit" comes from the Sanskrit root *dal* and means "broken, ground-down, downtrodden, or oppressed." "Dalit" refers to one's caste rather than class; it applies to members of those menial castes which have born the stigma of "untouchability" because of the extreme impurity and pollution connected with their traditional occupations. Dalits represent a community of 170 million in India. One out of every six Indians is Dalit, yet due to their caste identity Dalits regularly face discrimination and violence which prevent them from enjoying the basic human rights and dignity promised to all citizens of India.

India's Constitution abolished "untouchability," meaning that the dominant castes could no longer legally force Dalits to perform any "polluting" occupation. Yet sweeping, scavenging, and leatherwork are still the monopoly of the scheduled castes, whose members are threatened with physical abuse and social boycotts for refusing to perform demeaning tasks. Migration and the anonymity of the urban environment have in some cases resulted in upward occupational mobility among Dalits, but the majority continue to perform their traditional functions. A lack of training and education, as well as discrimination in seeking other forms of employment, has kept these traditions and their hereditary nature alive.

This book provides a systematic analysis of the incidence and extent of the practice of untouchability in contemporary India. While the evidence presented in this book suggests that the more blatant and extreme forms of untouchability appear to have declined, discrimination is still practised in one form or another. The content of this book will be highly useful for students and researchers in the fields of sociology and anthropology.

Sadanand Paswan

Contents

1

The Caste System

The phenomenon of Caste has aroused more controversy than any other aspect of Indian life and thought. Some see India's caste system as the defining feature of Indian culture and some have dismissed it as a colonial artefact. Since the days of the British rule, both historians and anthropologists referred to India as a 'caste society'. Obviously this is an overstatement of the importance of caste. But for many leading personalities, caste was, and is, a real force in Indian life. As explained by experts in the field such as Dr. Susan Bayly, caste is not the essence of Indian culture and civilization. It is rather a contingent and variable response to the enormous changes that occurred in the subcontinent's political landscape both before and after the colonial conquest.

The New Shorter Oxford English Dictionary defines Caste as,

> "A Hindu hereditary class of socially equal persons, united in religion and usually following similar occupations, distinguished from other castes in the hierarchy by its relative degree of purity or pollution."

The term Caste is commonly used to refer to two distinct concepts of corporate affiliation: the 'Jati' (birth group) and the Varna (order, class or kind). The term Jati is used for the units of thousands or sometimes millions of people with whom one may identify oneself for such purposes as marriage. There are thousands of titles associated with specific Jatis in different parts of the country: Rajput, Chamar and Jat– these terms have come to be widely recognised. But these terms are unfamiliar to people outside a limited geographical area. In contrast to this profusion of Jatis or birth-groups, the concept of Varna involves a scheme with only four divisions. Thus what would now be called Hindu society is conceived of as being divisible into four very large units which transcend specific regional associations. These are: Brahmana, Kstriya, Vaisya and Sudra. They are commonly understood as a ranked order of precedence. Then there is another caste called the 'fifth' one (called Pañcama), the so-called 'untouchable' (the hill and forest population who are called tribals, inclusive). This group occupies a place below, outside this Varna scheme.

The Brahmanas are commonly identified with those who fulfil the calling of priests and spiritual preceptors. The Ksatriyas (etymologically, the 'protectors') are usually rulers and warriors. The Vaisyas are those who have commercial livelihood, and are associated with other producers and wealth-creators as well. The Sudras are toilers and artisans. People belonging to the 'fifth' group perform 'unclean' services such as cremation, killing animals for food, etc.

1.1. Caste in Theory and Practice

Those sharing a common caste identity may subscribe to at least a notional tradition of common descent, as well as a claim of common geographical origin and a particular occupational ideal. For instance, an individual claiming Brahman parentage is not obliged to follow a priestly or preceptorial livelihood. A man professing princely descent automatically is not expected to wield a sword. But those claiming Brahmin or Ksatriya origin do not expect others to think that their ancestors were humble labourers or providers of menial service, as would be the case for an individual identified by a low-caste Jati designation such a Paraiyan or Chamar. In theory at least, civilized 'caste Hindus' regard it as wrong and unnatural to share food or have other intimate social contact with those who are dissimilar to them in terms of caste. The implication is that to be of a high or low caste is a matter of innate quality or essence. This is what is stated in many Indian scriptures dealing with caste ideals. But in real life, these principles have often been widely contested and modified. The implication would be that all who are born into the so-called 'clean' castes, rank as high and pure, regardless of wealth, achievement or other individual circumstances. Dr. M.N. Srinivas has brought in the 'theory of

Sanskritization', an historical process of a group moving upward socially through the embrace of the high or 'Sanskritic' practices, as opposed to local or popular forms of social and religious practices. Thus in his view, caste-society is mobile and fluid, rather than static and inflexible.

Caste is explained by many specialists as a system of elaborately stratified social hierarchy that distinguishes India from all other societies. It has achieved much the same significance in social, political and academic debates as 'race' in the United States, 'class' in Britain and 'faction' in Italy. It has thus been widely thought of as the paramount fact of life in the subcontinent, and for some, it is the very core or essence of south Asian civilization.

1.2. Early Beginnings

The Purusa Sukta of the Rgveda 5000 B.C.) contains the first symbolic reference to the emergence of the four castes, Brahmanas, Rajanyas (Ksatriyas), Vaiyas and Sudras, from the mouth, shoulders, thighs and feet respectively of the Cosmic Being. Interpretation then came into play, claiming that these castes are in the descending order of importance. As a matter of fact, the Hindu castes are not related to heredity or birth. What is implied in this symbolic description of the emergence of the four castes is that human society is given its 'voice' (mukham), 'order' (bahu), 'form'(uru) and 'change' (pad) respectively. The vocational choice was mainly need-based and circumstantial, in terms of the availability of labour in certain places and certain times.

Manu the Law Giver explains the principle of caste as a universal law of life. The key principle of 'caste Hindu' thought is understood as the code of duty, religious law and right human conduct which defines the path to virtue (Dharma) and spiritual fulfilment for all humankind. According to Manu, the source of this Dharma is the Will of the Divine Creator who gave each of the four human archetypes or Varnas a distinct moral quality, and a calling to follow. God, the 'lustrous one', made 'separate innate activities' for the different orders of humanity, says Manu.. He called these, 'Varnas' and laid down their duties and responsibilities so as to make life in society comfortable and meaningful. He also laid down the Asrama Dharmas duties of celibates (brahmacarins), householders (grhasthas), forest-recluses (vanaprasthas) and ascetics (samnyasins). The caste system was designed and expected to make social life a well-knit, self-dependent unit, implying of course, mutual dependence.Everybody was expected to contribute his mite to the wellbeing of the society at all levels.

Manu also explains that the classification of castes based on profession, does not disqualify the members to intermarry. He speaks of *anuloma*–type of marriages (in the descending order) according to which a man belonging to the higher order may marry a woman belonging to the lower order. The Varna classification was of course, not rigid or inflexible. In the Ramayana for instance, Paraurama who was a Brahmin by birth but behaved as a Ksatriya. Visvamitra who was a king by birth became a Brahmin by virtue of his spiritual attainments. Drona and Krpa in the Mahabharata were Brahmins by Jati but became Ksatriyas by profession.

The Bhagavadgita (ch.I. 38 ff) glorifies the sanctity of caste. Without caste, there would be corruption of humanity's most precious standards of domestic honour and sexual propriety (v. 41). In IV.13 the Gita makes it clear that this system of four divisions (caturvarnyam) is based on the division of gunas and activities corresponding with those gunas. Ch.XVIII (v. 41) elaborates that all occupations are important and correspond to various needs of the segments of society and are dispensed according to ability (svabhava) on the basis of qualifications (gunas). The duties relating to each adopted vocation are also listed (vv.42-44). It is pointed out in XVIII (vv. 45-46) that no matter what a person's duty or task is, one attains perfection or heavenly bliss if he is fully dedicated to it and performs it with pleasure and interest as if it were a service to the Lord Himself.

It is thus clear that there was no 'rigidity' in regard to the caste divisions in ancient times, but it became unfortunately, a point of discord in course of time. Narrow walls were raised between one community and another. The Brahmanas, supposed to be the repositories of sacred knowledge, with the favour of the ruling class (ksatriyas) became the wielders of absolute power in religious domain. The affected party was the Sudra or the working class and the Pañcama (outcaste).

The sole cause of discord and animosity that affected various sections of society is nondiscrimination between the two segments 'Jati' (caste by birth) and 'Varna' (caste by profession). One may claim to have been born in a particular Jati and consider oneself as Suddha' (pure) or 'Subha' (auspicious). But the division in terms of caste by profession (varna) remains flexible. E.g., professions as those of Doctors, Lawyers, Engineers, Professors and Musicians. Those born in any Jati can take up any of the above professions. That was the original import and intention of ancient scriptures and law-texts. But in India, in the middle ages, people began to think of only one type of caste, i.e., caste by birth or Jati. An individual began to think of himself or herself as superior or inferior to others. This is the chief cause of malady in India. All the ruling parties in the country, since the dawn of Independence, both at the Centre and in different States, have been missing this point and are as a matter of fact, widening the rift between one Varna and another. It is time this truth is brought out in bold relief, publicised and popularised by all our statesmen, politicians, social reformers, educationists, religious and spiritual leaders, heads of monasteries and other organizations if they are really interested in creating an egalitarian society.

1.3. Emergence of Caste

To be frank, the emergence of caste cannot be reduced to any single causal factor. In contrast to other areas of Asia, the paramount fact of Indian history has been the subcontinent's remarkable array of contrasting ecologies, languages, religions and political systems, as well as its great political fluidity, with persistent oscillations between prosperity and dearth, commercialisation and subsistence, pastoralism and peasant agriculture. One striking element of Indian life has been the presence of very large subordinated populations who have been identified as distinct from other Indians culturally, morally and even biologically. These are the people called 'tribals' and 'untouchables'. These cultural, ethnic and historical diversities are reflected in the profusion of different meanings that Indians have given to the term Caste or caste-like groupings with which they have identified themselves.

1.4. Later Stages

In the post-Mughal period, the religious atmosphere in India tended to show what may be described as 'casteless' and anti-Brahmanical signs. The religions during this period and even before, derived their support from the Bhakti traditions inspired by great teachers like Ramanuja, Guru Nanak, Caitanya and Kabir. Also, the fourth Asrama of ascetics is supposed to be 'casteless' in the sense that they are above the denominations of caste. By the 16th century, the rise of Muslim-ruled kingdoms in the Deccan and North, spread the teachings of Islam to both humble and elite groups. After the decline of Mughal power in the early 18th century, Muslim *pirs* (well-versed in mysticism and devotional traditions known as Sufism) continued to be revered by both Muslims and non-Muslim Hindus. These *pirs* or cult saints attracted constituencies which were similar to the followings of the Hindu bhakti teachers and Sikh gurus, and which shared many of their ideas and spiritual practices. Thus, from these sources also, Indians encountered messages of devotion to a Deity which was to be seen not only as transcendent, but also as dissolving all divisions of rank and hierarchy through practices of personalised mystical devotion. The teaching of devotional approach (bhakti) simply gave to the ordinary caste-Hindu, an experience of mystical and apparently 'casteless' union with the Divine.

But at the practical level, the position did not change. The lay adherents did not deny or give up claims for the validity of their caste distinctions. Especially where marriage was concerned, lay initiates who worship through the personal 'guru' rather than a Brahmin ritualist would still accept that the 'untouchable' was radically different from the devotee of respectable caste origin. Many bhakti sects denied initiation to 'unclean' groups. Some allowed only those of Brahmin birth to become gurus. Further, the activities of these 'conversion' faiths and 'sampradaya'-networks gave rise to assertive countermovements like Bengal's early 19th century Dharma Sabha organisations which rallied self-professed preservers of orthodox faith to the defence of Brahmanical authority. In many cases both before and during the colonial period, battles took place in the Bengal between organized groups of Hindu 'modernisers' and 'traditionalists'. This only helped to heighten the awareness of Jati and Varna concepts for people of varying social backgrounds, both before and after the colonial era.

From the later 19th century all the ideas about caste were given new impetus by their collision with two new forces in Indian life. The first of these was the encounter with notions of individual rights and nationhood which derive primarily from the writings of Western social theorists of the period. The second was the increasing self-confidence of the large and growing Indian intelligentsias which had been expanding rapidly since the 1950s. Beginning in the late 19th century, controversies about whether caste was a degenerate social evil or an embodiment of progressive spirituality and nationhood were pursued both in the liberal English Journals, especially the *Indian Social Reformer* (founded in 1890), and in pronouncements by defenders of orthodox Hindu tradition. Those who involved themselves in these debates included such celebrities like Swami Dayananda Sarasvati, founder of the Arya Samaj (1875) and Swami Vivekananda, founder of the Ramakrishna Mission Movement (1897). Many other important social and political leaders also played an active role, most notably M.G. Ranade and other leaders of India's most influential pre–1st World War 'reformist' voluntary association, the National Social Conference.

Those who participated in these debates did not accept the existence of hierarchical 'Jati' and 'Varna' affinities as neutral facts of Indian ethnography. In their view, the values and solidarities to which they attached the English term 'caste' raised issues requiring 'public men' (and sometimes women) to take a stand in the rapidly proliferating print media. What they wrote was an explicit challenge to those orientalists who saw caste as an immoral institution which had prevented Indians from acquiring the bond of a universal ethical code, thus debarring them from the achievement of nationhood. By the end of the 19th century three basic views of caste had emerged:

— *The incubus view* that caste in all its forms is a divisive and pernicious force, and a negation of nationhood;

— *The golden chain view* that 'caste' as a Varna is to be seen as an ideology of spiritual orders and moral affinities, and as a potential basis for national regeneration;

— *The idealised corporation view* that Jati is to be seen as a concrete ethnographic fact of Indian life, a source of historic national strengths and organised self-improvement or 'uplift'.

The National Social Conference (1887) was founded by the Bombay High Court Judge M.G. Ranade (1842-1901) and the Madras Civil Sevant R. Raghunatha Rao (1831-1912). The supporters of this Conference were expected to endorse the so-called uplift for untouchables, as well as the education of women, the banning of child marriages and the abolition of penitential seclusion for widows. Those who participated in the 1909 Conference declared that Caste was an alien and slavish institution which had been created in relatively recent times under pernicious ethnological and historical circumstances. Caste values were the badge of a 'degraded' and unfree people and a source of 'irksome and painful customs' which had rigidified a once free and open social order, 'trenching on the liberty of anterior times and 'shackling' Indians within a 'prison house' of superstition and social oppression.

Swami Vivekananda (1863-1902) condemned the oppressive treatment of the so-called untouchables and other subordinate castes. He re-echoed contemporary Western ethnological themes in his remarks about the 'natural differences of ability and character' that separated persons of unlike Varna. His views became a source of inspiration to Mahatma Gandhi in dealing with the problem of Casteism. Swami Vivekannda wrote: 'Each caste has become, as it were, a separate racial element. If a man lives long enough in India, he will be able to tell from the features what caste a man belongs to'. 'Two different races mix and fuse, and out of them rises one strong distinct type. This tries to save itself from admixture, and here you see the beginning of caste. Look at the apple. The best specimens have been produced by crossing, but once crossed, we try to preserve the variety in tact. 'Caste has its bad side, but its benefits outweigh its disadvantages.'. 'It is in the nature of society to form itself into groups.

The publications of Mahatma Gandhi in 1920s and 1930s contain passionate polemics about the doctrine of untouchability as a 'horrible and terrible' stain on the Hindu faith, as an 'evil' and an 'insult to religion and humanity'. His insistence on 'religious' solutions to the problems of untouchability lay behind his adoption of the term

'Harijan' (meaning, son of Hari, i.e., God). This term became widely used since 1930s though in recent times, its use has been condemned by self-styled representatives of low-caste groups.

Since the 1970s, many campaigners have sought to replace it with the word Dalit (the oppressed) which has connotations of modernity and militant class struggle rather than pious self-effacement, implied by the term Harijan. After Independence in the year 1947, important Hindu temples were declared open to Harijans. Even today, law and pubic policy are said to be anything but 'casteless'. But there are flaws and inconsistencies in this procedure. For example, in the Punjab, the members of the Khatik caste were deemed eligible for Scheduled Caste benefits. But in the neighbouring Uttar Pradesh, this same community was classed as 'forward', rather than as 'backward'. So attempts were made in some States to 'de-Schedule' several of the broadest regional Harijan communities. Even now, some of the leading national news papers publish long columns of 'matrimonial classified' asking for brides or grooms of a particular community or caste. Marriages between people of substantially different caste background are still as rare in the countryside as they are in the cities. Further, in both towns and nucleated village settlements there are still older housing areas containing single-caste residential streets. These include the 'Brahmin-only' streets surrounding many Hindu temples as well as the concentrations of impoverished Harijan-untouchables who still live apart from the so-called 'clean'caste populations in their own separate hamlets and urban slum enclaves.

Thus the making of caste-society in India has involved a sequence of complex but intelligible changes, notably in the areas of religion, state power and material environment.

1.5. Present Situation

Even after fifty years of Independence, Caste continues to be a major theme in Indian politics. Many political parties try to make caste an issue in the electoral arena and cash in. They denounce it as a social evil and attack others for being 'backward-looking' and 'casteist'. Many aspects of the contemporary caste-life in India echo the principles found in classical Indian religious scriptures. But in the West, neither race nor class can be related to any comparable body of codified texts and teachings. For all its diversity and its points of comparison with schemes of social differentiation to be found in other parts of the world, Caste stands alone, as a mode of thought and action. This distinctiveness is undeniable, even though caste certainly has much in common with other complex 'invented traditions', most notably those of nationhood and ethno-religious community. India's nationalist and communal religious ideologies have both interacted with the ideas and experiences of caste, sometime reinforcing their claims and sometime challenging them, but never fully overriding or replacing them.

The Government, in the name of creating a casteless, secular society, and to compensate the injustice meted out by the so-called higher castes to the oppressed, down trodden, economically poor, educationally backward masses of India, created a plethora of 'new'castes. These new castes are classified as Backward Classes, Schedule Castes and Scheduled Tribes. Tribal people are included in the Scheduled Tribes. These new castes are 'protected' by the Quota System or Reservation Policy for widening their educational and employment opportunities. The Tamil Nadu Government has created one more Community called the 'Most Backward Class/Community' so as to benefit certain other groups.. These people are preferred to all other groups for getting admissions to Schools, Colleges and Universities, and also for getting selected for different types of jobs. The higher classes have been called the 'Forward Classes'; and people belonging to this group face a tough challenge in what is called an 'open competition'. This 'reservation policy' has been in vogue for quite some time and will continue indefinitely for some more years. No deadline has been set for this policy officially. The resultant picture is that merit gets the back seat and people using their rights of reservation are benefited at all levels, however unqualified they may otherwise be.

1.6. Solution to Caste-based Discrimination

There is no magic wand by which we can create a 'casteless' society overnight. We have to take the horn by his bulls and try to solve the problem. It is rather, a problem with our own understanding and interpretation of Caste. There is nothing wrong as such with the concepts of Caste as understood and practised by the wise of yore. As pointed out earlier, one has to draw a distinction between Jati (caste by birth) and Varna (caste by profession). Indians wherever they live, should understand that there is no clash of interests between one Varna and another or between one Jati and another. So long as one can identify himself or herself as belonging to a particular birth-group and believe that they belong to a 'pure' origin, there is nothing wrong, so long as they do not harm others verbally or physically on the ground that they belong to a lower Jati and that they are not equal in social, religious and other matters. One should not and need not make much fuss about this factor. Then the division of society into the four Varnas and the distribution of labour is what should really cause worry to many. Even here, there need be no discord or dispute so long as the social needs are provided by different people who are proficient in different fields. A man of Brahmin Jati, for example, may be proud of his lineage and parentage; but he may, by virtue of his educational qualifications and aptitude become an engineer or marine biologist and contribute to those departments of study. He may if he so desires, join military forces and combat the enemies. He may still retain his Brahmin identity.

Towards the end of the 20th century and on the threshold of the 21st century, inter-caste, inter-racial and intercontinental marriages have become quite common. A Brahmin boy may, for instance, marry a non-brahmin girl. A Hindu girl may marry a Muslim boy. Or an Indian may marry a French or English. In a majority of cases, there may be a cultural and commensal change. Those who were vegetarians are fast becoming non-vegetarians and vice-versa. Drinking wine is no longer a taboo in many Hindu families. Some do it openly and others, due to some compulsions, do it secretly. This is to point out that the original divisions of society into Jati and Varna are fast losing their relevance and sanctity. The worst affected parties are the parents of the orthodox Hindu bent of mind. They are unable to make their daughters and sons stick to their old identities and habits. Nor are they able to live away from them. They have to ultimately yield to the wishes of their children, and be content that at least they themselves are able to preserve their identity. On the top of this, many Hindu ascetics (samnyasins) are crossing the seas and visiting foreign countries for preaching their religion and philosophy to the Hindus living abroad, which was once considered highly unorthodox and objectionable. Therefore there is change everywhere – in the thinking of people about caste, community, religious and philosophical values, and the like. Nothing is wrong so long as we do not wrong others. Nothing is objectionable so long as there is no compulsion, hatred, animosity, ill-will and hypocrisy. The world is created by God in a wonderful and mysterious way. Diversity is the Art of Nature; but Unity is the Heart of God. This is what the Rgveda declared ages ago: *'ekam sad vipra bahudha vadanti'*(What exists is one but wise men call it by different names). Let people practice what they think is right and good for them; but let them not fight in the name of religion, philosophy, race, caste, class, community, faction, cult, group or political affiliations. All have their own place, their own grace and role to play in making the world beautiful and habitable. Let there be an understanding of the basic values of life.

References

Ambedkar, B. R. "Castes in India." In *Dr. Babasaheb Ambedkar, Writings and Speeches,* edited by Vasant Moon, vol. 1. Bombay: Education Department, Government of Maharashtra, 1979.

Broken People: Caste Violence against India's Untouchables. New York: Human Rights Watch, 1999.

Chokhamela. *On the Threshold: Songs of Chokhamela.* Translated by Rohini Mokashi-Punekar. Delhi: Book Review Literary Trust, 2002.

Deliège, Robert. *The Untouchables of India.* Translated by Nora Scott. Oxford: Berg, 1999.

Dumont, Louis. *Homo Hierarchicus: The Caste System and Its Implications.* Translated by Mark Sainsbury, Louis Dumont, and Basia Gulati. Rev. ed. Chicago: University of Chicago Press, 1980.

Jha, Vivekananda. "Stages in the History of Untouchables." *Indian Historical Review* 2 (1975): 14–31.

2

Cultural Identity of Dalits

The word 'Dalit(s)' comes from the Sanskrit–root 'dal' and means 'held under check','suppressed', or 'crushed', or, in a looser sense, 'oppressed'. Dalits are communities of the people deprived of all that are needed to lead a normal and dignified life as human beings. The Historical exclusion of Dalits from the main stream of the Indian society has been done systematically for various reasons. They are institutionally deprived of their civil, political, economic, social, and cultural rights in every aspect of life. Dalits number approximately 240 million in South Asia and more than 160 million of them live in India.

The major reason for the suffering of the Dalits is due to the Indian caste system that classifies them as untouchables.To be born a Hindu in India is to enter the caste system, one of the world's longest surviving forms of social stratification. Embedded in Indian culture for the past 1,500 years, the caste system follows a basic precept:

— *The Brahmins:* The priestly class came from the head of God. They are eligible for learning and teaching and perform sacrifices. The others cannot teach and perform sacrifice.

— *The Kshatrias:* The warrior class came from the shoulder of God. They are eligible for learning. Their work is to protect the people by waging war against the enemies.

— *The Vysias:* The trading class came from the thigh of God. Their work is to trade and feed the above two classes.

— *The Sudras:* The servants came from the feet of God and their work is to do all menial works to the above three classes. They are not entitled to learn anything.

Other sub-castes are more than 3000 in number, with the "Untouchables" or "Dalits" at the bottom and outside. They are the slaves of the above groups and they are absolutely forbidden to learn and teach.

The code of conduct that deprives them of these rights was written three thousand years back. One may wonder why this is still in practice. The tragedy is that although untouchablity was abolished by law 1950 in India, yet the Dalits experience the agony of untouchability very deeply in all walks of life: Social, Economical and Political. One cannot understand the pain of being a Dalit unless he experiences it.

2.1. Social Status of Dalits

Today, Dalits make up 16.2% of the total Indian population, but their control over resources of the country is marginal, less than 5%. Close to half of the Dalit population lives under the Poverty Line and even more (62%) are illiterate. Among the Dalits most of those engaged in agricultural operation are landless or near landless agriculture labourers. The total household income for Dalits was of Rs. 17,465 in 1998 a mere 68% of the national average. Less than 10% of Dalit households can afford safe drinking water, electricity and toilets, which is strikingly indicative of their deplorable social condition. Moreover, Dalits are daily victims of the worst crimes and atrocities, far outnumbering other sections of society in that respect too, and in spite of the many cases that go unreported for fear of further retaliation. Between 1992 and 2000, a total of 3,34,459 cases were registered nation wide with the police as cognisable crimes against Dalits. After 57 years of Independence it is but evident that India is still very much afflicted by the cancer of the caste system. Dalits remain the most vulnerable, marginalized and brutalised community in the country.

Characterized as untouchables, they are discriminated against, denied access to land, forced to work in degrading conditions, and routinely abused at the hands of the police and higher-caste groups.

Condemned to labouring in the fields of high-caste families in return for a subsistence diet, millions are undernourished and exploited by landowners, officials and moneylenders.

In many Indian village tea-shops in which Dalits are still forbidden to drink out of the same glasses used by people of high caste.

In certain villages they are prevented from 'contaminating' entire streets by being forbidden to walk in shoes or ride bicycles.

Even after getting independence from British in some village Dalits were not allowed to have doors as the land lords could enter any time to force and enjoy the women.

Dalits have historically been allocated occupations that are considered demeaning or polluting by others - an estimated one million Dalits are manual scavengers who clean public latrines and dispose of dead animals and 60% of Dalits are dependent on casual labour. Literacy rates too present a bleak picture with only 37% of literate Dalits.

To be a Dalit today means having to live in a subhuman, degraded, insecure fashion: Every hour, two Dalits are assaulted. Every day, three Dalit women are raped, and two killed. In most parts of India, Dalits continue to be barred from entering Hindu temples or other holy places although doing so is against the law. Their women are banned from wearing shoes in the presence of caste Hindus. Dalit children often suffer a form of apartheid at school by being made to sit at the back of the classroom.

2.2. Reservation Policy for Dalits

The Reservation policy of the government could not be benefited fully by the Dalits that their poverty ridden conditions do not allow their children to go for higher education. Education has been crucial in shaping life of Dalits and taking them out of the morass of traditional caste based occupation but so far educated Dalits have been joining government /organised sector jobs was facilitate through reservation and affirmative action policies. The potential for absorption in this sector of employment is going to be small in future the existing employment is going trends also point a bleak future for unskilled and less skilled labour but there will be demand for skilled labour on account of technological development. The share of Dalit students receiving professional training is at the negligible level of 3.74% presicely for this reason the number of jobs even within the government and the organised sector continue to remain vacant because suitable Dalit candidates with recognized and professional / technical qualifications are not available.

As per 1991 census 62.52.59 Dalits are illiterate and 79.88 Dalits are illiterate and 79.80 Dalits School children drop out by middle level. While the situation has improved in 2001 still about half of Dalits may be illiterate and as many Dalit children may be dropping out before completing middle level.

Many of the legislative measures have not benefited Dalits to any appreciable extent. In fact, sincere and strict implementation of laws relating to land reforms, particularly the land ceiling law, which aims to distribute surplus land to the landless, would have greatly enhanced the socioeconomic conditions of Dalits who constitute a substantial proportion of the agricultural labour. Above all the discrimination and injustice done to them the physical assault and violence is vital problem they face through out India.

Dalits are denied access to land; their legitimate and traditional fishing rights in ponds are taken away; they are denied access to roads and often their living space, the Cheri on the outer fringes of the village, is encroached upon by the 'caste Hindus'; their access to clean drinking water is virtually nonexistent and their wells are often poisoned during anti-Dalit riots; the majority of Dalits are agricultural labourers with low wages and long stretches of unemployment.

However, these deprivations and discrimination are not just economic; they are also social, cultural and political. Illiteracy among Dalits is very high and this is exploited in more ways than one. There is a delicate line of social behaviour, transgression of which brings in immediate and often brutal reprisals. Smoking in front of 'caste Hindus' or walking in the main part of the village wearing chappals can invite violence. But the most brutal forms of reprisal— including 'honour killings' of the couple by 'caste Hindus'—seem to be reserved for inter-caste marriages involving a Dalit.

2.3. Dalits and Political Freedom

The discrimination are also political in nature. Often their right to vote is taken away through violent means; in some cases there is violent reprisal—by the police—because Dalits decide to boycott elections in protest. In elected panchayats with reservations for Dalits, elections are either not allowed to be held, or, when held elected Dalit panchayat members are not allowed to function. In some cases, the denial of these rights has taken the form of murder of Dalit panchayat members. Political rallies by Dalits are not allowed to take off or severely restricted.

There is very little solace for a Dalit in religion or even in death; various types of discrimination continue in these spheres. The religious rights of the Dalit to worship are often severely restricted. And the burial grounds for Dalits often lack proper approach roads and attempts to reach these grounds through land belonging to 'caste Hindus' often invite reprisals.

The fact that Dalits have to face such deprivation, discrimination, and violence in all their intensity and range from 'caste Hindus' is perhaps explicable in terms of the central role caste plays in our society. But these articles also bring out the role more often than not, nefarious played by various organs of the state in this. The police have often been brutal in their dealings with Dalits.. The administration has been insensitive, to say the least. Atrocities against Dalits and instances of Dalit assertion are treated essentially as law and order problems, not social ones. The devious ways in which the administration tries to scuttle various programmes and measures instituted by the State for the benefit of Dalits.

To conclude the various atrocities against the Dalit people we can look in to a case in which the judgement was as follows.

Four years after the murder in broad daylight of K. Murugesan, president of Melavalavu panchayat in Tamil Nadu's Madurai district, his brother Karuppaiah, vicepresident Mookkan and three other members of the panchayat, all Dalits, justice has run its course. On July 26, 17 of the 41 accused were convicted and sentenced to life imprisonment by the Principal District and Sessions Judge of Salem, A.S. Ramalingam. The court acquitted 23 of the remaining accused. One of the accused died during trial. The case was transferred to the court in Salem from the Madurai Sessions Court on orders from the Madras High Court.

The massacre, which took place on June 30, 1997, was widely viewed as a stark instance of caste Hindu violence against Dalits in Tamil Nadu. The victims were pulled out of a bus and hacked to death. Murugesan's head was cut off and thrown into a well 400 metres away from the spot of the murder.

The incident, seen also as a manifestation of upper-caste intolerance of Dalit empowerment, marked the culmination of a series of protests by sections of caste Hindus in Melavalavu against the 1996 government notification reserving the panchayat for Dalits. Initially, Dalits, who mostly depended on caste Hindu landholders for their livelihoods, were threatened with a social and economic boycott. Dalits who filed their nominations had to withdraw in the face of threats from caste Hindus and the elections were rendered in fructuous. When elections were held later, booth-capturing necessitated a re poll. Although Murugesan was elected president, he was not allowed to function as one. Accompanied by the vice-president and other members of the panchayat, he went to Madurai and submitted a petition to the District Collector seeking protection so that they could discharge their duties. The attack took place on their way back to Melavalavu village.

2.4. Culture of Dalits

Dalit history reveals that the Dalit community had a rich culture of its own. Here, Dalits who are the children of the soil found ways of expressing their identity through folk arts and classic arts in oral and written forms. But these rich cultural treasures were stolen from them by oppressors. Their cultural heritage was desecrated and destroyed and a foreign culture was imposed upon them. The upper caste oppressors saw to it that the Dalits would never produce a culture of their own.. The others ingeniously used the art form and the various traits of their culture to oppress and dehumanize the Dalits.

Thus culture which is supposed to give a meaning system and value system to a society was made into an instrument of oppression and domination. This manipulation of culture to dehumanize the Dalits has continued down unabated through the centuries even till today. The Dalits have neither the money power nor the political clout to make their voices heard. It is the upper caste that determines what the Dalits should think and how he should act and how he should see his status in the society.

By the use of electronic media and the print media, the upper caste society has successfully preserved its dominance and has tried to convince the world that the so-called low caste people are indeed low people. What is even more outrageous is the attempts to make the Dalits themselves believe and accept that they are low and worthless only to be despised and cast out to become the outcastes.

Despite the prejudice of people of high caste, those at the gutter level of the Hindu hierarchy is reclaiming their music. It is becoming a source of powerful resistance, the basis of new and revolutionary identities. As Dalit women come together to share and find solutions to their problems at meetings of self-help groups in villages throughout India, they learn that they are not to blame for their individual problems. They become 'conscientized' in the term coined by Paolo Freire, the Brazilian revolutionary educator to the fact that their problems are rooted in an oppressive social structure. With this realization comes a new sense of self and community as they band together to fight for fair wages, access to clean water, electricity and land rights. Their cultural expressions reveal how they are longing to break hierarchies, articulate aspirations that are political and economical.

Important characteristics of all the traditional lore that has been transmitted for centuries together in the forms of oral narratives, songs, music, tales, proverbs myths, legends, ballad, lullabies, Field songs, performing arts are as follows.

— Explaining the agony and the sorrow of their life styles.
— Trying to communicate to their community members in a subtle way
— Seeking consolation for the sufferings.
— Expecting a change that will liberate them.
— Directly or indirectly call for the unity among them.

In the state of Tamilnadu there were local Dalit heroes among the Dalit communities. These individuals either man or women would have tried to counter the dominance of upper caste people and got killed in doing so. These individuals become a hero and in due course the Dalits make them as their gods. There are many ballads sung in praise of these heroes. These ballads will express their anger and in the same time induce the new generation to take up the role of the deliverer. The ballads will begin with the details of birth and family details.Good qualities of the hero will be brought out and the cause of his death will be mentioned and sadness will prevail at the end with highlighting the loss of the hero.

As landless labourers the Dalit women will sing in the paddy fields while transplanting the seedlings.Every day life situations will be represented in their songs. Mocking the landlord satirically can be noticed in their songs. Those mocking elements may not be easily understandable for an outsider whereas it is communicated for enjoyment among the labourers. Fear prevents them from making direct mockery. The lullabies sung by the Dalit women express the state of their lively hood to their infants. Asking the babies to sleep the main lyrics of those lullabies will be of explaining to the child that it has entered in to a inhuman system of living where there is only sorrows and sufferings. It will curse the fate of birth and blame the god for allowing the child to grow in the unjust system. She will weep with the child narrating the bad situations of her life.

Mostly all forms of traditional cultural expressions are derived out of their day to day living conditions. Whether it is ritual or non ritual they recorded the ordeal of Dalits and longed for the attention of their own communities as well as others.

An individual or a community's identity,attitude and patterns of behaviour are formed and expressed in the forms of arts and aesthetics is not merely by the environment, in which one is part of,but importantly developed visa –a vis attitudes of significant others. It is this significant others that play a crucial role in the formation of one's identity. In other words an individual's self understanding and estimation would not develop in vacuum. It rather develops in mutuality of interaction and essentially depends on others treatment. With this understanding we can look in to the pride and dignity of the Dalit artists.

For many educated Dalit youths believe that practising of Dalit art forms bring shame and insult to their identity. The art folk drumming in pan Indian scale is connected mainly to Dalits and tribal communities. Since the folk drums are made out cow skins this art form was considered as some thing low and impure by the upper caste people. Here we have to note that the upper caste people do not eat beef and consider Dalits as beef eaters. Hence the art of folk drumming was predominantly used with funeral processions. But the modern day political processions and temple festivals and other types carnival use this art choreographed to suit to different occasions.

The emergence of Dalit liberation movements and other Dalit political parties and NGOs working for the upliftment of Dalits have given a new impetus for the art of drumming. Drumming for a social change is the new way of expressing their art form in various festivals held in India.No more it is considered as funeral music but music of liberation. The vibrations that it brings help them to arouse their feelings of agitation and recording their expression through their cultural resource. This folk drumming has the tremendous effect of crowd pulling at public meetings and gatherings.

Their singing, drumming, strumming and dancing are redefining their perspective. On the other hand alternative communication like third theatre, street theatre, puppet show, etc., is also widely spreading. Dalit's search for alternative media is in fact the search for a counter-culture that will stand as a paradigm to protect human existence; rewrite history and evolve a new culture of love and caring.

References

Mendelsohn, Oliver, and Marika Vicziany. *The Untouchables: Subordination, Poverty, and the State in Modern India.* Cambridge, U.K.: Cambridge University Press, 1998.

Moon, Vasant. *Growing Up Untouchable: A Dalit Autobiography.* Translated by Gail Omvedt. Lanham, Md.: Rowman and Littlefield, 2001.

Singh, K. S. *The Scheduled Castes.* Delhi: Oxford University Press, 1993.

Valmiki, Omprakash. *Joothan: An Untouchable's Life.* Translated by Arun Prabha Mukherjee. New York: Columbia University Press, 2003.

Zelliot, Eleanor. *From Untouchable to Dalit: Essays on the Ambedkar Movement.* 3rd ed. New Delhi: Manohar, 2001.

Zelliot, Eleanor, and Rohini Mokashi-Punekar, eds. *Untouchable Saints: An Indian Phenomenon.* New Delhi: Manohar, 2004.

3

Caste-based Oppression

Caste-based oppression in India lives today in an environment seemingly hostile to its presence: a nation-state that has long been labelled the "world's largest democracy;" a progressive and protective constitution; a system of laws designed to proscribe and punish acts of discrimination on the basis of caste; broad-based programs of affirmative action that include constitutionally mandated reservations or quotas for Dalits, or so-called "untouchables;" a plethora of caste-conscious measures designed to ensure the economic "upliftment" of Dalits; and an aggressive economic liberalization campaign to fuel India's economic growth.

On December 27, 2006, Indian Prime Minister Manmohan Singh became the first sitting prime minister to openly draw a parallel between the practice of "untouchability"—the imposition of social disabilities on persons by reason of their birth in certain castes—and apartheid. In a speech delivered at the Dalit-Minority International Conference in New Delhi, Prime Minister Singh explained that, "Dalits have faced a unique discrimination in our society that is fundamentally different from the problems of minority groups in general." He pledged support for affirmative action programs specifically targeting Dalits, stating that India's government "is deeply and sincerely committed to the equality of all sections of our society and will take all necessary steps to help in the social, educational and economic empowerment of dalits."

The analogy is an apt one on many levels, and an uncomfortable one on others. Like South Africa, those who sit atop the caste pyramid are a numerical minority. When combined, the population of Dalits, "tribals," "Other Backward Classes," and religious minorities far outnumber those of "uppercaste" Hindus. But the analogy reveals something far deeper, that the system of "untouchability" in India continues to operate as though a form of legal apartheid were effectively still in place.

3.1. Condition of Dalits in India

In many ways the Dalit condition naturally invites such comparisons, and in others it is a singular category, cutting across the Indian subcontinent, but categorically different than discrimination on the basis of race. To begin, the visual cues that accompanied apartheid in South Africa, or racial discrimination in other parts of the world, are lacking in India. Caste is like oxygen—it is both invisible and indispensable. While the absence of obvious racial cues does not prevent the system from functioning to the detrimental exclusion of those who fall below the "pollution line," a general lack of Western familiarity with a nonracial paradigm does frustrate international attention and intervention.

The Indian government has taken great pains to insulate itself from international scrutiny by repeatedly pointing out that this is not discrimination based on race, as though such confirmation nullifies the abuse in question. Their protests ignore the fact that the prohibition of "racial discrimination" under international law, and in particular the International Convention on the Elimination of All Forms of Racial Discrimination, Article 1, applies to discrimination on the basis of descent. Regardless of how the abuse is defined, its noxious and pervasive character should be sufficient to invite international attention and condemnation.

Though scholars have pointed to the racial dimensions of caste, this is not a Black and White issue, or a clear Black and Brown issue. The caste system is one of *graded inequality* that invites people to share in the spoils of iniquity even as they suffer from it. By offering individuals a rank in a pecking order, the system strengthens itself and keeps the equality revolution at bay.

India is also an example of injustice in the extreme: the numbers affected are greater, the poverty is deeper, the atrocities are an every day affair, and enforced servitude and segregation is the norm. The population of Dalits equals more than half the population of the United States. A majority of Dalits live on less than US$1 per day. Every week, thirteen Dalits are murdered and five Dalit homes are destroyed. Three Dalit women are raped and eleven Dalits are assaulted every day—a crime is committed against a Dalit every eighteen minutes. Aspects of the contemporary Dalit reality therefore find greater resonance with the 1950s American South, American slavery, and, as noted above, South Africa under apartheid. But, as discussed below, a number of contemporary commonalities do exist.

The cross-fertilization of ideas between India and the United States on approaches to ensuring equality is not new, nor is it surprising. As two of the world's largest democracies and as common law countries with a profound history of *de jure* discrimination, India and the United States have learned much from one another. The very language of the Indian Constitution borrows heavily from the U.S. Constitution. During his time at Columbia University, Dr. B.R. Ambedkar—architect of the Indian Constitution—was inspired by such legal constructs as the Fourteenth Amendment. As written by one commentator: "Ambedkar's revolution for the emancipation of untouchables was significantly influenced by American ideals of equality."

In 1947, the constitutional drafting committee's advisor B. N. Rau visited the United States and solicited the views of leading American judges and scholars. Almost every fundamental right in the Constitution of India finds its corollary in its American counterpart. Moreover, according to some scholars, the process of drafting the Constitution of India took into account not only the textual wording of the American provisions, but also the eventual interpretation of those provisions offered by American courts.

Both countries also continue to be mired in the politically charged debate around affirmative action as either a suitable remedy to compensate for past injustices or as a means to level a playing field tilted in favour of whites and "upper-caste" Hindus. Indian judges have often cited U.S. affirmative action decisions and law review articles in their opinions, although U.S. case law has not been cited as legal precedent. Indian Supreme Court Justice Matthew in the 1975 case *State of Kerala v. Thomas* noted the following in reference to the landmark U.S. case *Brown v. Board of Education*:

> **Beginning most notably with the U.S. Supreme Court's condemnation of school segregation in 1954, the U.S. has finally begun to correct the discrepancy between its ideals and its treatment of the black man.... These actions, while not producing true equality or even equality of opportunity logically dictated the next step: positive use of government power to create the possibility of real equality.**

It comes as no surprise that the richness of the field of comparison has invited critical and thoughtful comparative legal scholarship on the Indian and American experience with affirmative action. Less well-considered are the contemporary struggles faced by both movements to counter the mechanisms and rhetoric through which the objectives of that legal framework now stand to be defeated.

The narrative of oppression, and of racist and casteist denial, is strikingly similar from continent to continent and each country's equality project is decidedly unfinished for similar reasons.

Inviting American scholars and advocates to turn to India and the lessons it offers to illuminate their own racial justice project is not an anomaly, it is the natural continuation of a long tradition of inspiration and solidarity shared between Indian and American civil rights leaders and movements.

In 1936, Howard Thurman, a famous black preacher and educator, visited Mahatma Gandhi in India—who at the time was waging India's civil disobedience campaign against the British—to discuss issues of racial segregation and voting rights in the United States. Better known is the fact that Martin Luther King, Jr. utilized the Gandhian concept of "Satyagraha" or "nonviolent direct action" in his teachings and leadership. Less well known, but equally significant, is the relationship Ambedkar forged with W.E.B. Du Bois during the founding year of the United Nations.

The similarity of their situations was not lost on either individual. In efforts to take the struggle for racial justice to the international level, Du Bois used Ambedkar's example in appealing to the Secretary of the National Association for the Advancement of Colored People ("NAACP") to lodge a petition with the newly formed United Nations General Assembly concerning the plight of American Negroes.

Formed in the Indian state of Maharashtra in the 1970s, the Dalit Panthers aligned themselves ideologically to the Black Panther movement in the United States. During the same period, Dalit literature, painting, and theatre challenged the very premise and nature of established art forms and their depiction of society and religion. Dalit Panthers visited "atrocity" sites, organized marches, election boycotts, and rallies in villages, and raised slogans of direct militant action against their "upper-caste" aggressors. Panther leaders were often harassed and removed from districts for speaking out against the government and Hindu religion. And like the Black Panthers, the Dalit Panthers became frequent targets of police brutality and arbitrary detentions. Intellectual solidarity between Dalits and African-Americans has been found in the school of discourse called "Afro-Asian Traffic," which finds commonality between the two groups in their similar experiences of slavery.

Like the civil rights struggle that began in the 1950s and was led by African-Americans, Dalits in the twenty-first century are forming human rights movements, challenging local governments, and demanding equal access to services and equal protection before the law, often in alliance with international partners. In 2001, African-American and Dalit activists found themselves sharing the same contested space at the World Conference against Racism in Durban, South Africa. Both groups faced the racist and casteist denial of their respective governments who either refused to allow consideration of their concerns in the international forum or diluted their delegation's involvement to the point that their participation was rendered meaningless.

As the battle lines are drawn once again in the debate around affirmative action in both countries, the same ideologies are used to discredit the state's use of race or caste-conscious measures to ensure real equality of opportunity for minorities in the United States and Dalits and other "lower-caste" groups in India. Meritocracy, equality, efficiency, and liberalism are the catchwords that resonate in both countries to either defeat or redefine constitutional pronouncements that were heretofore invoked to ensure substantive equality on the basis of race or caste. Affirmative action is attacked as either having sufficiently served its purpose, or as not being up to the task of alleviating a broad-based social problem. In the latter category, the alternatives that are offered in its place rarely find traction, let alone implementation in policy terms. Reservations, once the mask that India wore to hide the real face of caste oppression, are now being attacked as an affront to (formal) equality and a barrier to achieving a caste blind society. Yet formal equality assumes a level playing field—which it certainly is not for minorities in the United States or for Dalits and other marginalized communities in India. As critical race theory scholar Crenshaw notes in the context of the rhetoric of color blindness in the United States, this remarkable strategy is a "breathtakingly bold act of cooption" wherein color blindness "now delivers its reputation and historical capital to a specious claim that the journey to the promised land is nearly complete."

African-Americans and Dalits are also now made to compete against other marginalized communities in their respective countries for sufficient attention to their demands and their rights. It seems the small slice of the pie reserved for non-whites and non-"upper-caste" Indians has not grown much bigger, and attempts to broaden the collective share invites swift protest and condemnation in the conservative media, on the streets, at the polls, and in the courtroom. Regrettably, the attendant claims of women in both struggles, and the compounded discrimination they face, get lost in the debate.

Like the United States, India exhibits a temporal tension between striving for equality as a space where caste categories (or, in other countries, racial categories) do not matter, and the need to continually identify and name the categories that have been used to create hierarchy or exclusion for the purposes of ensuring social inclusion. Such a tension is reflected at the level of policy, of social movements, and of political discourse, both for and against caste-conscious measures to ensure social inclusion.

In both countries, caste or race-based stigma has not been erased by upward class mobility. Even for the minority of Dalits who have managed to defy their religiously proscribed economic lot, social oppression has not fallen away. As poignantly noted by a Dalit surgeon,

> It is India's most shameful paradox—this country has made almost unimaginable progress in nearly every sphere of human life, but the one thing unchanged is the condition of its dalits and backward

> communities. I am a microsurgeon specialising in hand and spinal reconstruction, and am [a Member of Legislative Assembly] from Bihar, but I still remain very much a dalit—a dhobi, to be precise—open to routine humiliation from the upper castes.

The inter-category diversity among Dalits that comes about as a result of the creation of a new Dalit middle class is cited not as the success of affirmative action that it represents, but as the reason to now defeat the affirmative action project. Class operates in both countries as a displacement strategy. And in both countries the criminal justice system and its application to particular groups suffers from the twin malaise of over and under-enforcement. Dalits are routinely rounded up for crimes committed in their vicinity, yet summarily ignored when they themselves are the victims of abuse.

Like the United States, India's social transformation project is stunted by its increasing dependency on courts as a source of redress; its recourse to the legislature and courts is seen as the dominant avenue for social reform. The disproportionate focus on proportional representation—or policies that aim to increase the representation of marginalized groups in the legislature, institutes of higher education, and now the private sector—is where this conversation gets debated and defeated. Left out of consideration is the broad range of possible race or caste-conscious measures that exist on paper but are neglected or undermined in practice. Even more neglected is the work that must be done on both continents to dismantle the racist and casteist mindsets that fuel the discrimination and generate inequality.

The social transformation project—that began in India with adoption of the constitution in 1950, and in the United States with the civil rights struggle leading up to and following the landmark case of *Brown v. Board* in 1954—has left some with greater opportunity and political mobility but has "transformed" little. The "Dalit ordeal" is an example of a comprehensive legal framework with little to no execution. The "African-American ordeal" is an example of an emasculated legal framework that sees little hope of revival. The gap between constitutional vision and social reality is therefore far greater in India where the progressiveness of the constitution and the broader legal framework is belied by its almost complete under-enforcement. The rule of law lives in the shadow of the rule of caste. Though crafted as a bulwark against caste discrimination, the juxtaposition of egalitarian laws against an inherently unequal system acts as an open invitation to frustrate constitutional intentions.

As a case study, the condition of Dalits in India brings into clear view the limitations of the law and economic growth as antidotes to inequality. India's high levels of poverty concentrated among particular social groups, its epidemic of violence meted out in the name of upholding caste-based norms and traditions, and the prevalence of Dalit segregation, exploitation, and untouchability as the rule, rather than the exception, all expose the ways in which discrimination wears poverty as its mask.

Poverty is deceptive. It makes one conclude that all suffer from it equally. Poverty also masks a lack of political will to change the status quo by shifting the debate to a lack of resources. But a closer look at India's poverty reveals the discrimination inherent in the allocation of jobs, land, basic resources and amenities, and even physical security. A closer look at victims of violence, bonded labour, and other atrocities also reveals that they share in common the lowest ranking in the caste order. Poverty in India is, of course, not limited to Dalits, but as is the case with African-Americans in the United States, if you are a Dalit in India, you are far more likely to be poor. Moreover, the poverty endured is abject, violent, and virtually inescapable.

In both countries, economic progress has not led to equitable growth. In the United States— which is the most economically powerful country in the world—and India—whose economic growth is celebrated as a success of the ethos of economic liberalization—the rising tide has not lifted all boats; rather, it has caused many to drown, in some cases all too literally. Just as African-Americans bore the brunt of Hurricane Katrina in 2005 due to their concentration in the areas where the flooding was worst, as well as the lethargic response of the U.S. federal government, Dalits too were twice victimized in India's recent natural disasters—first by nature, and then by the apathy of the state. Dalits are particularly susceptible to loss of life and property in times of natural disasters due to the precarious conditions in which they live. A survey conducted by the National Campaign on Dalit Human Rights ("NCDHR") following catastrophic flooding in the eastern state of Bihar in August 2007—which affected 14 million people in the state and killed 2,253 in the region—found that Dalits were the worst hit. Relief rarely reached Dalits, testifying to the fact that "[t]he culture of discrimination which runs through Indian society intensifies in times of crisis." In some cases, Dalits were forced to wait for their share of relief supplies until all other groups had received aid.

Even during moments of shared hardship, communities are divided by race or caste. Similarly, caste-based inequality, like racial inequality, survives dramatic economic growth. Even as India celebrated its triumphant testing of nuclear weapons, exploding them underground in the deserts of Rajasthan, Dalit manual scavengers were being manually lowered into open sewers without protective gear to unblock toxic and noxious sewage. In India, the rise of a nuclear state and a technological powerhouse has been accompanied by the rise of the number of manual scavengers in the country today. The militarism and jingoistic nationalism of both governments has also depleted state coffers in the name of ensuring "national security" and fighting the global "War on Terror"—a fight in which both states are now staunch allies—to the detriment of the poor in both countries who enjoy neither physical nor economic security.

Inequality, Indian-style, is a valuable case study for a variety of reasons: it exposes the pitfalls of relying on the "rule of law" as a self-fulfilling prophecy, or on the "neutrality" of the state as a guarantor of social justice. The case of Dalits in India also serves to counter prevailing global narratives that an insufficiency of resources is solely to blame for the economic woes of the dispossessed, or, its sister argument, that allowing for aggressive market reforms in the name of promoting economic growth will reduce poverty and lead to equitable development. The treatment of Dalits as "untouchables," regardless of their educational attainment or their economic class, also serves to summarily reject the argument that "success," as measured by one's level of education or income, can work to displace the stigma associated with caste or will do away with discrimination and inequality all together. Such lessons are particularly apt for general inquiries into the need for and/or legitimacy of affirmative action. Inasmuch as affirmative action around the globe is under attack as an affront to liberalism and "meritocracy," the intrinsically anti-merit nature of the caste system offers an alternative space in which conversations about "merit" can take place.

India also presents a unique challenge for those human rights lawyers and advocates who operate exclusively in the framework of international human rights law as a mechanism for achieving social change. International human rights laws and mechanisms, with their over-reliance on the role of the state, and their almost unquestioned faith that the right laws will do the trick, are ill-equipped to take on systems that define equality in the inverse, and in which human beings are born inherently *unequal*. Finally, a closer look at caste, worthy of academic inquiry in its own right, provides a powerful reminder that race and ethnicity are not the sole dominant constructs around which social and economic oppression is organized to the detriment of a sizeable population of the world.

3.2. System of Social Hierarchy

India's caste system is perhaps the world's longest surviving and most rigorously enforced system of social hierarchy. The caste system encompasses a complex ordering of social groups on the basis of ritual purity. Caste is descent-based and hereditary in nature. It is a characteristic determined by one's birth into a particular caste. Caste denotes a traditional system of rigid social stratification into ranked groups defined by descent and occupation. While the particular ranking of castes may vary among regions, the extremes of the spectrum are fixed with Brahmins sitting atop the hierarchy and Dalits, or so-called untouchables, at the very bottom.

The caste system is an intrinsic part of Hinduism, the dominant faith practised by Indians. According to Hindu scripture, individuals are born inherently unequal into a graded caste-based structure that defines their status and opportunities in life. Caste-based discrimination is also openly practised by Sikhs, Christians, and Muslims against Dalits who have converted to these faiths in an effort to escape their persecution.

Though the origins of the caste system have long been a subject of dispute, as has the question of whether it tracks racial groupings, the following theories are worthy of note. Caste is said to have its basis in the Hindu religion, as it is referred to in scripture. In the *Bhagavad Gita*, Lord Krishna proclaims:

"The four castes have been created by Me;"

Similarly, the *Manu-Smriti* sets out the main castes as each having been created from a different part of God's form, and codifies the respective God given duties of each of these castes. Altérnative sociological theories posit the caste system as a ritual solution to the Vedic cultural preoccupation with distancing oneself from pollution. A popular, but contested, suggestion has been that this Vedic culture arrived in India with the migration of the Indo–Aryans, from whom the Brahminic "upper castes" are allegedly descended. Still others have focused on the role of British colonial rule in cementing caste-based divisions.

Differences in status are traditionally justified by the religious doctrine of *karma*, a belief that one's place in life is determined by one's deeds in previous lifetimes. Traditional scholarship has described this more than two thousand-year-old system within the context of the four principal *varnas*, or large caste categories. In order of precedence these are the Brahmins (priests and teachers), the Ksyatriyas (rulers and soldiers), the Vaisyas (merchants and traders), and the Shudras (laborers and artisans). A fifth category falls outside the varna system and consists of those known as "untouchables" or Dalits; they are often assigned tasks too ritually polluting to merit inclusion within the traditional varna system.

Though most closely associated with Hinduism, the practice of untouchability—the social imposition of particular disabilities against individuals deemed to be untouchable—permeates all major religions in India and the entire subcontinent. Within the four principal castes, there are thousands of sub-castes, also called *jatis*; endogamous groups that are further divided along occupational, sectarian, regional, and linguistic lines. Collectively, all of these are sometimes referred to as "caste Hindus," those falling within the caste system. The Dalits are described as varna-sankara, falling outside the system. They are considered so inferior to other castes that they are deemed polluting and therefore "untouchable." Even as outcasts, they themselves are divided into further sub-castes and practice untouchability against those ranked below; the discrimination is wholly internalized giving way to what Dr. Ambedkar termed a system of "graded inequality."

Whereas the first four varnas have over time enjoyed significant occupational mobility, a majority of Dalits in India continue to involuntarily inherit occupations assigned to the caste into which they are born—occupations deemed too filthy or polluting for others to carry out.

3.3. Living Below the "Pollution" Line

In much of South Asia and India in particular, caste has become co-terminous with race in the definition and exclusion of distinct population groups on the basis of their descent. For over 167 million Dalits or "untouchables" in India, caste remains the determinative factor for the attainment of civil, political, social, economic, and cultural rights.

The practice of "untouchability"—the imposition of social disabilities on persons by reason of their birth into "untouchable" castes—continues to blight the lives of millions of Indians today who are relegated to life below the "pollution" line. The manifestation of such oppression has taken and continues to take many forms. Age-old customs included prohibiting Dalits from walking public streets lest their "polluting" shadow should fall on an "upper-caste" Hindu, and requiring Dalits to mark themselves with black bracelets; string a broom around their waists so as to sweep the "polluted" dust they walked on; or hang an earthen pot around their necks "lest [their] spit falling on the earth should pollute a Hindu who might unknowingly happen to tread on it."

Modern India has improved little by way of untouchability practices. Dalits are still prohibited from entering temples, are segregated into Dalit ghettoes, and in some areas are still forced to get off their bike or take off their slippers when walking past non-Dalit homes—gestures that force Dalits to repeatedly self-affirm their inferior status. Caste divisions between Dalits and non-Dalits dominate in housing, marriage, employment, and general social interaction—divisions that are reinforced through the practice and threat of social ostracism, economic boycotts, and physical violence. Dalits are denied access to land, forced to work in degrading conditions, and routinely abused at the hands of the police and "higher-caste" groups that often enjoy the state's protection. In what has been called India's "hidden apartheid," entire villages in many Indian states remain completely segregated by caste. As noted by Ambedkar, "India is admittedly a land of villages and so long as the village system provides an easy method of marking out and identifying the untouchable, the untouchable has no escape from untouchability." Every village has its ghetto, and the ghetto is where the Dalits live.

"Untouchability" relegates Dalits to a lifetime of discrimination, exploitation, and violence, including severe forms of torture perpetrated by state and private actors. Because of the castes into which they are born, Dalits are forced to work in "polluting" and degrading occupations and are subject to exploitative labour arrangements such as bonded labour, migratory labour, and forced prostitution. Dalit children are vulnerable to trafficking and the worst forms of child labour in these and other areas. Dalits are also discriminated against in hiring and in the payment of wages by private employers.

Migration and the anonymity of the urban environment have in some cases resulted in upward occupational mobility for Dalits, but the majority continues to perform its traditional or "polluting" functions. A lack of training and education, along with the discrimination faced in seeking other forms of employment, has kept alive these traditions and their hereditary nature. A majority of the Dalit rural workforce subsists on the menial wages of landless agricultural laborers, earning less than US$1 per day. Those in urban areas work mostly in the unorganized sector. India's much touted system of reservations or constitutionally reserved quotas for scheduled castes assists less than 1 percent of the Dalit population. In all forms of labour, women are consistently paid less than men, compounding the dual discrimination of caste and gender detailed below.

Segregation between Dalits and non-Dalits is routinely practised in housing, schools, and access to public and private sector services. Ninety-nine percent of Dalit students are enrolled in government schools that lack basic infrastructure, classrooms, teachers, and teaching aids. Government schools by and large teach in local languages, as opposed to private schools—whose students are predominantly "upper-caste"—that teach in English. Their inability to speak English further disadvantages Dalits in the private sector and the global market. Dalit children also face abuse from teachers and non-Dalit students as well as segregation both in the classroom and in the provision of midday meals. Dalit schoolchildren and teachers also face discrimination from "upper-caste" community members who perceive education for and by Dalits as both a waste and a threat. Their hostility toward Dalits' education is linked to the perception that Dalits are not meant to be educated, are incapable of being educated, or if educated, would pose a threat to village hierarchies and power relations.

Indian economist Sukhadeo Thorat analyses data generated by primary surveys conducted in four regions of India as well as data generated by the National Commission for Scheduled Castes and Scheduled Tribes' all-India annual reports. He argues that the regional data generated by the primary surveys is important because it underscores severe caste-based abuses that may not have been reported to the local authorities and have been left undocumented. The studies highlight persistent patterns such as: denial of Dalits' access to water; refusal of essential and/or public services to Dalits, or provision of such services in a discriminatory fashion; physical violence against Dalits; and Dalit political disenfranchisement. Thorat concludes that "upper-caste" social behaviour in rural India is governed by the norms and codes of the traditional caste system. Consequently, Dalits are separated from other communities, denied freedom of movement, and otherwise ostracized from shared social activities.

The practice of economic exclusion and discrimination is also evident in the differential pricing for Dalits in the sale and purchase of items ranging from raw materials to finished goods, and in Dalits being denied the ability to purchase land for both agricultural and non-agricultural use. A study published in 2006 on the forms and prevalence of "untouchability" in rural India—based on an extensive survey of 565 villages in 11 Indian states conducted in 2001-2002—confirmed the extent of "untouchability" practices in rural India today. But contrary to conventional wisdom, "untouchability" is not an exclusively rural phenomenon perpetuated by the uneducated masses. Egregious incidents of caste-based discrimination and abuse at the New Delhi-based All India Institute of Medical Sciences ("AIIMS"), the country's premier medical college, and other institutions of higher education bear testament to the depth and breadth of anti-Dalit sentiment in education and illustrate that such discrimination transcends the urban/rural, educated/non-educated divide.

3.4. Endogamy

Strict prohibitions on inter-dining, inter-living, and general social interaction come together with the practice of endogamy as the means for which the caste system is the end. Prohibitions on intermarriage are not only a hallmark feature of the caste system—designed to ensure rigid social norms of purity and pollution—but are essential to maintaining its very existence. As a result, inter-marriages between Dalits and non-Dalits frequently become flashpoints for conflicts and can result in extrajudicial punishments that include the public lynching or killing of couples or their relatives, rape, public beatings, and economic sanctions. Many such punishments receive "official" sanction from the "upper-caste" dominated *panchayats* (village councils). The prevalence of on-line matchmaking sites, which explicitly offer to match individuals according to their caste (both within India and abroad) provides a clear example of the practice of endogamy in its twenty-first century avatar.

3.5. Dalit women —Double Discrimination

Caste discrimination has a unique and specific impact on Dalit women who endure multiple forms of discrimination. Dalit women are especially vulnerable to violence by the police and private actors. As the majority of landless laborers, Dalit women come into greater contact with landlords and enforcement agencies than "upper-caste" women, rendering them more susceptible to abuse. Landlords use sexual abuse and other forms of violence and humiliation against Dalit women as tools to inflict "lessons" and crush dissent and labour movements within Dalit communities. Vulnerability to sexual violence also results from Dalit women's lower economic and social status, leading many of them to turn to prostitution for survival.

Dalit women have unequal access to services, employment opportunities, and justice mechanisms as compared to Dalit men. In relation to employment opportunities, Dalit women are allotted some of the most menial and arduous tasks and experience greater discrimination in the payment of wages than Dalit men. In relation to services, Dalit women have less access to education and health facilities, ensuring that their literacy, nutrition, and health standards fall far below that of Dalit men and non-Dalit men and women. The number of Dalit women in decision-making positions is also very low, and in some central services Dalit women are not represented at all. Benefits of various development programs for Dalits, such as distribution of land and other productive assets, have essentially gone to Dalit males and have failed to improve the status of Dalit women. Investment in projects targeted to the development of Dalit women is also far lower as compared to those for men.

The practice of *devadasi*, in which a girl, usually before reaching the age of puberty, is ceremoniously dedicated or married to a deity or to a temple, continues in several southern Indian states including Andhra Pradesh and Karnataka. Literally meaning "female servant of god," *devadasis* usually belong to the Dalit community. Once dedicated, the girl is unable to marry, forced to become a prostitute for "upper-caste" community members, and eventually auctioned into an urban brothel. The age-old practice continues to legitimize the sexual violence and discrimination that have come to characterize the intersection between caste and gender.

3.6. Manual Scavengers

Dalit women make up the majority of manual scavengers—a caste-based occupation wherein Dalits remove excrement from public and private dry pit latrines and carry it to dumping grounds and disposal sites. Indeed, the "occupation" of manual scavenging is the only economic opportunity available to many Dalit women hailing from scavenger sub-castes, with the result that more Dalit women and girls work as manual scavengers than Dalit men. Manual scavengers are situated at the very bottom of the graded inequality structure of the caste system and as a result face discrimination from other non-scavenger caste Dalits who treat them as "untouchables," creating an unquestioned "'untouchability' within the 'untouchables'" The entrenched discrimination against manual scavengers makes it difficult to find alternative employment and even more difficult to convince scavengers that they are able to take on, or are "worthy of performing," different occupations.

"Though long outlawed, the practice of manual scavenging continues in most states, and will continue as long as dry latrines are used." Similarly, dry latrines will continue to be used as long as there are Dalits forcibly designated to clean them.

> In 2002-03 the Union Ministry for Social Justice and Empowerment admitted the existence of 6.76 lakh (676,000) manual scavengers in India and the presence of 92 lakh (9,200,000) dry latrines, spread across 21 States and Union Territories.... According to unofficial estimates, the number of manual scavengers in India may be as high as 1.3 million.... Manual scavengers are employed by private and public employers, including the military engineering services, the army, the railways, and other organs of the state.

Manual scavengers work under extremely hazardous conditions. A manual scavenger from Paliyad village, Ahmedabad district, Gujarat, described how in the rainy season,

> Water mixes with the feces that we carry in baskets on our heads, it drips onto our clothes, our faces. When I return home, I find it difficult to eat food.... But in the summer there is often no water to wash your hands before eating. It is difficult to say which [season] is worse.

Manual scavengers are routinely exposed to both human and animal waste without the protection of masks, uniforms, gloves, shoes, appropriate buckets, and mops, resulting in severe health problems. "Many scavengers have died of carbon monoxide poisoning while cleaning septic tanks." "More than 100 die every year due to inhalation of toxic gases or drowning in excrement." "The fear of being fired by municipality officials keeps manual scavengers from demanding higher wages or sanitary instruments."

The persistence of the outlawed and inhuman practice of manual scavenging speaks to the resilience of caste-based discrimination. That human beings should continue to clean human waste and be lowered into sewers in a country that boasts of technological innovation and prowess demonstrates the stranglehold of caste in India today—a system set up to *enforce* the poverty of those it considers "outcaste."

3.7. Untouchability in All Walks of Life

Although "untouchability" was officially abolished under Article 17 of the Constitution of India, the practice remains determinative of the social and economic outcomes of those at the bottom of the caste hierarchy. Though "untouchability" is normally considered as a religiously prescribed system of separating the pure from the impure, it is, at its heart, a system to support and sanction an exploitative economic order. As a result, Dalits in India today continue to rank below other social groups in all major social and economic indicators. While Dalits have achieved some gains across a variety of indicators in the six decades since independence, their socioeconomic development continues to lag significantly behind non-Dalits. Broadly speaking, the gap between Dalits and non-Dalits in education, health, income, and land ownership has either remained constant or widened.

The practice of "untouchability" in schools has contributed to an alarmingly high dropout rate and illiteracy level among Dalit children, particularly Dalit girls. According to the 2002 India Education Report, school attendance in rural areas in 1993-94 was 64.3 percent for Dalit boys and 46.2 percent for Dalit girls, compared to 74.9 percent among boys and 61 percent for girls from other social groups. According to a 2001-2002 report prepared by the Indian government, "the dropout rate in Scheduled Castes during 1990-91 was as high as 49.35 percent at primary stage and 67.77 percent at middle stage and 77.65 percent at secondary stage." The statistics for higher education are just as alarming—the same government report states that enrolment of Dalit students at graduate, postgraduates, and professional/research/PhD levels is "abysmally low," at 8.73 percent, 8 percent, and 2.77 percent respectively. The 2001 population census reveals that the literacy gap between Dalits and non-Dalits remains significant at 54.7 percent for Dalits as compared to 68.81 percent among other groups.

Discrimination in schools and the resulting dropout rates for Dalit children are intimately linked to child labour. Illiteracy results in a lack of gainful employment options for Dalits. Even educated Dalits face discrimination in the labour market, as seen through the systematic exclusion of Dalits from jobs that they are considered too "impure" or unintelligent to perform. Selective inclusion of Dalits in various employment sectors still results in unequal treatment in the payment of wages, in different terms and conditions applied to their work (including the number of hours worked), in discriminatory treatment in the workplace, and in the prevalence of compulsive or forced work governed by traditional caste related obligations.

There are an estimated 40 million bonded laborers in India, of whom 15 million are children. The vast majority of these laborers are Dalits or tribal community members. Bonded labour is sustained by the caste system, in particular through the traditional expectation of free labour and/or inadequate remuneration for work, and by the lack of Dalit ownership of land. Bonded labour also results from indebtedness to employers or moneylenders on whom Dalits must rely because of inadequate wages and because of the reluctance of institutional agencies to lend to the poor in general and to Dalits in particular. Landlessness encompassing a lack of access to land, inability to own land, and forced evictions constitutes a crucial element in the subordination of Dalits. When Dalits do acquire land, their right to own property including the right to access and enjoy it is routinely infringed.

As a result of their poverty and discriminatory treatment, Dalits also fare poorly in health indicators. Over half of India's Dalit children are undernourished, 18.5 percent are classified as "severely underweight," while 8.8 percent die before their fifth birthday. Dalits are often refused admission to hospitals, access to healthcare, and medical treatment. Those who do gain access frequently receive discriminatory treatment. In addition, caste-based occupations that Dalits are made to perform, such as manual scavenging and forced prostitution, frequently expose Dalits to serious and sometimes fatal health hazards.

3.8. Dalit's Status in Liberalized Age

Beginning in 1991, and under the direction of the International Monetary Fund ("IMF") and World Bank's Structural Adjustment Programme, India's New Economic Policy introduced dramatic shifts in macroeconomic policy and aggressively pursued the privatization of industries and the liquidation of policies and controls in economic planning and regulation. While these reforms may have ushered in an era of astounding progress in the areas of technology, infrastructure, machinery, space, and even nuclear research, much of this progress has meant little to Dalits; most continue to live in grinding poverty, lacking food security, and without the basic amenities of electricity, sanitation, and safe drinking water. Almost two decades later, economic reforms in India cling faithfully to the flawed "trickle down" theory—a theory that holds even less relevance for Dalits for whom few benefits can permeate the caste ceiling or trickle below the "upper-caste" stranglehold on the fruits of economic growth. Unprecedented economic growth has coincided comfortably with a post-reform reversal in poverty reduction trends. Economic liberalization, for Dalits at least, may be fuelling economic inequality.

As liberalization leads to a capital-intensive mode of production requiring a greater proportion of highly skilled workers to manage automated production processes, a large migration of unskilled labour to the agricultural sector has led to lower wages for agricultural workers as a whole. In addition to a reduction in agricultural subsidies, Dalits are also affected by the increased acquisition of coastal lands by multinationals (via the central government) for aquaculture projects. Dalits are the main laborers and tenants of coastal land areas and are increasingly being forced to leave these areas to live as displaced people as foreign investment rises.

A reduction in the budget and fiscal deficit, devaluation, privatization, the elimination or reductions in subsidies, and export promotion have all contributed to inflation. As is true the world over, inflation hits the poorest the hardest. With most of their earnings spent on food, shelter, and clothing, any rise in prices has had a direct negative effect on Dalits' level of consumption. A lack of purchasing power is compounded by the devaluation of currency and has led to a rise in prices for general essential imports.

Empirical studies seem to confirm that poverty rates are uniformly higher in Dalit households (as compared to "higher-caste" households). Eighty-five percent of Dalits live in rural areas while over 75 percent of Dalits perform land-connected work; 25 percent as marginal or small farmers and over 50 percent as landless laborers earning less than US$1 per day. Though only 16 percent of the population, Dalits comprise 60 percent of those below the poverty line.

According to government estimates in 2000, the unemployment rate for Dalits and tribal groups was double that of non-Dalits/tribals. Additionally, public sector divestment to private owners is estimated to have left two hundred thousand Dalit employees jobless. Dalits continue to be significantly under represented in most professional strata and their representation in India's high industries, exports, imports, and electronic industries sectors is dismal. Economic liberalization has not translated into economic liberation for Dalits and other marginalized communities in India. The market, in short, has not served as an equalizing mechanism. Economic reforms must be scrutinized for the work that they leave undone and for the inherent assumption that such work can be done by either economic or legal means. Legal reforms to address caste-based inequality and discrimination, though astounding in their vision and reach, have been sabotaged in their implementation due to the conflation of casteism and corruption.

3.9. Constitutional Rights of Dalits

The Constitution of India, often heralded as a landmark document, was inspired by the emancipatory vision of its chief architect Dr. B.R. Ambedkar—a Dalit leader who himself suffered severe discrimination and who sought to ensure equal protection and substantive equality for Dalits in independent India. As a document, the constitution combines broad social purpose, stemming from the social content of the Independence Movement, with practical administrative detail, based on the Assembly members' experiences in government and on the events around them. Ambedkar cautioned against adopting too "Western" a vision of what constitutional democracy in India should look like. According to Ambedkar,

> [Such a system failed] to realise that political democracy cannot succeed where there is not social and economic democracy. Democracy is another name for equality. Parliamentary democracy developed a passion for liberty. It failed to realise the significance of equality and did not even endeavour to strike a balance between liberty and equality, with the result that liberty swallowed equality and has left a progeny of iniquities.

Indian constitutionalism attempts, however imperfectly, to balance liberty and equality interests and in so doing foreshadows the delicate balance between formal and substantive conceptions of equality in international human rights law. Chief among these fundamental rights is the right to equality. Article 14 of the Constitution of India reads:

> "The state shall not deny to any person equality before the law or the equal protection of the laws within the territory of India."

An exception clause allows for affirmative action measures under some circumstances.

> "Nothing in this article... shall prevent the state from making any special provision for the advancement of the socially and educationally backward classes of citizens or for the Scheduled Castes and Scheduled Tribes."

The clause marks a significant departure from the American model on which India's equality provision is based and constitutionalizes the validity of affirmative action in the Indian context. The Indian model is also one of substantive equality. If formal equality aims at equal opportunity, then substantive equality aims at equal results by considering the social structures in which equal results would not necessarily result from formal equality guarantees.

The Court has interpreted Article 14 on a number of occasions as charging the state with ensuring that there is equality among equals. In *State of Kerala v. Thomas*, the Supreme Court noted that,

> The guarantee of equality before the law or the equal opportunity in matters of employment is a guarantee of something more than what is required by formal equality. It implies differential treatment of persons who are unequal.... Formal equality is achieved by treating all persons equally... But men are not equal in all respects. The claim for equality is in fact a protest against unjust, undeserved and unjustified inequalities. It is a symbol of man's revolt against chance, fortuitous disparity, unjust power and crystallised privileges.

As noted above, Article 17 of the constitution abolishes the practice of "untouchability" and punishes the enforcement of any disability arising out of the practice. Article 21 guarantees the right to life and liberty. The Indian Supreme Court has interpreted this right to include the right to be free from degrading and inhuman treatment, the right to integrity and dignity of the person, and the right to speedy justice. Article 23 prohibits traffic in human beings and other similar forms of forced labour. Since the majority of India's forty million bonded laborers belong to scheduled castes, Article 23 is especially significant for them. Similarly, Article 24 provides that no child under the age of fourteen shall work in any factory or mine or engage in any hazardous employment.

Article 43 calls on the state to secure to all workers, agricultural, industrial, or otherwise, a living wage and conditions of work ensuring a decent standard of life. Article 46 comprises both development and regulatory aspects and stipulates that:

> "The State shall promote with special care the educational and economic interests of the weaker sections of the people, and in particular, of the Scheduled Castes and the Scheduled Tribes, and shall protect them from social injustice and forms of exploitation."

As the article falls under the category of directive principles and not fundamental rights, it cannot be enforced by the state's courts. Article 15 prohibits discrimination on the grounds of religion, race, caste, sex, or place of birth while Article 15(4) empowers the state to make any special provisions for the advancement of any socially and educationally backward classes of citizens, or for scheduled castes and scheduled tribes.

Article 330 provides reservations for seats for scheduled castes and scheduled tribes in the Lok Sabha (the House of the People), while Article 332 provides for reservations in the state legislative assemblies. Through Article 16(4) the state is empowered to make "any provision for the reservation of appointments or posts in favour of any backward class of citizens which, in the opinion of the State, is not adequately represented in the services under the State." Accordingly, under constitutional provisions and various laws, India grants Dalits a certain number of rights, including reservations (quotas) in education, government jobs, and government bodies. India's policy of reservations is an attempt by the central government to remedy past injustices related to "low-caste" status.

To allow for proportional representation in certain state and federal institutions, the constitution reserves 22.5 percent of seats in federal government jobs, state legislatures, the lower house of parliament, and educational institutions for scheduled castes and scheduled tribes. An amendment to the constitution also enables reservations for scheduled castes and scheduled tribes in village councils (*panchayats*) and municipalities, with no less than one-third of reserved seats to be allocated to scheduled caste and scheduled tribe women. Notably, no other reservation programs provides for a sub-category of reservations for women. Reservations have also been provided for "Other Backward Classes" ("OBCs")—a group of castes officially recognized as having been traditionally excluded but who, unlike Dalits, are not treated as "untouchables." Under the premise of proportional representation, OBCs are entitled to 27 percent reservations in public sector employment and higher education.

3.10. PROTECTIVE LEGISLATION

In addition to constitutional provisions, the government of India has pursued a two-pronged approach to narrowing the gap between the socioeconomics status of the scheduled caste population and the national average: one prong involves regulatory measures which ensure that the various provisions to protect their rights and interests are adequately implemented, enforced and monitored; the second focuses on increasing the self-sufficiency of the scheduled caste population through financial assistance for self-employment activities through development programs to increase education and skills.

The protective component of this strategy includes the enforcement of those legal provisions that make up the Protection of Civil Rights Act, 1955, and the Scheduled Caste and Scheduled Tribe (Prevention of Atrocities) Act, 1989; of other state and central government laws; and of "positive discrimination" through reservations in the arenas of government employment and higher education. These protective measures are monitored by the National Commissions for Scheduled Castes and Scheduled Tribes. The development measures for the educational, social, and economic "upliftment" of scheduled castes are administered by the Ministry of Social Justice and Empowerment.

3.10.1. The Protection of Civil Rights Act

With an eye to eradicating pervasive discrimination practised against scheduled caste members, the central government enacted the Protection of Civil Rights Act, 1955 ("PCR Act") to enforce the abolition of "untouchability" under Article 17 of the constitution. The

PCR Act punishes offences that amount to the observance of "untouchability." These include, *inter alia*, prohibiting entry into places of worship, denying access to shops and other public places, denying access to any water supply, prohibiting entry into hospitals, refusing to sell goods or render services, and insulting someone on the basis of his or her caste.

Perhaps the greatest deficiency of the PCR Act was the fact that abuses against Dalits were not limited to name-calling or denial of entry into public spaces: violence was a defining characteristic of the abuse. Thirty-four years after the introduction of the PCR Act, the Scheduled Castes and Scheduled Tribes (Prevention of Atrocities) Act of 1989, was enacted purportedly to bring these other forms of abuse to an end.

3.10.2. The Scheduled Castes and Scheduled Tribes (Prevention of Atrocities) Act

In 1989 the Scheduled Castes and Scheduled Tribes (Prevention of Atrocities) Act was enacted to prevent and punish caste-based abuses, to establish special courts for the trial of such offences, and to provide for victim relief and rehabilitation. Its enactment represented an acknowledgement on the part of the government that abuses, in their most degrading and violent forms, were still perpetrated against Dalits decades after independence. A look at the offences made punishable by the Act provides a glimpse into the retaliatory or customarily degrading treatment Dalits may receive. The offences include: forcing members of a scheduled caste or scheduled tribe to drink or eat any inedible or obnoxious substance; dumping excrement, waste matter, carcasses or any other obnoxious substance in their premises or neighborhood; forcibly removing their clothes and parading them naked or with painted face or body; interfering with their rights to land; compelling a member of a scheduled caste or scheduled tribe into forms of forced or bonded labour; corrupting or fouling the water of any spring, reservoir or any other source ordinarily used by scheduled castes or scheduled tribes; denying right of passage to a place of public resort; and using a position of dominance to exploit a scheduled caste or scheduled tribe woman sexually.

3.11.3. Additional Social Welfare Legislation

In addition to the acts described above, a number of other statutes aim to eradicate exploitative labour arrangements in which Dalits are frequent victims. The Employment of Manual Scavengers and Construction of Dry Latrines (Prohibition) Act, 1993, prohibits the employment of manual scavengers or the construction of dry (non-flush) latrines and punishes such offences with imprisonment and/or a fine. The Bonded Labour System (Abolition) Act, 1976, seeks to abolish all agreements and obligations arising out of the bonded labour system, release all laborers from bondage, prohibit the creation of new bondage agreements, and order the economic rehabilitation of freed laborers by the state. Other relevant acts include the Inter State Migrant Workmen (Regulation of Employment and Service Conditions) Act, 1979, the Child Labour (Prohibition and Regulation) Act, 1986, the Minimum Wages Act, 1948, and the Equal Remuneration Act, 1976.

3.11. Economic Development of Dalits

The government of India has also attempted to increase the self-sufficiency of the scheduled caste population through financial assistance for self-employment activities and through development programs designed to increase education and skills. Included among these are post-matriculation scholarships for scheduled caste students (which purportedly reach over 20 million students), special education development programs for scheduled caste girls with low literacy levels, hostels for scheduled caste girls and boys from rural or remote areas (designed to facilitate access to education), and a centrally-sponsored assistance scheme for scheduled caste development corporations, which provide eligible scheduled caste families with low-interest loans and financial assistance for a variety of economic development schemes.

Pursuant to Articles 38, 39, and 46 of the constitution a Special Component Plan ("SCP") was introduced in 1979 with a view to "achieving overall development of SCs/STs (Scheduled Castes/ Scheduled Tribes) and to raise them above the poverty line." The SCP is "an umbrella programme under which all schemes implemented by State and Central Governments are dovetailed for addressing different needs of the Scheduled Castes," and is used by the Central Government to direct funds to critical areas of need to ensure the developments needs of the scheduled caste population. The Ministry of Social Justice and Empowerment's Planning, Research, Evaluation, and Monitoring Division ("PREM") is charged with assessing the effectiveness of these welfare programs. Through PREM, the Ministry provides grants to research institutions, professional organizations, and universities to study its scheduled caste welfare programs.

The plethora of laws and programs outlined above, that collectively comprise India's affirmative action package for Dalits, stand in perverse contradiction to the social realities that Dalits face.

3.12. Rule of Law Vs. Rule of Caste

The Rule of Law in India lives in the shadow of the Rule of Caste. If law is understood as a set of rules backed by sanction, then both the legal system and the caste system can lay claim to the mantle of law with one significant difference: the caste system operates more efficiently, more swiftly, and more punitively than any rights-protecting law on the books. Political theorist Hannah Arendt lamented the "poignant irony" of the discrepancy between regarding as "'inalienable' those human rights, which are enjoyed by citizens of the most prosperous and civilized countries, and the situation of the rightless themselves." The rightless, in Arendt's opinion, were those stateless individuals who had been deprived of what she saw as the most fundamental of all human rights: the right to membership in a political community. According to Arendt, without citizenship status, inalienable rights do not come into effect. Devoid of such membership with a people or a state, individuals lose "the very qualities which make it possible for other people to treat [them] as fellow [human beings]."

If citizenship is understood as a bundle of rights that includes, *inter alia*, the rights to personal liberty, personal security, equality before the law, freedom of speech and conscience, the right to own property, and the right to political participation, then Dalits fall far short of that bundle. As a system of law, the caste system relegates Dalits into an almost permanent state of exception. If castes are understood as nations, then as outcastes, Dalits are rendered stateless in their own country. As shown below, the rights enshrined in the constitution and implemented through a plethora of legislation are not meant to serve them. As victims of both over- and under-enforcement of the law, Dalit existence is defined by the extremes of brutality and neglect.

3.13. Brutality Against Dalits

India's National Human Rights Commission ("NHRC")—a body that India characterizes as the apex national institution to protect human rights and redress grievances has characterized the law enforcement machinery as the greatest violator of Dalits' human rights. According to the NHRC, custodial torture and killing of Dalits, rape and sexual assault of Dalit women, and looting of Dalit property by the police "are condoned, or at best ignored."

Under a theory of collective punishment, the police will often subject entire Dalit communities to violent search and seizure operations in search of one individual. Dalit communities may also be perceived by the police as inherently criminal. Dalits and other poor minorities are disproportionately represented among those detained and tortured in police custody because most cannot afford to pay police bribes. Police officers' deeply embedded caste bias (most officers belong to the "upper castes") and a general lack of familiarity with legislative protections for Dalits further compound the problem. Dalits, including those arrested for minor offences, are often held in custody for long periods of time, occasionally at distant and isolated locations to avoid publicity, where they are frequently deprived of food and water, subjected to verbal abuse and humiliation, severe beatings, sexual perversities, and demeaning acts. Often the injuries inflicted can prove fatal.

Dalit activists are also accused of being "terrorists," "threats to national security," and "habitual offenders," and frequently charged under the National Security Act, 1980, the Terrorist and Disruptive Activities (Prevention) Act, 1985 ("TADA"), and even older counter insurgency laws such as the Indian Explosives Act, 1884. Dalit activists are often subjected to specious prosecutions, falsified charges, and physical abuse and torture following arrest.

3.14. Under–enforcement of Dalits' Rights

Media, non-governmental, and official reports reveal that the police have systematically failed to protect Dalit homes and Dalit individuals from acts of looting, arson, sexual assault, torture, and other inhumane acts such as stripping and parading Dalit women and forcing Dalits to drink urine and eat feces.

According to legal scholar Alexandra Natapoff, under-enforcement as a phenomenon "deserves a more central role in the evaluation of the evenhandedness and democratic legitimacy of the criminal system." Though articulated in the context of the United States, her conclusion, that under-enforcement "offers important insights into the government's relationship with vulnerable groups in the context of the criminal system," is equally applicable to the Indian context. As Natapoff contends,

> Over- and under-enforcement are twin symptoms of a deeper democratic weakness of the criminal system: its non-responsiveness to the needs of the poor, racial minorities, and the otherwise politically vulnerable. Because of this weakness, justice and lawfulness are distributed unevenly and unequally across racial and class lines, and some people can trust and rely on law enforcement while others cannot.

In what Natapoff defines as "underenforcement zones," "the state routinely and predictably fails to enforce the law to the detriment of vulnerable residents," with the result that "[f]or residents of these zones, lawfulness is spread unevenly throughout daily life and the legal system is at best unpredictable." For Dalits in India, the under-enforcement "zone" may be as wide as India itself.

3.14.1. Under-enforcement of Protective Legislation

In 2004, the NHRC released the findings of an in-depth examination of the implementation of protective legislation for scheduled castes. The report is a strong indictment of the government's failure to carry out its promises to protect Dalits from atrocities and violations of their fundamental rights and to grant remedies for rights' violations. NHRC concluded that there is virtually no monitoring of the acts' implementation at any level. Political leaders have also played a significant role in hindering the implementation of the Prevention of Atrocities Act.

The Protection of Civil Rights Act and the Prevention of Atrocities Act together represent the most important pieces of legislation for the protection of Dalits. The potential of these laws to bring about social change, however, has been severely hampered by their under-enforcement due to institutional prejudice and police corruption. State governments have made no serious efforts to identify areas where the practice of "untouchability" is prevalent, have done very little to make public the provisions of the acts, and have failed to periodically survey the acts' effectiveness.

According to the 2001-2002 Annual Report on the Prevention of Atrocities Act, 30,022 cases were registered under the Act in 2001 and 27,894 cases were registered in 2002. As staggering as these statistics are, they represent only a fraction of the violence committed against Dalits. Systematic non-registration or improper registration of atrocities contributes to under-reporting. Additional failures in investigation once a case is registered also help ensure low conviction rates. According to the Annual Report, only 2.31 percent of cases brought under the Act in 2002 resulted in convictions. The low rate of convictions, compared against the high number of atrocities reported against Dalits, is often attributed to the caste bias of prosecutors as well as other organs of justice, including the judiciary, and to the law enforcement machinery's lack of familiarity with provisions of the relevant legislation.

Dalit women are more likely to suffer violence and especially sexual violence, and are least likely to get redress in the courts. Rape cases are not prosecuted in good faith and Dalit women suffer both caste and gender discrimination in the courtrooms. Prosecutorial failures in the context of cases involving rape against Dalit women also serve to encourage the use of rape as a tool to punish and silence Dalit communities.

3.14.2. Under-enforcement of Social Welfare Legislation

A plethora of social welfare legislation has been enacted with the goal of eradicating exploitative economic arrangements in which Dalits are frequent victims. Land reform legislation has additionally been passed to help free Dalits from their perennial landless condition. Pervasive under-enforcement, however, along with significant loopholes in the acts themselves, has severely undermined the effectiveness of these laws and their accompanying rehabilitation programs.

While the Bonded Labour System (Abolition) Act, 1976, seeks to abolish all agreements and obligations arising out of the bonded labour system, the extent to which bonded laborers have been identified, released, and rehabilitated in the country is negligible. Rehabilitation programs for individuals who have been released from bonded labour are similarly undermined by their failure to secure substantial alternative employment, implement rehabilitation immediately after release, and ensure timely provision of benefits.

The prevalence of the practice of manual scavenging has not been alleviated by the Employment of Manual Scavengers and Construction of Dry Latrines (Prohibition) Act, 1993, or its rehabilitation program. To the contrary, the number of dry latrines has increased since 1989. Despite the fact that the Act was intended to be fully implemented by October 2, 2002, only 151,930 out of the total 676,009 manual scavengers identified as of 2004 by the NHRC have been retrained, while only 394,638 have been rehabilitated. The NHRC has concluded that the objectives of these and other relevant labour laws have been soundly defeated due to the inadequacy and unresponsiveness of the law enforcement machinery, as well as the economic and social dominance of the offending employers.

Land reform laws that were intended to provide reparations for the historic landlessness of Dalits have failed due to: a lack of political will and bureaucratic commitment; loopholes in the laws; the tremendous manipulative power of the landed classes; excessive interference of courts; and problems in ensuring that oral tenancies are truthfully recorded in land records so as to enable implementation of the land to the tiller policy.

While India has adopted measures to abolish forced prostitution and "rehabilitate" *devadasis*, these efforts have been largely unsuccessful. Legislative initiatives are poorly implemented. The societal perception of *devadasis* as women who are sexually available to men makes it more difficult for them to approach the police with complaints of sexual violence. Moreover, the police themselves have been known to exploit *devadasis*.

3.14.3. Under-enforcement of Economic Development Measures

According to the National Human Rights Commission, the beneficial impact of programs aimed at ensuring Dalit development have been hindered by inadequate investment of public resources; nonutilization or diversion of funds earmarked for Dalit development; a lack of programs specifically targeted to Dalit development; poor preparation of such projects; and a lack of monitoring of development programs leading to the failure of many such programs to reach their target groups. The anti-Dalit bias of personnel in charge of implementing these programs has also hindered their effectiveness.

Moreover, Dalits rarely participate in the formulation and implementation of development projects. Many Dalits are also unaware of the existence of such programs, further restricting their participation. The Special Component Plan described above—a potentially powerful mechanism for ensuring Dalit economic empowerment—has itself been thwarted in its application and implementation by administrative agencies at the central and state level. According to the National Campaign on Dalit Human Rights, during the past five-year plan period, an average of 2 billion Euros (US$ 2.96 billion) per year was illegally diverted from these funds. According to some estimates, over the course of the past quarter-century a total of US$93.75 billion has been siphoned from Dalit development programs.

3.15. Casteism and Corruption

While the near epidemic of over and under–enforcement speaks to a lack of political will on the part of the state to ensure Dalits' rights, it also serves to counter common assumptions about why such abuses persist. The notion that a dearth of resources are to blame for the lack of socioeconomics development of Dalits is belied by the siphoning of close to $3 billion a year away from funds that were meant to advance Dalit economic empowerment. Secondly, the brutality of the police toward Dalits makes clear that they are not merely uninterested in securing redress for anti-Dalit crimes; they view Dalits as criminals and derelicts at best, and subhuman at worst. Local police chiefs have been known to indoctrinate recruits to hate Dalits, and Dalits may be denied entry into police stations. What security do Dalits have when they cannot even step foot into the very office that represents their first line of defence, or worse, when they are tortured or raped by those meant to defend them?

What has alternatively been called a "lack of political will" or "police corruption" benignly represents something far more pernicious. The words "police" and "corruption" seemingly go hand in hand in India; one can hardly avoid using one word without uttering the other. But what is meant by corruption in the context of caste is woefully misunderstood. While petty bribes do certainly play a role, especially when most Dalits can ill-afford to pay them, the lack of "will" to enforce the law is not due to passive apathy but to active complicity in the caste system. The nexus between political leaders and "upper-caste" community members accounts, to some extent, for these failures and for the disincentive to address violations by private actors. That which is under-enforced is done so at the behest of the privileged castes to whom the police and the judiciary owe their caste loyalty and who have a vested (karmic and economic) interest in keeping the system in place. Those who are brutalized represent individuals who are simply meant to be treated that way.

Just as police officers refuse to register complaints brought by Dalits, Dalits as complainants "are often treated with indifference by local judges." The caste composition of the police and the judiciary is a significant part of the impunity equation. Dalits are severely under-represented in the higher ranks of the police, the prosecutors, and the judiciary. The reservations regime, discussed below, does not extend to the judiciary —with the result that, in 2002, the Supreme Court had only one Dalit out of twenty-six judges, while the High Courts had 25 Dalits out of 625 positions. In January 2007, that Dalit judge, Justice K.G. Balakrishnan, became the first Dalit to rise to the position of Supreme Court Chief Justice. According to recent studies based on available data, 47 percent of India's Chief Justices and 40 percent of all other judges have been "high-caste" Brahmins, who constitute only 6.4 percent of the population.

Caste discrimination also does not cease once a Dalit is appointed to a judicial position, as discriminatory attitudes prevail among judges themselves. The depth of anti-Dalit sentiment in the judiciary is particularly well illustrated by an incident that took place in

July 1998 in the state of Uttar Pradesh, where, as the *Times of India* reports, an Allahabad High Court Judge had his chamber "purified with Ganga *jal*" (water from the River Ganges) because it had earlier been occupied by a Dalit judge.

When the law enforcers become the criminals and the judiciary treats its own colleagues with untouchable contempt, then something far more insidious is at play. The police, and in some cases the judiciary, do not owe their allegiance to the rule of law, but to caste. Casteism must then be viewed as a form of corruption, and a force that invites corruption, rather than something separate from it. Those who occupy a variety of positions in the public administration—from the police, to prosecutors, to district collectors, to judges, and to government bureaucrats responsible for implementing social welfare programs—are so deeply entrenched in the casteist mindset that the system cannot be anything but corrupt and the state is anything but neutral. The brutality and apathy of state agents is matched by the brutality of the dominant castes. This could only be so if they were one and the same.

3.16. Caste Entrenchment

In India's perennial struggle between the rule of law and the rule of caste, violence is the trump card that ensures the rule of caste always wins out. Violence against Dalits in India has reached epidemic proportions. Between 1992 and 2005 a total of 398,644 cases involving crimes against Dalits were registered throughout the country. These include the crimes of murder, rape, kidnapping, robbery, and arson, among others. Police statistics averaged over the past five years indicate that every week 13 Dalits are murdered, 5 Dalit homes (or possessions) are burned, 6 Dalits are kidnapped or abducted, and that every day 3 Dalit women are raped, 11 Dalits are assaulted and a crime is committed against a Dalit every eighteen minutes.

As noted above, these statistics represent only a fraction of the violence committed against Dalits. A lack of police cooperation (including denying Dalits entry into police stations), fear of reprisals, systematic non-registration or improper registration of atrocities cases, and additional failures of investigation have all contributed to underreporting and to the staggering acquittal rates associated with these crimes. Despite these obstacles, fifty-seven atrocities cases are officially registered in police stations across the country every day.

Violence is a principal weapon in sustaining economic and caste-based discrimination against Dalits. Dalits' attempts to enforce their rights, alter village customs, defy the social order, or to demand land, increased wages, or political rights often lead to violence and economic retaliation on the part of those most threatened by changes in the status quo. Dalit communities as a whole are summarily punished for individual transgressions; Dalits are cut off from community land and employment during social boycotts, women bear the brunt of physical attacks, and the letter of the law is rarely enforced. Over the course of just one week in September 2007, a number of atrocities made the headlines.

On September 20, it was reported that a Dalit man, a sixty-year-old landless labourer, was beaten to death by landowners in the eastern state of Bihar over a "land-related dispute." Two days later in the northern state of Uttar Pradesh, a Dalit woman, whose son was accused of eloping with an "upper-caste" girl, was set on fire and killed. The following day it was reported that police had failed to register a First Information Report ("FIR") against suspects in the case of a Dalit boy who was forced to set himself ablaze in the northern state of Punjab. On September 26, newspapers reported that in the central state of Madhya Pradesh, a Dalit labourer was reportedly tied to a tractor and dragged, sustaining severe injuries, for refusing to plow the fields because he was sick. That same day, it was reported that the suicide of a Dalit Ph.D. student from the Indian Institute of Science in the southern state of Karnataka was alleged to have resulted from caste-based abuse and harassment.

The atrocities outlined above are revealing on many fronts and speak to the degrading, retaliatory, and violent nature of abuse against Dalits; to the impunity enjoyed by perpetrators of such acts; to the geographic spread of such cases; and perhaps most disturbingly, to the fact that these abuses are all too commonplace. A review of cases reported in any other week would likely yield the same results and even then would grossly underestimate the prevalence of such abuses, the majority of which never get reported to the police or make national headlines.

Tellingly, in that same week and in the week that followed, a number of headlines spoke to both the initiatives taken by the government to purportedly protect Dalit rights and to examples of Dalit protest and Dalit activists' engagement with the state machinery in an effort to demand their rights. The headlines, among others, read: "National Human Rights Commission issues notice to police for failure of action;" "Dalit Commission constituted in state;" "Collector for speedy disposal of atrocity cases;" "Cells to deal [with] Dalit issues;" "SC/ST orgns to campaign for reservation in Kerala;" "SC/ST hostel students go on an indefinite fast;" "Protestors block Delhi-Dehradun National highway;" "PIL [Public Interest Litigation] moved in HC [High Court] by Dalit outfit."

Hidden beneath the headlines are the parallel stories of resilience and retaliation. It has been suggested that the rise in violence against Dalits since the early 1990s is a direct reaction to increasing resistance on the part of Dalits to defy the social order and demand their basic rights, on the streets and in the courtrooms. The retaliation, which in many instances is directed at entire Dalit communities, seeks to send a clear message that Dalits should not dare to step outside their karmically prescribed duties and occupations. The very nature of the violence signals the dehumanization of Dalits as lesser humans and speaks to the use of violence as caste entrenchment. The use of sexual violence against Dalit women signals the perception of Dalit women as "sexually available," while the use of economic boycotts ensures that a relationship of economic dependency between Dalits and their "upper-caste" employers remains intact.

In the overwhelming majority of cases, the sheer brute force with which caste rules are enforced, and against entire Dalit communities, acts as a form of collective punishment. As noted above, punishment from the law enforcement machinery against perpetrators of such acts is comparatively nonexistent. The contradiction is not ironic; it is the logical outcome of that which justifies the violence itself. The observance of "untouchability" and the punishment of those who dare step out of their ranking as "untouchables" are acts "of religious merit, the nonobservance of which is a sin." If the act of discriminating and punishing is seen as just, and laden with economic incentive, then how can just punishment be punished? Seen in this light, the impunity perpetrated by the police—who are products of the same hierarchical system—is not impunity from the vantage point of caste, but a form of justice in observance of a wholly different set of laws.

Atrocities of the nature outlined above do not find a home in the collective conscience of the nation. Though the state may respond with the pro forma setting up of commissions to investigate particular atrocities, or with administrative agencies mandated to address the lack of justice to Dalit victims, the outcry from the general public is deafeningly silent. This of course begs the question, "Why?" Some may posit that such cases, by the sheer force of their volume turn outrage into apathy, compassion into fatigue, and normalize that which should be anything but. Others may live in wilful blindness and fail to connect the dots between acts of violence to draw the clear line that such violence helps preserve: the line between the "pure" and the "polluted." Some may offer counter-narratives that pigeonhole such incidents into rural pockets, blame them on a few bad apples, or worse, blame the victims for the violence they surely invited upon themselves. These and other narratives help reconcile such tragedies more comfortably with one's idea of what India represents: a secular liberal democracy (and the world's largest at that), a multicultural tapestry of cultures and religions, and a booming economic powerhouse.

The Idea of India is, of course, in the eye of the beholder. As has been said about the caste system itself, India is "Superman's heaven and the common man's damnation." Some have begun to tell the Tale of Two Indias, wherein inequalities are further polarized by globalization's steady march, and where Indians are anointed into the Billionaire's Club, while farmers commit suicide to escape their vexing poverty. But the equation is not so simply divided between the "Haves" and "Have-Nots." For caste has turned India into many nations and has kept India from realizing true nationhood. If nationhood is defined as the success of securing citizens' allegiance to the nation above all else, then surely India has failed in its nation-building project. For Indians, the nation comes a distant second to caste, religion, and region.

Then there are those who, even while acknowledging the Two India paradigm, argue that reservations will only serve to "enshrine caste differences" and "prevent India from reaching its full potential." For such critics, the vision of the future India can only be realized through the creation of educational opportunities for all, regardless of caste, and through equality of opportunity in a "meritbased system." Reservations, in turn, are emblematic of a "divide-and-rule" approach that has the "potential to break up India."

Ironically, those at the bottom of the caste system would likely make the very same argument with one important difference: it is not reservations that divide and rule or get in the way of equality of opportunity; it is the caste system itself. Set against the backdrop of the "untouchability" mindset described above, and the abuses and inequalities that it foments, reservations *create* the possibility of a meritocracy and of equality of opportunity, albeit imperfectly, rather than undermine it. The space into which reservations enter, the space of caste, is antithetical to "merit" because under the caste system respect and ability (or lack thereof) is determined not by natural talent, but by the karmic *non*-accident of one's birth into a particular caste.

As the reservations debate careens into the corporate board room, many now argue that India will lose its competitive edge and sacrifice efficiency if the private sector comes under the purview of reservations and opens the door to "non-meritorious" candidates. Caste-based affirmative action in India, a constitutional right, is now portrayed as antithetical to the meritocracy that India purportedly represents. An overhaul of the terms of the reservations debate is long overdue.

3.17. The Reservation Debate

The reservations policy has not proved in and of itself to be a sufficient remedy for caste discrimination against Dalits in India. Though reservations have helped support a Dalit political awakening, they are limited in their reach. The reservations policy benefits only a minute percentage of Dalits in the country—high illiteracy and drop out rates among Dalits mean that very few are able to avail themselves of constitutional rights in public sector employment and education. A number of key sectors also continue to remain outside the purview of the reservation policy; and caste-based discrimination continues to be practised in the sectors where reservations are secured, leading to under-enforcement.

Problems of enforcement and reach are, however, effectively sidelined in the anti-reservations debate. Reservations are now at the center of a storm of critique that projects reservations as undermining "meritocratic ideals" and reinforcing caste-based divisions. There has also been widespread public opposition to reservations for Dalits in local government bodies (often leading to violence) and in highly coveted government jobs and seats in higher education because of the economic security these jobs are perceived to offer. While reservations to state legislatures and the lower house of parliament have ensured greater Dalit representation in political bodies, these reservations have not necessarily translated to greater protection of Dalit rights. Finally, the already limited reach of reservations is increasingly undermined by economic liberalization and its attendant outsourcing of public sector jobs to the private sector where reservations, for the time being at least, cannot reach.

3.17.1. Limited Reach of Reservations

It is not incorrect to say that for some things are getting better. Dalits have achieved positions of economic and political prominence unimaginable prior to independence. Thanks in large part to greater opportunities created by reservations, Dalits are now engineers and surgeons and feature prominently on the political landscape. The expanding power base of Dalit and "low-caste" political parties, the election of Dalit and "low-caste" chief ministers to state governments, and even the appointment of a Dalit as president of India in July 1997 all signal the increasing political prominence of Dalits, but cumulatively have yet to yield any significant benefit for the majority of Dalits. Indeed, one could argue, as sociologist Jogdand does, that the reservations have really only provided "individual social mobility at the expense of group stagnation," in that gains at the singular level are only loosely tending towards the uplifting of Dalits as a whole.

The examples of a Dalit chief minister, a former Dalit president, and the current Dalit Chief Justice of the Supreme Court of India are called upon to symbolize far more than they represent— evidence of real equality for Dalits in India today. Such figures are on the fingertips of those who critique accounts of widespread untouchability, exploitation, and violence against Dalits as "unbalanced." How the identification of a handful of examples balances the treatment of over 167 million people as subhuman is left unquestioned as the curious mathematical feat that it represents. As is often the case in other countries, the existence of the exception is enough to swallow the rule. Rather than strengthening the argument that such *few* examples confirm the sluggish pace of change, they are offered as proof positive of the success of legal reform.

According to a 1996 estimate, only 1.1 million out of the then population of 138 million Dalits were employed in sectors that fell under the domain of reservations, a paltry 0.8 percent. With the privatization of public sector industries since the advent of economic reforms in India in the early 1990s, that percentage has likely declined. For the minute percentage that has been able to escape the confines of poverty, reservations represent the only viable path to economic liberation and the embodiment of hope for many Dalits that a slice of the economic pie is "reserved" for them. Reservations are an entry point, an opening of the door to institutions that were historically sealed shut by the caste system.

Though limited in their reach and their effect, research suggests that reservations for Dalits in political representation, public employment, and education have benefited those whom the policies were able to reach. Supporters of reservations argue that without affirmative action Dalits would not be able to penetrate the caste ceiling in education and employment that results from entrenched anti-Dalit biases. They add that there are no objective standards of merit applicable to all groups within society, given that dominant groups shape traditions within which they make judgments of merit. Further, they support reservations on the basis of national diversity, arguing that different views should be represented in national institutions to promote diversity, which ultimately benefits the social and the political life of the country.

Supporters also point to evidence that reservation policies have been successful in some areas. Reservations in local government bodies, such as village councils or *panchayats*, for example, have enhanced the delivery of local public goods to disadvantaged groups. Similarly, reservations in higher education have afforded greater opportunities to Dalit students. While the reservation policies tend to benefit the so-called "creamy layer" of the Dalit population, the average socioeconomic status of Dalit students is still significantly lower than that of other students. As a result of reservations, these students are able to secure better career opportunities than they would have in the absence of reservation policies.

3.17.2. Under-enforcement of Reservation Policies

The few who have been able to avail themselves of the benefit of reservations must still wage a hard-fought battle to overcome the stigma of their "untouchable" status. Caste-based occupational distribution is reinforced in reserved government employment. The National Human Rights Commission reports that Dalits occupy 65.57 percent of the total government posts for *safai karmacharis* (sweepers) and only 16.7 percent of non-sweeper posts. Dalits are also discriminated against when being considered for promotions. Reservations in higher education continue to be met with a great deal of resistance leading to under-enforcement. In the country's 256 universities and approximately 11,000 colleges funded by the University Grants Commission (an apex body of the Government of India), Dalits and tribal community members comprise only 2 percent of the teaching positions—about 75 thousand teaching positions reserved for these communities remain vacant.

Dalit students also continue to face discrimination in higher education and are limited in their employment opportunities upon graduation. In September 2006, amidst anti-reservation protests, allegations of caste-based discrimination and intimidation surfaced at the All-India Institute of Medical Sciences ("AIIMS"), India's premier medical institute. In written complaints submitted to the director of the Institute, two first-year Dalit students complained of casteist remarks and various forms of harassment and intimidation from senior "upper-caste" students. The complaints were accompanied by a memorandum signed by forty students recounting similar incidents of harassment and intimidation.

Graduating from an eminent institution also does not guarantee suitable employment for Dalits. Despite earning a Masters degree in economics from Gujarat University, the best job twenty-four-year-old Arvind Vaghela could get was as a road sweeper. Vaghela's story underscored the experience of many other university-educated Dalits. In his city of Ahmedabad;

> "[n]early 100 of its council sanitation workers have degrees in subjects ranging from computing to law, but cannot get better jobs because they are Dalits."

Such outcomes are the result of intentional discrimination in hiring decisions, and the lack of "social and cultural capital" enjoyed by Dalits. As noted in a recent study by economist Deshpande and sociologist Newman, "social and cultural capital (the complex and overlapping categories of caste, family background, network and contacts) play a huge role in urban, formal sector labour markets." As a result, Dalits' historic exclusion and disadvantage continues to undermine their advancement even where they are just as qualified and competent as their "upper-caste" peers.

Where political reservations are concerned, strict party politics has, according to one commentator, resulted in "accommodating rather than forceful, articulate and independent" Dalit elected representatives. More fundamentally, violence and intimidation are used to prevent Dalits from standing for election in local government bodies. In October 2005, a Dalit woman, Prabhati Devi, was burned alive for contesting a *panchayat* (village council) election against an "upper-caste" candidate in Mirzapur district in Uttar Pradesh in defiance of a local politician's warning not to contest. Those Dalits who are in positions of public office are also often unable to properly discharge their public functions due to intimidation, threats, and physical violence at the hands of "upper-caste" community members.

Additionally, Dalits who convert to Christianity or Islam lose their "scheduled caste" status and the few benefits it affords. While the Constitution of India grants certain constitutional rights to Hindu, Buddhist, and Sikh Dalits, the same benefits do not extend to Dalits who convert to Christianity or Islam, even though they are ultimately unable to escape their discriminatory treatment as "untouchables." At this writing, a petition challenging the constitutional validity of the 1950 Presidential Order limiting reservations to Hindu, Buddhist, and Sikh scheduled castes was pending before the Supreme Court.

Despite the obvious problems associated with the effective implementation of reservations, equality on paper has helped usher in a new conservative discourse. Fuelled by proposals to introduce reservations in the private sector and expand the scope of reservations in higher education, such a discourse skips the step of situating reservations in the context of the social and unequal reality that Dalits face, and moves straight to critiquing the continued "privileging" of particular groups on the basis of their caste as a mechanism that reinforces difference.

3.17.3. Reservations in the Private Sector

Economic liberalization in India with its underlying philosophy of increased reliance on market forces, a dismantling of controls, and a drastically reduced role of the state has resulted in a shrinking of the public sector. The reservations model is therefore affecting and able to assist fewer people, inasmuch as government-related jobs are being drastically reduced. Though poorly monitored and enforced, there is, as noted above, evidence to support the notion that Dalits have benefited from the quota system. Substantial divestment in the public sector, including the proliferation of joint ventures formed between public sector undertakings and private companies, both domestic and foreign, serves to severely undercut the reach of the reservations policy. According to Dalit theorist Dr. Anand Teltumbde,

> Even if such entities technically remains a PSU [Public Sector Undertaking] and follows the reservation policy sincerely, it would still have little or no scope to absorb the dalits in its staff. Whatever may be the strategic considerations, the fall out of this process practically amounted to shutting the doors of these new age companies to the dalits and to potential neutralization of the reservation policy.

Reservations in educational institutions and scholarships for Dalit students represent a critical component in Dalit socio-economic development. Economic reforms have, however, led to a freezing in grants to many institutions. The privatization of social services is turning education and health services into commodities only affordable to the rich. A blind faith adherence to privatization as the lone path that India must take, combined with the pretext that reservations undermine India's ability to compete in the global market, is seamlessly "superimposed on... traditional caste prejudice" to all but seal reservations' ominous fate. In response, sectors within civil society and some government actors and agencies have supported a proposed extension of reservations to the private sector.

The National Commission for Scheduled Castes and Scheduled Tribes has stated that the private sector, which continues to enjoy government patronage through concessional land, financing, and excise and sales tax relief should also be brought under the purview of the reservation policy. Indian economist, Sukhadeo Thorat, has argued in favour of extending reservations to the private sector to redress market discrimination against Dalits. According to Thorat, caste-based market discrimination not only exacerbates inequality but is also "retrogressive for economic growth." Thorat and Newman argue that discrimination here should be understood as the result of social exclusion of Dalits. The restrictions placed by caste on Dalits' ability to participate in the market, and the fact that the benefits of an exploitative market outweigh the intangible costs to Dalits, mean that we cannot simply rely on a competitive market to self-correct discrimination. Strong opposition to the private sector proposal remains, however, from both private employers and certain political parties. Private employers have criticized the government for failing to provide Dalits adequate opportunities in education and for imposing upon the private sector the obligation to employ individuals they deem unqualified.

India has indeed failed to provide Dalits adequate opportunities in education. The notion that more must be done to increase educational opportunities and ensure nondiscrimination in the classroom for Dalits and other marginalized communities can hardly be refuted. But the notion that non-meritorious individuals are now being hoisted upon the private sector must be unpackaged for the casteist thinking that it represents.

3.17.4. Caste as Anti-merit and Anti-power Sharing

Opposition to reservations often centres around the "meritocratic ideal" that "positions in society should be based on the abilities and achievements of the individual rather than on characteristics such as family background, race, religion or wealth." Critics add that reservation policies are inherently divisive and serve only to solidify caste divisions. Instead of lowering the caste barriers, they argue, reservation policies accentuate caste identity and lead to greater social stratification. Opponents have also called for greater reliance on economic indicators of "backwardness," rather than on caste, and have criticized the reservation policies as strengthening "anti-Scheduled Caste attitudes."

The idea that reservations are a *threat* to meritocracy is a farce. The road that begins with Dalit students being made to clean toilets at schools and sit at the back of classrooms, and ends with Dalit students facing ongoing harassment from their peers in institutes of higher education, while examiners stroke students' backs to check whether they are wearing the sacred Brahmin thread, is hardly one that is paved with meritocratic ideals.

The caste system is by its very nature antithetical to merit inasmuch as it assigns value on the basis of birth and not individual aptitude. Similarly, hirings and promotions are dictated not just by the academic credentials of particular candidates, but by the ability of those individuals to effectively deploy caste-based networks that, as in the public administration, corrupt the ability of the private sector system to operate neutrally.

Moreover, if market efficiency is furthered by the freedom of individuals to develop their capacities to the point of choosing their occupations, then that very principle "is violated in the caste system in so far as it involves an attempt to appoint tasks to individuals in advance, selected not on the basis of trained original capacities, but on that of the social status of [his or her] parents." And what could be more inefficient than the denial of opportunity to individuals, in the millions, who are told from birth to death that they will never amount to more than that which has been previously ordained for them? As an economic organization, "caste is therefore a harmful institution, in as much as it involves the subordination of man's natural powers and inclinations to the exigencies of social rules." By denying so many the freedom to choose their profession, caste also becomes "a direct cause of much of the unemployment we see in the country."

Reservations or quotas are critiqued for their inflexibility, but the rigidity of the caste system, against which more fluid options find no traction, does not get scrutinized. Time frames for bringing reservations to an end are proposed as though giving legal remedies a deadline will automatically lead to discrimination's time-bound demise.

Reservations as a form of power sharing in India take on new significance given that the caste system is organized around the idea of power consolidation and is, in its division of labour according to caste, antithetical to the very notion of a meritocracy. The absence of choice in employment is also quite stark in the Indian context wherein one's caste, or more specifically one's membership in an "untouchable" caste, remains determinative of one's occupation. Dalits throughout India are forced into an involuntary monopoly over occupations considered too filthy or polluting for others, occupations over which they ironically exert 100 percent reservations. *Inequality* of opportunity is the social norm and one that the state has stepped in to legislate against in order to secure equality of respect and concern for its most marginalized inhabitants. Left to its own devices, Indian society would no doubt swallow Dalits whole. Until now at least, the Indian Supreme Court has agreed.

3.17.5. Indian Supreme Court Jurisprudence on Reservations

According to comparative constitutional law scholar Jacobsohn, each nation's constitution contains a vision of the kind of polity it seeks to preserve and to become, which combines distinctive aspects of the country's political culture with features of a universal culture of constitutionalism. Jacobsohn refers to the gap between the ideal espoused in a constitution and the societal status quo as the "disharmonic jurisprudential context," within which courts have incentives and opportunities to learn from the constitutional approaches of other countries, although they may also incur costs in doing so. Indeed the Indian judiciary has on numerous occasions triumphantly stepped into such a disharmonic context to attempt to harmonize India's constitutional vision with the abysmal condition of Dalit social reality (borrowing in some cases from the American experience). The jurisprudence of the Indian Supreme Court has to date lent much credence to this ethos. In *ABSK Sangh v. Union of India*, Justice Chinnappa Reddy noted that,

> [W]hen posts... are reserved... to members of Scheduled Castes, Scheduled Tribes and other socially and economically Backward Classes it is not a concession or privilege extended to them, it is in the recognition of their undoubted fundamental right to equality of opportunity... and to secure to all its citizens, justice, social, economic and political and equality of status and opportunity... to ensure their participation on an equal basis in the administration of the country.... Every lawful method is permissible to secure the due representation of SCs and STs in the public services.

In that same case, Justice Krishna Iyer noted:

> Trite arguments about efficiency are a trifle phoney.... The fundamental question arises, as to what's "merit" and "suitability?" Elitists, whose sympathies with the masses have dried up, are from standards of Indian people, least suitable to run the government and least meritorious to handle the state business.... Unfortunately, the very orientation of our selection process is distorted and those like the candidates from Scheduled Castes whom from their birth, have a traumatic understanding of the conditions of agrestic India, have in one sense more capability than those who lived under affluent circumstances and are callous to the human lot of the sorrowing masses.

As the following discussion shows, implementing this understanding of Dalit's social reality is far from straightforward. As challenges to the constitutional validity of reservations grow, the limits of the Supreme Court's ability to reconcile the state's duty to take positive action with its duty to ensure the right to equality are increasingly tested.

3.17.5.1. Caste vs. Class, and the "Other Backward Classes"

The period starting in the early 1990s is significant not only because it launched the era of economic reforms, but also because it saw the entry of "Other Backward Classes" ("OBCs") into the reservations conversation—an entry that has resulted in much confusion and backlash, including against Dalits, and has paved the way for Class to enter the Caste debate. OBCs or so-called backward castes are identified as those whose ritual rank and.occupational status are above "untouchables," but who themselves remain socially and economically "depressed." Few groups in independent India have made progress on a scale comparable to the OBCs, including in the arenas of politics and land reforms. Yet the inclusion of so many heterogeneous groups within the OBC category has both made for its enormous size and has complicated its demands for reservations.

In *Indira Sawhney v. Union of India*, which challenged the constitutionality of then-Prime Minister V.P. Singh's decision to implement 27 percent reservations in government employment for OBCs, the Supreme Court affirmed that caste may still be used as a criterion for determining backwardness, as long as the caste is primarily socially and educationally backward, as determined by empirical evidence. Furthermore, in order to ensure that the most disadvantaged would benefit from reservations, the Court spelled out a means test, or the "creamy layer" test, which imposed an income limit to exclude those eligible for OBC classification. The Indian government subsequently implemented a more complex means test to be applied to individuals and their families who attempted to claim backward status. This test takes into account a variety of indices of social, educational, and economic disadvantage, such as parents' professional status, and the claimant's occupation and wealth as calculated by agricultural landholdings.

Notably, the Supreme Court's determination of "scheduled caste" status embodies the critical recognition that one's membership in a Dalit caste *per se* subjects individuals to a particularly egregious form of discrimination ("untouchability") *regardless* of one's socioeconomics status, and merits positive action and special attention by the state. By contrast, the determination of "Other Backward Classes" recognizes the socioeconomic gains achieved by many members of backward castes in India—who are not subject to "untouchability" practices—and circumscribes constitutional protections more strictly to those in greatest need by using empirical evidence of economic status.

In December 2005, the Ninety-third Amendment, which inserted Article 15(5) into the Indian constitution, expanded reservations for OBCs to include private colleges, while the Central Education Institution (Reservation in Admission) Act of 2006 provided for 27 percent reservations for Other Backward Classes ("OBCs") in higher educational institutions in the country. When combined with the percentage of seats already reserved for scheduled castes and scheduled tribes, a total of 49.5 percent of seats would be reserved in national public universities. In April 2008, a five-judge constitutional bench in the Supreme Court upheld the 27 percent OBC quota in government-maintained and funded institutions, stating that the Ninety-third Amendment—which empowers the Central Government to make reservations for "socially and educationally backward classes," scheduled castes, and schedules tribes in educational institutions — does not violate the Constitution's "basic structure." Meanwhile, the implementation of the Central Education Institution Act has been stayed by a two-judge bench hearing, which in light of the importance of the questions of law raised in this case referred it for hearing to a higher bench.

At issue in the latter case is whether the Ninety-third Amendment confers on the government the "unbridled power" to make provisions for certain groups without indicating the circumstances under which such reservations can be made, or limiting the duration of such provisions thereby violating the right to equality and the basic structure of the Constitution of India. Petitioners have argued that there is currently no accepted definition of who constitutes the "socially and economically backward classes," adding that the use of data that is either obsolete or based entirely on caste statistics further perpetuates the caste system. A related contention involves the scope of Article 15(5) and whether allowing for reservations in institutions of higher education abandons the significance of merit altogether, adding that such reservations in speciality institutions had been struck down by the Supreme Court in earlier decisions. Finally, the petitioners have argued that the current Act does not take into account the concept of excluding the "creamy layer" from the reservations policy.

While the category at issue is that of OBCs, the issue of whether Dalit candidates should also be subjected to the "creamy layer" test has now entered the fray. Moreover, the public discourse and ensuing protests have conflicted the Dalit and OBC categories in the symbols used to decry the Amendment and the Act. In the spring of 2006, for instance, thousands of students across the country went on strike to protest the expansion of reservations in higher education. Under the banner of "Youth for Equality," "[m]edical students in Delhi, dressed in their white coats, took up brooms and swept the streets to suggest that they will become untouchable 'sweepers' if the policies are implemented." Students at the All India Institute of Medical Sciences also burned copies of Dr. Ambedkar's books in protest, videotaped the incident, and circulated the video on campus as a means of intimidating Dalit students who were no strangers to name-calling, abuse, and harassment. Oblivious to the irony of degrading Dalits as sweepers while simultaneously marching under an equality banner, or burning the books of the author of the constitution whose equality language now buttresses their fight—an act no less horrific for Dalits than the burning of crosses in front of African-American homes by the Klu Klux Klan—the anti-reservations protests in India are a microcosm of the global trend to co-opt the language of equality for wholly unequal ends.

3.18. Caste vs. Human Rights

On November 25, 1949, in an address to members of the Constituent Assembly, Dr. Ambedkar declared:

> We must make our political democracy a social democracy as well. Political democracy cannot last unless there lies at the base of it social democracy. What does social democracy mean? It means a way of life which recognizes liberty, equality, and fraternity as the principles of life.... On the 26th of January 1950, we are going to enter into a life of contradictions. In politics we will have equality and in social and economic life we will have inequality. In politics, we will be recognizing the principle of one man–one vote and one vote–one value. In our social and economic life, we shall by reason of our social and economic structure, continue to deny the principle of one man-one value.

The Constitution of India now in 22 parts, with 395 articles and 12 schedules embraces an aggressive state role in ensuring both formal and substantive equality (equality of result) in India. Even with its more than 117,000 words, and the volumes of laws to which it has given birth, it has yet to yield its promised result for Dalits. As noted above, the mere presence of laws and constitutionally mandated affirmative action programs has served to mask widespread, egregious, and often violent forms of *de facto* discrimination. In 1943, Ambedkar commented that,

> The idea of making a gift of fundamental rights to every individual is no doubt very laudable. The question is how to make them effective? The prevalent view is that once rights are enacted in a law then they are safeguarded. This again is an unwarranted assumption. As experience proves, rights are protected not by laws, but by the social and moral conscience of society.

The drafting of the Indian Constitution in 1947 and 1948 also coincided with the promulgation of the Universal Declaration of Human Rights ("UDHR") in 1948 and as such emulates the UDHR in a number of ways. Ambedkar's words apply with equal force to the corpus of human rights law to which the UDHR has given birth and which prohibits discrimination in its many forms and calls on the state to take positive measures to ensure equality in effect.

Nowhere is this tussle between law and social conscience more pronounced than in the context of caste. The caste system is inimical to human rights and to the vision of human equality as defined under various international instruments. Article 1 of the UDHR, the foundational document of the international human rights legal regime and the calling card of the international human rights movement, proclaims that,

> "[a]ll human beings are born free and equal in dignity and rights. They are endowed with reason and conscience and should act towards one another in a spirit of brotherhood."

By contrast, Dalits are born unequal and slotted into a system of graded inequality wherein the inequality is so ingrained that Dalits themselves practice untouchability against other Dalits below them in rank.

As Thorat notes, inasmuch as the caste system and the institution of untouchability continue to govern social behaviour in India, "it makes the enforcement of human rights difficult, if not impossible." Thorat adds:

> The provisions in the Constitution and law are secular and equal but the customary rules of the caste system and the institution of untouchability are based on the principle of inequality in social, economic, cultural and religious sphere.... People continued to follow the latter because it provides immense privilege and serves their social, political and economic interests.

What then are we to make of the challenge that the caste system presents to human rights law and human rights lawyers? The implications of such a system are vast and counter intuitive to those who reach for the law as a triggering mechanism for social transformation: in sum, legal measures will make little difference unless and until the inequalities embedded in the social structure of the caste system are confronted head on.

The Constitution of India, with all its celebrated virtues, does not take on this challenge. The constitution explicitly prohibits "vertical" distinctions (i.e., the hierarchical distinctions of caste) while tolerating "horizontal" distinctions (i.e., differential treatment for different religions). The limitations on these vertical prohibitions, however, are seldom considered. The constitution explicitly outlaws "untouchability," calls for the social, educational, and economic advancement of scheduled castes, and extends constitutionally reserved positions for members of scheduled castes. It does not, however, abolish the caste system *per se*, only the most extreme injustices associated with it.

Such limitations necessarily beg the questions: will an "untouchable" ever cease to be so as long as there is a Brahmin whose claim over priesthood and even the judiciary is near absolute? What rights does a Dalit have if the privilege of "upper-castes" remains unchecked? And what rights would "uppercastes" have left if Dalits were truly treated as equal? Seen in this light, the active and pernicious subordination of the rule of law to the rule of caste is not surprising; rather it is the logical outcome of a general failure to challenge Brahminism, in the same manner that white supremacy remains institutionally unchallenged in the West. Legally, Dalits may be "former untouchables" but there is no "former Brahmin," legally or otherwise.

Judicial interventions in the context of caste, though commendable in a number of respects, continue to "disaggregat[e] an issue with religious significance to take account of the various ways it may impinge on secular concerns." Though courts have to date allowed the government "to achieve modern secular goal[s] of helping disadvantaged groups," they do so without interrogating the broader caste categories. The "untouchable" does not exist in isolation from the greater caste structure; rather he or she is socially constructed in order to ensure "upper-caste" privilege. Privileges or rights assigned or denied to a particular caste are determined by that caste's relationship to other castes. The question human rights lawyers must therefore start asking is not simply who is disadvantaged by discrimination, but who stands to benefit from it.

Even with its inherent limitations, a faithful application of the Constitution of India as human rights and constitutional scholar, Upendra Baxi, reminds us would be a recipe for complete social revolution. According to Jacobsohn, Baxi sees India as having both a written and unwritten constitution where the written is the social justice ideology of the document, while the unwritten is the "antireform ideology of the privileged classes and castes, who, [Baxi] argues, have been quite successful in entrenching their version as constitutional orthodoxy."

Defenders of each system have burned the words of the other in effigy: just as medical students burned the writings of Dr. Ambedkar in anti-reservation protests in 2006, in 1927, Ambedkar set fire to the *Manu Smriti*, the ancient Hindu law book that Ambedkar believed sanctified and authorized the cruel treatment of Dalits. Both acts seek to annihilate that which symbolically stands between those who are aggrieved and that which they seek. For anti-reservations protestors, Ambedkar and his thoughts are the embodiment of undeserved Dalit "privilege," while for Dalits, the *Manu Smriti* stands in as the veritable Brahmin Bill of Rights.

Even acts of simple revolution like the decision to extend reservations to include other "lowercaste" categories have contributed to the resurgence of the Hindu Nationalist movement in India. The movement's emphasis on cultural nationalism is seen as both an attempt to unite Hindus under one cultural, nationalistic banner and as an effective means of "maintaining the status quo in social and economic privilege."

The success of the anti-reform project is so profound that laws are openly and confidently flouted by those who wear their "upper-caste" status as a badge of superiority and preach the virtues of caste to audiences full of reverence. Rules of caste come pouring out of the mouths of school children who learn from a very young age that these norms must be obediently followed, while families openly and exclusively court marriage proposals (in India and abroad) from families of the same caste.

Any project of social transformation, whether rooted in the language of human rights, human dignity, or in the language of equality, must set its sights on the twin goals of eliminating inequality and discrimination wherein discrimination is understood not simply as a legal term but as a hierarchical mindset that allows race- or caste-based abuses and inequalities to comfortably and openly flourish. Instead of reaching for these twin goals, we have arrived at a moment where social transformation and mobilization is subordinated to imperfect judicial and legislative action and affirmative action policies are narrowly defined and easily defeated under the rubric of liberalism.

The conventional strategies adopted thus far do little to counter such a mindset, which in turn ensures the failure of even the most aggressive legal and economic approaches to achieve equality. The constitution and the law remain paper tigers with little effect; economic growth has been unevenly distributed along caste lines; reservations, already limited in their reach, increasingly offer diminishing returns; and the broader affirmative action project threatens to be defeated, ironically, using the nomenclature of rights and equal protection.

Whatever the limitations, reservations have helped create a Dalit middle class. But the creation of a Dalit middle class has not created a revolution, nor does upward class mobility work to eliminate the stigma attached to one's "untouchable" status. Dalit journalist Chandraban Prasad perhaps the only nationally prominent Dalit journalist poignantly reminds us that even as select Dalits migrate into higher class and occupational categories as a result of reservations, Dalit tea shop vendors are nowhere to be found. Though non-Dalits may grudgingly accept marginal economic success among Dalits, they will not dine with them, allow their children to marry them, or even be served a cup of tea by Dalit hands.

3.18.1. Human Rights' Flawed Trickle-down Theory

Until recently, attention to India from international human rights nongovernmental organizations ("NGOs") focused on the symptoms of the caste system (e.g., bonded labour, forced prostitution, and police corruption) without diagnosing the disease. Simultaneously, international interventions on caste (and racial) discrimination were limited to inquiries regarding the mechanisms of protection offered by the state, without asking for evidence of their effective enforcement. U.N. human rights treaty bodies have now begun to ask for such evidence while domestic agencies have invested greater energy into exposing gaps in protection.

For the human rights movement, what began as a failure of diagnosis has now transmuted into a failure of strategy. The international human rights framework holds as its organizing principle the promotion of a system of laws, universal in their application, but delivered by the state. Inherent to this strategy is an over-reliance on the state as a neutral agent of social change and the assumption that like economic growth, international laws and admonitions directed to the higher echelons of the state will trickle down to the rest of the population. The primacy the human rights movement has given to the system of laws and the state's implementation of these laws merits closer scrutiny, most especially in the context of the caste system. The social and religious sanction, when combined with the economic incentives, all but ensures that the practice of "untouchability" is perpetuated. In turn, attempts to alter the status quo are met with violent recrimination. Where then does that leave the law and the state?

3.18.2. Role of the Law and the State

The introductory paragraph to Narendra Jadhav's family biography, *Untouchables: My Family's Triumphant Escape from India's Caste System*, proclaims:

> Every sixth human being in the world today is an Indian, and every sixth Indian is an erstwhile untouchable, a Dalit. Today, there are 165 million Dalits (equal to more than half the population of the United States) and they continue to suffer under India's 3,500 year-old caste system, which remains a stigma on humanity. However, Dalits are awakening. We are struggling against caste discrimination, illiteracy, and poverty; our weapons are education, self-empowerment, and democracy.

The plight of Dalits in India serves to highlight the paradoxical role of the state in a society that is, in its natural state and left to its own devices, inherently unequal. The role of the state in such a context is to institutionalize checks and balances and intervene against the natural inclinations of the dominant groups for the protection of the dominated. But reaching for the state lands us in a double bind: without government intervention, the system could not dismantle itself, but we incorrectly assume that the state is a neutral actor. The state's law enforcement and administrative machinery is itself constructed along the hierarchy of caste.

Even if we were to assume that the state was both neutral and faithful in its implementation of the law, we still must ask whether the law can be a vehicle for social change, or does it simply divert attention away from the social condition it masks and act as a safety-valve to diffuse pressure for real reform. Moreover, can the law take away that which it did not create? If equality is understood as a value as opposed to a law, then can the state as a non-emotional body ever address it? Any program of affirmative action, no matter how broadly defined, implemented, and enforced, will not work to remove the underlying prejudice as long as it conceives of "the oppressed" as its sole target.

3.18.3. The Touchables

If the human rights framework is to be critiqued for presuming that the state will ensure that the laws will trickle down, then it must also be scrutinized for setting its sites on those at the "bottom." The downward trajectory of human rights sets its sights on the wrong target and invariably assumes that the persona to be reclaimed is that of the "untouchable victim." As noted by Ambedkar,

> It is usual to hear all those who feel moved by the deplorable condition of the Untouchables unburden themselves by uttering the cry, "We must do something for the Untouchables." One seldom hears any of the persons interested in the problem saying, "Let us do something to change the Touchable Hindu."

Affirmative action policies, as currently envisioned and advanced, fail to sufficiently transform the racist or casteist hierarchy itself. And what of the fact that the very existence of these policies help to strengthen and cement the very identities that we seek to fight against? Affirmative action may alleviate inequality but it will not break discrimination, and in the process may end up strengthening the discrimination itself by cementing identity formation along racial or caste lines.

Affirmative action (whether under the mantle of the constitution or human rights law), must be conceived in a way that is compatible with the goal of social transformation while recognizing that affirmative action, as currently constructed, is a necessary but insufficient tool for social transformation. The gap between affirmative action and social transformation can perhaps be overcome to some extent by reframing affirmative action policies to reflect the salient fact that rights and privileges are negotiated, assigned, and denied not just in the courtroom, the police station, or even the legislature, but in nonformal social spaces where "upper-caste" privilege and "upper-caste" rights are rarely contested on legal or moral grounds. According to Thorat:

Non-formal institutions; social, religious as well as economic, involve a framework of social behaviour of their own, which may not be in consonance with the principles enunciated by the United Nations, or the Constitution of a nation in which case different sets of values may result in conflicts. It implies that unless inequalities embedded in the social, economics and cultural structure of the Hindu society are addressed, the legal measures will make little difference in providing access to human rights to the dalits in India.

The caste system may be understood as an example of what critical theorist Michel Foucault termed disciplinary power. Viewed in this light, caste oppression can be seen as inhering in diffuse power relations that arise out of socially entrenched practices (including discourse) which have become the "norm." These practices "discipline" individuals by imposing categorized identities on them and others, and set those categories within a hierarchy. Foucault argued that the liberal conception of rights was useless as a means of resisting disciplinary power, as it conceived of domination as negative *repression* by the state, thus overlooking the identity-*constructing* effect of disciplinary power relations which do not emanate from a single, central source, but pervade all of society. He argued for a "new form of right" that concerns itself not with setting limits on state intrusions against the private autonomy of an abstract subject, but altering the constructive effects of disciplinary power. Ambedkar was keenly aware of the necessity of a solution that confronted caste as a constructive power of this kind; as he saw it, caste as a discipline was rooted in religious ideology and he made an effort to tackle it at the level of discourse.

Among Ambedkar's most salient contributions was to define the caste system as not simply a division of labour, but a *division of laborers* that is neither spontaneous nor based on natural aptitudes, and which prevents mobilization because of the system of graded inequality in which it inheres. Perhaps the greatest threat comes not from those who oppose affirmative action or Dalit rights, but from the internalization of the mentality of graded inequality. "Untouchability" among "untouchables" is a well documented practice, seen especially in the treatment of manual scavengers by other Dalits. As noted in the Mandal Commission Report,

> "[t]he real triumph of the caste system lies not in upholding the supremacy of the Brahmin, but in conditioning the consciousness of the lower castes in accepting their inferior status in the ritual hierarchy as part of the natural order of things."

While the task of mobilizing Dalits to claim a uniform Dalit identity in place of the hierarchical structure they inherited and impose is ongoing, the impetus does not and cannot come from the state. The state and any actor tasked with the project of translating the human rights vision into reality must set its sights on the (un)consciousness of the privileged castes. Yet what program exists to ameliorate the pathetic mentality of the bigot? Once the "touchable" condition is problematized, then perhaps the quotas would apply to them leaving the remainder and majority of seats and positions open to the majority of the nation.

3.18.4. Economy of Human Rights in the Free Market

An over-reliance on the law and the state has rendered other paths and options for the realization of human rights virtually obsolete. While the state must continually be held accountable vis-à-vis its obligation to respect, protect, and fulfil human rights, an almost myopic focus on the state ends up also ceding to it too much power and fosters a perpetual state of dependency. In India, as elsewhere, the state cannot be seen as the sole locus for social change. While the linking of reservations to broader social welfare strategies exists on paper, even those paper promises are being shredded by economic and ideological liberalization.

Ideologically, caste categories are constructed and imposed to organize exclusion, yet when those very categories are used as a basis to claim remedies to ensure inclusion, the categories magically disappear and we are invited to revel in the fantasy of a caste or color-blind nation that through the very proclamation of equality has achieved an imaginary break with the past.

Economically, the persistence of massive poverty in India and its concentration among particular social groups suggests that, without "wide spread purchasing power," the free market perpetuates castebased exploitation. An alternative prescription offered by Dalit economists involves *greater* investment in agriculture and public services and positive discrimination for disadvantaged classes that must be expanded to sectors currently out of reach and must include due attention to the implementation of the directive principles of the constitution. These policies and programs, they add, must seek to effectuate those principles through caste-conscious interventions in primary education, housing, and healthcare. A similarly aggressive role of the state is promoted by human rights advocates.

Yet, the free market ideology stands in fierce opposition to the notion that the state must take positive action to ensure substantive equality for its marginalized citizens. The prevailing legitimacy of the free market ideology within India also serves to legitimize preexisting anti- Dalit sentiment. The outsourcing of public sector functions to the private sector, unaccompanied by the simultaneous outsourcing of human rights obligations to non-state actors, dismantles both the obligation and the infrastructure of programs that support social inclusion, and along with it, any hopes of Dalit advancement. Less frequently noted, but equally pernicious, is the signalling to Dalits that their hopes for social inclusion, centuries overdue, may now be dashed long before they were ever fully realized.

But the iniquities of liberalization must be delinked from the potential benefits of globalization. Inasmuch as globalization represents the influx of outside forces into the Indian scene, and insofar as it has helped build solidarity among anti-discrimination activists across the world, globalization allows Dalit activists to reach beyond the state to foreign actors and the international community to press their claims.

Social scientist Ramaiah cautions against unequivocally accepting criticisms of globalization and instead draws attention to its potential to empower Dalits in ways that the state has failed. Legal scholar Chimni supports such a view and finds that Dalit intellectuals tend to see the threat of oppression by globalization as secondary to oppression by caste adding that much of the Dalit movement has successfully galvanized international pressure to force some change in their status. Indeed the very success of the demands for private sector reservations may hinge on the willingness of foreign investors, who are not steeped in the same caste culture, to both participate and take the lead in creating a space for Dalit employment in sectors from which they have, to date, been excluded.

That foreign investors, aid agencies, and governments are now more attuned to the deleterious role that the caste system plays in undermining both human rights and uniform economic development is a result of the work done by international and Indian advocates using the language and tools of human rights. The next and necessary step is for human rights advocates to step out of the constraints of the trickle-down legal regime and support the advancement of Dalits rights from the bottom up.

3.19. Casteism and Social Change

The law as a mechanism for achieving social change has fallen drastically short of delivering on its paper promise of ensuring equality. While legally sanctioned forms of caste-based discrimination have been largely abolished, discrimination and inequality persists, adapts, and even thrives in environments seemingly hostile to its growth environments that outlaw *de jure* discrimination and seek to ensure nondiscrimination and substantive equality through the availability of constitutional remedies, protective legislation, and social welfare programs. As with other countries with a history of institutionalized or legalized racism or casteism, the dismantling of *de jure* discrimination complicates the project of making visible ongoing and structural forms of discrimination. India's remarkable affirmation of Dalit rights through constitutional privileges and legislative protections is a double-edged sword. On the one hand, it lays the foundation for real social transformation. On the other hand, it masks the daily reality of *de facto* segregation, exploitation, and other forms of abuse by discouraging further scrutiny into the condition of Dalits.

The role of discourse in shaping and informing affirmative action policies and debates is in need of further examination. Despite the virulence of racism and inequality in the world today, the categorization of affirmative action as a program to address "historic" forms of discrimination is accepted, seldom debated, and now increasingly circumscribed. A variety of formal mechanisms ranging from protective legislation to affirmative action policies have not penetrated the caste-ceiling in any real sense, and the market has not proved to be an equalizing mechanism. Despite a large body of legislation and administrative agency mandates assigned exclusively to deal with the oppression of scheduled castes, the laws have benefited few and development programs and welfare projects designed to improve economic conditions for Dalits have generally had little effect.

In order to effectively redress entrenched discrimination against Dalits and ensure their substantive equality, the testing of these formal mechanisms against their actual impact in promoting basic human rights is a first and necessary step. Reservations create the possibility of a meritocracy in a system that is functionally anti-merit. Yet conversations about affirmative action stagnate around the question of whose disadvantage deserves protection and for how long, and fail to ask who stands to benefit from systematic social exclusion. Reservations alone constitute an insufficient remedy to the problem of caste discrimination in India. Controversy over the reservations scheme has also allowed the debate to predictably stagnate around the distribution of "privilege," taking the focus away from violations of basic rights.

To say that the road that we are on will eventually get us to a place where one's race and caste will no longer be determinative of one's claims over resources or one's very human personality is false. One's "untouchable" status continues to act as a bar to material progress, access to justice, and to development of human personality. The passage of time has not witnessed discrimination's elegant decline, but its sadistic entrenchment. Growing movements by Dalits to claim their basic human rights and their human dignity are increasingly met with large-scale violence and attempts to further remove Dalits from economic self-sufficiency.

While the stark disjuncture between constitutional vision and social reality quickly gives way to indignation, the call to action is still directed at the state, using top down approaches that assume a self-executing quality of the law. Human rights strategies must instead be informed by the twin goals of remedying the effects of discrimination and dismantling the discriminatory mindset. Without the latter, the equality project will by definition remain incomplete.

References

Ashok Kumar, E.N. Caste metamorphosis: the Korachas of Dharmapura. pp 187-211, in Simon R. Charsley & G.K. Karanth eds *Challenging Untouchability. Dalit initiative and experience from Karnataka.* New Delhi: Sage Publications Publications. 1998.

Brouwer, Jan . *The Makers of the World. Caste, craft and mind of South Asian artisans.* New Delhi: Oxford University Press. 1995.

Charsley, Simon R. Caste, cultural resources and social mobility. In *Challenging Untouchability. Dalit initiative and experience from Karnataka*, ed. Simon R. Charsley & G.K. Karanth. New Delhi: Sage Publications. 1998.

Deliège, Robert. Replication and consensus: Untouchability, caste and ideology in India, *Man* (n.s.) 27, pp 155-73. 1992.

4

Dimensions of Untouchability

Untouchability refers to certain practices of the "upper" castes such as refusing to touch or share water with people who have been called the "Untouchables" and who are today collectively called dalits. These sets of practices involve not only proscriptions on both groups of people but are often justified through notions of purity and related concepts. For many social commentators the practice of untouchability characterises the Hindu civilisation. But what exactly constitutes this practice? While there have been tomes written on the sociology and politics of this practice, there is little of significance on the philosophical foundations of this practice. Such a philosophical reflection is made all the more urgent given the magnitude of the problem and its direct impact on modern Indian society.

Touch is one of the five senses of the human body. While it is often believed that sight is the dominant sense, ancient traditions in different cultures emphasised touch as the most important sense. In particular, and of special importance in the context of untouchability, the Indian traditions considered touch as an important sense; in some schools, touch was the most important sense. This is also echoed in other philosophical and scientific traditions. Many biologists consider touch as the "greatest sense" in the body and skin as the most important organ. Paradoxically the skin was not studied in great detail till the middle of the last century. Also there is a surprising lack of the role of the skin in poetry and when found in prose most often it is associated with pathologies, such as blotches, pimples and so on. This is ironic considering the fact that while we can conceivably learn to live without our other senses such as seeing and hearing it is impossible to live without having the sensation of touch. Drawing upon the experience of Helen Keller, Montagu points out that "when other senses fail, the skin can to an extraordinary degree compensate for their deficiencies". Psychologically, the importance of touch has been widely recognised. Experiments on animals have shown that newborn babies who are not touched or licked by their mother have a greater mortality rate. As Jablonski notes, the special significance of skin, fingers and touch was not just in helping animals and humans find food but also in creating social bonds. The relationship between "care" and touching is also very important.

In the western tradition, Aristotle's views on touch have been influential. Aristotle's view on the senses is based on defining senses by reference to sense objects and in so doing he is also following Plato. Aristotle offers two criteria that were used to characterise touch: "contact criterion" and the "non–localisation criterion". Direct contact with a body characterises touch. In the *De Anima*, Aristotle notes that "all things that we perceive when in contact with them we perceive by touch" and "what is perceived by touch is directly contacted". The other senses such as seeing, hearing and smell "are *never* exercised through direct contact" whereas taste is only exercised thus and therefore, for Aristotle, taste is a form of touch. Touch was the most *basic* sense without which animals would not be able to survive but Aristotle believed that sight was the most *superior* sense.

In viewing touch as contact we might forget the presence of the medium which is essential for any idea of touch. To touch is to move towards an object, to bring surfaces into contact. Therefore, "to touch is to approach or to be approached". In the sensation of touch, the distance which characterises the objects of touch is forgotten and so also the ever present minute distance between surfaces of contact. Not only is this forgotten but without the constant recreation of this distance there is no possibility of sensing touch. We can understand the phenomenological significance of the act of touch in this context. What is the difference between touching a thing and being a part of that thing? The question of touching of a part to another part (both of which compose a whole) is different from the touching between two objects. What characterises this difference – the ever present space/medium/ body between the two objects which are in contact? Touch is more than contact because of the ever present, inerasable space between the objects of touch. It is this manipulation of this intervening medium that constitutes the different textures of touch. It is also this ever present medium which is untouchable in the act of touch. Thus, the idea of untouchability is always present, always contiguous to the act of touch. The notion of untouchability is all the more interesting because we are always in the process of touching even when we do not act to touch.

4.1. Untouchability in Indian Context

The Indian views on contact and touch offer a different set of possibilities to understand these terms. First of all, there is in general a clear distinction made between touch (*sparœa*) and contact (*saryoga*). Moreover, touch is a quality of substances. Qualities are those that inhere in substances only, are not in contact with anything and have something inhering in them. The last clause (of having something inhering) excludes universals satisfying other three conditions. (As another example of a quality, consider motion. Motion is a quality that inheres in material substances.)

Material substances have finite dimension, are capable of motion and defined in terms of contact. One standard classification of nine primary substances includes five which are material and four which are not. The five are earth, water, fire, air and internal organs; the four immaterial ones are time, spatial direction, *akaoea* and selves. Touch is a quality of substances; contact is another quality. Each of these four substances earth, water, fire and air has its own unique qualities. Only the earth is the unique locus of smell and water of cold touch. Similarly, fire is the substance whose quality is hot touch.

The NyayaVaisesika categorisation views the body as an entity, excluding the sense organs. Instead, the body is seen as the "locus of the sense organs". The body is the locus of motions caused by the self (in that body). Also, pains and pleasures associated with organs are experienced in the body and not in the senses. Each sense organ is composed exclusively of one of the five elements smell of earth, taste of water, touch of air, sight of fire, hearing of ether. Because of this unique constitution, the objects of perception have to be those which are either entirely or mostly composed of the element associated with that perception so we need fire (light) to see and so on. Furthermore, for the Naiyayikas, the sense organs are the ones which are found on the body but they are imperceptible.

Touch is a *guna* quality, like taste, smell and contact. It is a quality only for earth, water, fire and air whereas contact is a quality for all the nine substances including akaoea, time, place, self and internal organs. Furthermore, touch is perceived only through one sense organ but contact can be by two sense organs. Also, contact produces a variety of qualities including pleasure, pain, aversion, merit and demerit. However, touch does not produce these which contact does.

4.1.1. Role of Touch and Contact

In the context of untouchability, what exactly is the role played by these two different qualities of touch and contact? The notion of contact is much broader than that of touch. Contact is a quality that inheres in a pair of substances. This means that contact is a quality that is present in the "toucher" and the "touched". If two bodies are in contact with each other, then that contact is a symmetrical relation each body is in contact with the other. However, in the case of touch, there seems to be an asymmetry since the person who touches is at the same time not being touched by the object. Touch in this sense is a specific human sense unlike contact which is a specific kind of relation between any two entities. Furthermore, there are many different types of contact the *Advaitins* describe six types of contact.

Given the semantic complexity of contact and touch, we can see a potential problem in the use of the English word "touch", which in common usage often refers to some idea of contact. Particularly in the conventional understanding of untouchability, the contact with a person who is untouchable is what is seen to be defiling. But the point, for the Indian philosophers, is that touch is not about contact (which is a relation) but is a *quality that inheres in the object*. This means that the untouchable manifests the sense of "untouch" within the person. This means that the person is untouchable whether or not the person comes in contact with another person.

4.1.2. Naive Reading

Moreover, the physiological description of the body and the senses in these traditions should make us question any naive reading of touch. For example, for a medical tradition like Ayurveda, the model of the body is quite different as compared to its description in modern biology. Suoeruta, the famous surgeon of ancient times, classified the body into seven layers of skin. If skin is the organ of touch as we understand it now then which of these layers of skin are actually involved in the experience of touch? To compound this problem further, proponents of Sankhya and Advaita Vedanta describe the body in terms of both gross as well as subtle body.

Moreover, the sense organs are not to be equated with the biological eye, tongue, skin, etc. Even in Ayurveda, the sense organs which are the usual ear, nose, eye, tongue and skin are only "external appendages" and are merely the "seats of organs and not the subtle organs themselves". That is, the sense organs are themselves made of "subtle material" and the visible skin, for example, is only the seat of the cognitive sense organ corresponding to touch. Since the sense organs are subtle, in death they leave the body and it is the gross material body that decomposes. This means that the qualities associated with these sense organs are not restricted to the gross physical body because of which these characteristics continue to endure with the subtle body. There are implications of such views for understanding untouchability. For example, continuation of characteristics through the subtle body would be one way of explaining the hereditary continuity of untouchability. What this discussion alerts us to is the need to employ much wider categories in order to make sense of the notion of untouchability. Given that Indian philosophical views were reflected in social order in various ways, it will be useful to first of all interpret untouchability through categories specific to Indian cultural and philosophical traditions.

The view of the senses, the body and their relation to the world is described quite differently in the various Indian traditions. To engage with the phenomenology of untouchability it is necessary to explore the various nooks and corners of these discourses. In so doing, various interesting possibilities arise.

Skin is seen as the organ of touch in both the western and Indian traditions. How is the skin described and understood in classical Indian traditions? The skin has an important function that of encompassing and enclosing. It is intrinsically related to boundaries and surfaces. Glucklich uses these characteristics to make an insightful reading of dharma. He finds an inherent relation between dharma and skin since both of them have been symbolically conceived as boundary. Since the boundaries are sensed by the body in a particular way this implies, for Glucklich, that "dharma can actually be touched"! The narrative about the skin illustrates the complexity of its relation with touch. The seven layers of skin "are replicated in Hindu mythology and in village folklore, with the seven layers of the earth". The symbolism and mythology surrounding the skin, along with the theory of karma, suggests a reason for the view that the "skin is a primary register of the fruition of sins committed in previous births". Glucklich identifies two fundamental metaphors related to the human body: one of the body as a "microcosmic reflection of the world" and the other as a "selfenclosed space" in an antagonistic relation with the world. The first conception considers the skin in a spatiocosmological sense. Along with this is the "temporal metaphor of the skin as a map of character and moral disposition".

4.2. Dharma in the Context of Untouchability

The interpretation of dharma as boundary makes possible the invocation of dharma in the context of untouchability. Most importantly, it is primarily the skin which can do this job that is, if morality in some sense is to be ascribed to untouchability then it can only be done if they share a common characteristic in this case, the character of a boundary. In other words, it is because of these complex worldviews underlying body, sense, world and dharma that untouchability is chosen as the vehicle for transmitting specific moral or dharmic dictums. The many different properties of the skin all go to establish the nature of untouchability: the skin as the defining quality of a person means that a person whose skin is untouchable is himself an Untouchable (note the change from an adjective to a noun state in this process, the creation of a kind of people from an adjectival property of a skin); the skin as a "map of character and moral disposition" again illustrates how an untouchable's skin embodies certain moral properties; once untouchability is inscribed on an individual, then the impossibility of crossing the wall of untouchability. All these explain why it is touch that should be the primary sense in any such act of exclusion and proscription. Proscribing touch is not only biologically and psychologically the most damaging but it is also the only way that matches a much larger narrative of untouchability. This narrative, contrary to most accounts, is not really about the pure and impure as much as it is about the metaphysics of the body.

The Buddhist view of the body is also important here, especially in the context of untouchability. One reason is that the B Buddhists rejected a brahminical outlook towards individuals, society and god. The other reason is that following Ambedkar, Buddhism has become the preferred religion for many dalits. As mentioned earlier, the body has often been used as a metaphor for the world. For the Buddha, the body was indeed the world in that it is within the body that there is the arising and ceasing of the world. The belief in the impurity of the body in the Buddhist tradition seems to be all pervading. Right from birth to death the body is the site of impurity of various kinds. For example, in the *Ta-chih-tu Lun* a compendium of Madhyamika philosophy, most attention is given to the application of mindfulness of the body. Five impurities of the body are identified: womb, seed, body's nature, body's characteristics and corpse. Right from birth to death, impurity is what characterises the human body.

As Lang notes, for the Buddhists, understanding the body is important because it also helps to understand "how human beings remain trapped within them". One way to understand the body is to focus on the body during meditation, for example, to focus on the activities of breathing. Lang points out that such a meditative dissection of the body being mindfully aware of the body and its constituents eliminates the belief in self identity. Meditation on a corpse will illustrate the nature of impermanence, impurity and pain associated with the body.

In such practices, two important things happen: the negation of the self and recognition that one's own body is the site or locus of impurity. In a worldview such as this, it is impossible to place the burden of impurity on another human body while appropriating a discourse of purity on one's own body. There is no possibility of supplementation that becomes the hallmark of untouchability. In this sense, the metaphysics of Buddhism is indeed one that negates the metaphysics of untouchability.

The categories of western thought are not isomorphic with Indian ones and that distinct western categories do not remain so in the Indian view – note how categories such as logic and epistemology, metaphysics and epistemology, metaphysics and ethics do not remain distinct and separate in the Indian systems. So when Glucklich makes the important point that natural and moral concepts are interrelated in Hinduism it should be of no surprise. The implication of this interrelatedness is that natural "dirt" gets related to moral "dirt". Or that those who are morally "impure" also embody this impurity in their natural body. Thus, in literary descriptions of the *Candalas* they are described as "deformed, foul smelling and ugly"; these are characteristics which reflect and add to the notion of impurity associated with that community.

Something as universal as "water" also has different signification in these traditions. In the case of water, there is another hidden significance about touch itself. Bathing is to be in contact with water but the act of touch is not circumscribed by this physical contact. Contact is always more than the physical one. There are different modes present in every single physical contact one which is the physical, of course, but there is also a transcendent dimension. The use of language and invocation of words and chants as part of the bathing process suggests the transcendent contact of the body and words (or sounds, or language). This means that the perpetual gap characterising touch are also ones that cause complex theories of perception, touch and action in Indian thought. Since touch or contact between bodies is always more than physical contact, untouchability is not merely about physical touching but includes the other spheres inherent in touch.

4.3. Analysing the Idea of Untouchability

The idea of the untouchable is essential to the notion of touch. In the many philosophical traditions ancient Greek and Indian or contemporary we are often confronted with this paradox.

MerleauPonty invokes the idea of the untouchable through an analysis of touching and being touched. "Consider the example of my right hand touching my left. My body is involved in two processes simultaneously in this case: it is touching as well as experiencing feeling touched". For MerleauPonty, these processes cannot be coincident: not in the body or in the mind or consciousness. What and where does this possibility of this simultaneous experience reside if not in body or in consciousness? For MerleauPonty, it resides in the "untouchable".

> To touch and touch oneself… They do not coincide in the body: the touching is never exactly the touched. This does not mean that they coincide "in the mind" or at the level of "consciousness". Something else than the body is needed for the junction to be made: it takes place in the *untouchable*. That of the other which I will never touch. But I will never touch, he does not touch either … it is therefore not the *consciousness* that is the untouchable… The untouchable is not a touchable in fact inaccessible—the unconscious is not a representation in fact inaccessible.

The implication of this thesis is that,

> "to touch something is also and necessarily to be touched by it".

This model (related to what he calls as "reversibility") makes it possible to understand the relation between the self and the other. Just as much as there is a reversal in the roles of touching/touched so too is there a reversal between the self and the other. In that sense, the "Other functions as my mirror", which means that the self can take up the other's vantage point without coinciding with the other.

This idea of the untouchable captures an essential mark of the act of touching. The visible (touchable) and the invisible (untouchable) are in a reversible relation and in a fundamental sense it is the invisible (untouchable) that grounds the visibility (touchability) of the world:

> "It is the invisible *of* this world, that which inhabits this world, sustains it, and renders it visible".

In the same tradition but expanding much further, Derrida notes two aspects of the idea of the untouchable. First, Derrida suggests an intriguing relation between the untouchable and law. He makes this connection by beginning with "tact". In the notion of tact he discovers the first notion of a law:

> "The law is always a law of tact".

For Derrida, tact is something like "touch without touching". He goes on to add that in touching, "touching is forbidden: do not touch or tamper with the thing itself, do not touch on what there is to touch. Do not touch what remains to be touched, and first of all law itself which is the untouchable, *before* all the ritual prohibitions that this or that religion or culture may impose on touching". Derrida's concern with touch here arises from proscriptions such as those relating to touching another person, say a person of the opposite sex or somebody else's spouse.

These approaches illustrate a way of the matising untouchability, which is very different from the practice of untouchability in the Indian context. One difference is that the meanings of untouchable in the former case range from not being proper objects of touch (such as a concept or a law) to the notion of ever present incompleteness. Also, these examples assume the centrality of the autonomous subject. But in the case of untouchability as a practice, the impulse against touching is situated within the "object", the untouchable. And most importantly, the difference has to do with the objects of sense. Western philosophers invoke untouchability not in terms of objects of nontouch. In the Indian context, the creation of untouchables as a category precisely does this job of creating a discursive set of objects and these are objects of the sense of the nontouch or untouch. Therefore, just as there are objects of vision and hearing, there are objects specific to the sense of untouch these are the untouchables.

Not everything which is not touchable is untouchable. Space and time are two entities which are both untouchable and unseeable. Space, time, god, properties and so on are not objects of touch but they do not become objects of nontouch. They are not objects of the sense of nontouch and in this sense are not Untouchable. Very far objects that we see are untouchable, so are mirror images. And so is a stranger especially if this person is of the opposite sex, then she/he is untouchable in most contexts but is not *an* untouchable.

The very idea of untouchability, therefore, has many nested notions within it such as the notions related to impossibility, ought, negation, inability and so on. At the most basic level, untouchability as a social practice involves the possibility of touching and untouching. Untouchability as objects of the sense of nontouch is what captures this fundamental difference between not touching objects because of deleterious consequences (like fire), or presumed contagion (like diseases) and not touching an untouchable. In the case of fire or disease, there is no negation of the sense of touch. Often, a naive understanding of the practice of untouchability reduces the act of untouchability to such reasons for example, saying that one does not touch untouchables because they are involved in highly demeaning acts of cleaning human waste. But this is to misunderstand the phenomenology of untouchability because it reduces the act to some functional reasons.

Moreover, even for the untouchables there is no negation of touch as a sense. They can touch themselves, they can touch each other, they touch their children and so on. A clue to the larger philosophical problem can be found in the construction of the word itself.

Consider the use of the word untouchable—how does this compound really work? Does it mean untouchable? "Un" is a negation operator. But as we know with negation operators the meaning of the compound drastically changes depending on where the negation acts. In this case, does the negation act on the sense of touch or on the "ability" to touch? If the former, then it is the impossibility of touching (like touching space, say) but if the latter then it is the impossibility of the act of touching. In other words, does the word untouchable translate into "nottouch able" or "touch unable", that is, unable to touch?

The primary difference between these two formulations is that they point to two different types of inability. In the former, it is the inability placed on the object of touch the object of touch is such that it is inaccessible to the sense of touch (space or god), whereas in the latter it is such that the subject is unable to fulfil the act of touching. In the first case, it points to the nature of the object that is sought to be touched while in the second case it is the nature of the subject who is unable to touch. It is clear, therefore, that being an Untouchable points to the inability of the "toucher" rather than any inability of the touched person. *Thus, the real site of untouchability is the person who refuses to touch the untouchable.*

There are important consequences for the person who does not fulfil this potential of touching. The model of touching others is that of touching oneself. Thus, in the most primal sense of the term, denying oneself the fulfilment of touch leads to denying oneself the capacity to touch oneself. As much as touching fire causes burns, so also the denial of touching an Untouchable causes an inability to touch oneself in a certain sense. That is, the person who refuses to touch an Untouchable suffers from touchunability. This inability to touch is a characteristic of the toucher and not the touched. The moment one creates this inability to one's sense of touch one loses an important aspect of touch. The impact of not touching is on both the brahmin and the dalit both of them cannot fulfil the act of touching but they have different phenomenological experiences of the same. In the case of the former, it could be associated with psychological feelings of revulsion, power, rejection and so on whereas in the latter it is associated with feelings of humiliation, shame and so on. What in the phenomenon of untouchability causes this a symmetry of response even though the act of untouchability is symmetrical (the person who does not touch is also not touched)?

To be able to answer this and related questions, we have to go back and inquire into some aspects of the sense of touch. As mentioned earlier, there is no localised organ in the body which does the job of touching. The organ of touch is the skin. And if you do not like to touch something then you have to "close your skin". But closing the skin is to close the first means of contact with the world. As a variety of philosophers and biologists have pointed out, we cannot live without the skin although we can live without other senses. Simply put, the moment you close the skin you die.

Thus, it is the partial death/decay of the subject who practises untouchability that is the first consequence of practising untouchability. This happens not just because practising untouchability is morally wrong but because the person is denying himself a part of his ability, his capacity to engage with his own sense.

Unlike other senses, touch is an action. Our standard response towards objects is that we automatically reach towards them. But the untouchability experience conditions us to be more cautious towards touching in general. So the very act of touching becomes problematical because every act of touching becomes reflective. There is an important consequence of this: touching is no more an "automatic" sense but becomes a judgment. In so doing, it gets modelled on vision. In the case of vision we see objects on the one hand but we also see objects as something. "Seeing as" is a reflective process associated with perception. In the phenomenology of untouchability, we see a similar move that makes touching a matter of judgment. So touching now becomes "touching as". Such a judgment is not about "facts" alone; there is a moral code attached to it.

What distinguishes the phenomenological dimension of untouchability is the relation between *touching oneself* and *not touching another*. Not touching another is actually a manifestation of the problem of touching oneself this shift is precisely what makes untouchability in the Indian context unique. This is what differentiates it from other objects which are beyond the sense of touch. *That is, in the most essential sense untouchability is actually about the always present, potential untouchability not of another but of oneself.* This is most clearly manifested in the way the structure of untouchability unfolds in the Hindu practice.

4.4. Untouchability of Brahmins

Untouchability is a characteristic of the brahmin community. Quigley, for example, emphasises this characteristic in order to support a different reading of caste. He notes that brahmins "can *be* Untouchables, and Untouchables, as ritual specialists, are priests". His rereading of caste critiques Dumont's observation that the hierarchy in the caste system occurs through the opposition of the pure and the impure. He finds Dumont's characterisation of the opposition between spiritual authority (brahmins) and the temporal authority (of the kings), which leads to the essential disjunction between status and power, as not being empirically supported. Based on this, Dumont constructs brahmins and the untouchables as extreme contrasts.

Quigley argues that the fact that the notion of impurity is very much a part of a brahmin priest implies that one cannot use the pureimpure axis, following Dumont, to posit contrasts between different castes. Firstly, Quigley points out that there are at least six types of "brahmin personae" such as the renouncer, spiritual preceptor, nonpriest, a personal priest, temple priest and death priest. He then goes on to point out the various ways by which these brahmin priests become impure. He also points to the reaction of members of other communities who look down upon the brahmins, in terms of their impure status either in a accepting gifts or "who digest the sin, evil, and death of others".

Ambedkar was aware of the enduring idea of the impure among brahmins and other castes but he clearly points out to the many differences. He notes that there is only a notion of temporal "untouchability" in the case of brahmins and others who are in a state of impurity. There is no encoding of this state into one of a permanent stature. The acts of propitiation to get rid of the "impure" state are not available to the untouchables. To point out the brahmins too had moments of untouchability cannot allow one to equate them with the untouchables. Ambedkar conceptualises this difference in terms of the impure and the untouchable. So, what Quigley calls as untouchable in the case of brahmin priests, Ambedkar would call as the impure. Is there any merit to creating such a distinction? Ambedkar's distinction can be retained if we understand that *untouchability is not about impurity* as well as recognising that impurity is not untouchability.

4.4.1. Daily Rituals

First of all, note that the notion of "untouchability" among brahmins is not restricted only to priests in the act of accepting gifts or "accepting" death of others. The rituals concerned with impurity begin with daily acts. There are many texts which describe elaborate rituals of purification starting from the time one gets out of bed. It is also the case that there are states of *madi* when the brahmin is "untouchable" to others and these states accrue even when not associated with impurity. Almost all the moments of auspicious worship, festivals, marriages, daily prayers have some rituals of *madi* associated with them.

Madi is a characteristic of untouchableness. Certain rituals, which include most forms of prayers, have to be performed under this condition. A common ritual associated with *madi* is the following: the person who is doing a ritual must first of all wash his clothes and hang it to dry. Once it is dry it cannot be touched by any other person. The person who is "in" madi cannot wear the clothes unless he or she has had a bath. If the cloth has to be moved, it is often done with the help of a stick. If anybody else or the *madi* person touches the dried cloth before She/he has had her bath, the cloth will have to be washed again. When a person is in *madi* nobody, including his own children, can touch him. What this means is that during family rituals family members are completely untouchable till the ritual is completed.

Following Ambedkar, we can actually note the important distinctions in such states of "untouchability" of the brahmins. While one can designate such an individual as being in a state of "untouchability" the characteristics of untouchability are fundamentally different.

First of all, the individual voluntarily takes on the mantle of untouchability. If we have to invoke the language of purity, then one can say that untouchability in this case is a mark of greater purity and not of greater impurity.

Second, the fact that such an individual takes it upon himself to be an "untouchable" means that he is the autonomous agent for such a decision. Moreover, in most cases, such an individual can come out of this state.

Third, the punishment for transgression is not one that is similar to what is imposed on the involuntary untouchables. The brahmin's "untouchability" is that one does *not want* to be touched and is not that one is refused the touch. The touched touching dichotomy which informs this position is one that is characteristic of touch.

However, we should note here another class of brahmins who are "permanent untouchables" and these are the *Acharyas* (for example, in the Ramanuja tradition). These Acharyas are permanently untouchable but since their untouchability is already inscribed within the notion of superior untouchability they retain this superior nature. Such Acharyas, for example, will not eat food which is cooked even by their wives. They too, like the untouchables, gain their status of absolute untouchability through birth. The children (at least the eldest son) of Acharyas usually continue to be Acharyas. Even brahmins in a state of purity cannot touch these Acharyas, or watch them eat and so on. Untouchability for these people is not about attaining a state of untouchability and then coming out of it. It is hereditary, it is part of tradition and they are in a permanent state of being an untouchable, even to their family and kin. Here, it is not about purity and impurity but about a *state of being*.

4.4.2. Bipolarity among Untouchables

What should capture our attention is the bipolarity in those who are untouchables. Agreeing with Ambedkar, we can distinguish those caste individuals in moments of impurity as being in a transient state and hence not being an untouchable. But the special case of the Acharyas suggests something radically different. It is that the notion of being an untouchable is an essential and necessary component of being a brahmin. To be a brahmin is to be an untouchable, a permanent untouchable. For most brahmins there are only moments of untouchability and they do not have the discipline or practice to reach this state of permanent untouchability. But for the most exalted spiritual leaders the moments of untouchability are permanent. In fact, being a permanent untouchable, one that is passed on hereditarily, is what distinguishes these brahmin spiritual leaders.

Untouchability in the former case is obviously a positive virtue whereas in the latter case it is a negative "fact". What is it in the nature of untouchability that allows this accretion of value? And what is it that resists the inversion so that the positive virtue becomes a characteristic of all untouchables?

The importance of the idea of the "untouchable" among the brahmins is indicative of the essentiality of this notion to the very definition of what is it to be a brahmin. A brahmin is not one who belongs to a particular community this is merely the sociological interpretation of being a brahmin.

Being born into the community is not enough to be called a brahmin unless the male member undergoes the investiture of the sacred thread. Different subgroups then have other initiations that are needed before one can become a full-fledged member of this community. In the case of one sect of brahmins, it is necessary for a person to have undergone the panchasamskaram which includes the upanayanam (sacred thread). Unless a person has done the five *samskaras* he cannot perform most of the rituals. For example, a person who has not done these *samskaras* cannot cook in various rituals. Orthodox brahmins (of certain sects) will not eat food that is cooked by somebody who has not undergone these samskaras.

Thus, one becomes a brahmin in ways that are unique to that group. But the most important marker in becoming a brahmin has to do essentially with the possibility of being an untouchable to members of their own community. Moreover, the most exalted state is reached when one is in a permanent state of untouchability.

It is well known that membership to a brahmin community is not through hereditary alone. It is a necessary condition that one is born into a brahmin household but it is not sufficient. The sufficient condition that makes one into a brahmin is related to the idea of becoming an untouchable.

But then why is it that the brahmin's untouchability is valorised whereas the untouchability of the untouchables transforms into most inhuman forms of treatment? The philosophical answer lies in the notion of supplementation, a concept that has been effectively used by Derrida in a completely different context.

4.5. Untouchability and Supplementation

A sign is that which stands for something else. Our access to the signified is mediated through the representation through signs. But the dominant metaphysics underlying this process gives a primacy to that which is signified, because of which the sign is always placed hierarchically lower than the signified.

Derrida engages with this idea through the analysis of writing. In western thought, writing has dominantly been seen to be derivative to speech, which itself is derivative to an originary thought, an essence or presence. Whether it is Rousseau's comment that writing is a "dangerous supplement" to speech or a more virulent opinion that writing is evil, there is a continued tradition of suspicion towards writing. Derrida's critique of the binary of speech and writing where speech is seen to be "superior" to writing leads him to suggest that writing does not act as a mere "supplement" to speech.

A supplement suggests that there is a lack in what is supplemented. But it cannot just be a mere representation of this lack or absence. What this process of supplementation points to is the fact that the supplemented is incomplete and necessarily depends on the supplement. It is the supplement that brings to presence the signified. The consequence of this move is that the signified is not accessible to us other than through the presence of the signifiers every signified therefore is a trace of the signifier. In the case of writing, thought, which is supposed to be represented by writing twicere moved, is not completely accessible without writing. Not only is thought thus incomplete without the supplement it is also the case that the supplement adds to the original thought. It is the supplement which makes the originary possible.

Speech is not "independent" of writing; writing is not a mere supplementation of speech. As Culler notes, "the thing supplemented (speech) turns out to need supplementation because it proves to have the same qualities originally thought to characterise only the supplement (writing)". The logic of supplementation gives us various possible alternatives of the relation between the supplement and the supplemented. Barbara Johnson suggests the following possibilities: If A is the supplement to B, then the relation between A and B can be one or more of the following added to, substitutes for, superfluous addition to, makes up for the absence of, makes for deficiency, usurps the place of, corrupts the purity of, necessary for restoration of, as that which the other is lost without, is a danger to, is a remedy to, protects against direct encounter with, and so on.

Even this brief entry into the idea of the supplement points to its potential use in understanding untouchability in the Indian context. The popular understanding of caste privileges the axial polarity between the brahmins and the untouchables, also articulated along the pureimpure opposition. Like the speech/ writing binary or man/ woman, the brahmin/untouchable binary is not only a constructed opposition but one in which the latter is inferiorised with respect to the former. This allows us to consider the possibility that the untouchable acts as a supplement to the brahmin. It is moreover a "dangerous supplement" and one that is intrinsically "dangerous" to the signified, the brahmin. It moreover, to use one characterisation of Johnson's logic of the supplement, "corrupts the purity of" the brahmin. To use another characterisation, it "protects against direct encounter with" the brahmins. The discourse of the untouchable illustrates its construction as a supplement in these various descriptions.

Derrida's argument that the supplement is all that there is, that the supplement is to be found at the source, allows us to engage with the dominant discourse of untouchability in a different manner. The discourse on brahmins and untouchability clearly indicates that the notion of untouchability is seen as a supplement to the notion of a brahmin. However, the critical analysis of the supplement suggests that it is impossible to sustain untouchability as a "mere" supplement. It, instead, is to be found in the source the brahmin itself.

The example of the permanent untouch able among brahmins is an added illustration of the importance of the idea of untouchability among brahmins. To be the highest brahmin is to be an untouchable but not of the kind that characterises the untouchables. In other words, the necessity to construct a group called the untouchables arises in large part due to the inherent presence of the notion of untouchability in the very idea of a brahmin.

What then are the implications of this argument? It is first and foremost the recognition that untouchability as a notion is intrinsic to brahmins. And this notion of untouchability is not about the rituals associated with impurity. It is actually about the characteristics of the nontemporal, permanent and hereditary characteristics of untouchability.

The creation of a supplementary community of untouchables is a necessary consequence of the inability of brahmins to attain the "pure" state of untouchable. But in creating this supplement the pure state of untouchability that characterises the Acharyas, for example, is converted into a negative virtue. In other words, the untouchables are the supplemented Acharyas and this supplementation is needed for the possibility of having a community of brahmins whose members no longer carry the burden of "pure untouchability". Thus, if there were no creation of a supplemented class of untouchables there is no possibility of having a community of brahmins.

The untouchables are the supplemented brahmins in the final analysis. In Derridean terms, the brahmins are like speech and the untouchables are like writing. Ironically, the literal meaning of a brahmin is essentially related to speech and the dalits have been essentially reduced to possessors of a body the material substratum on which writing is possible. Speech is temporary, transitory and is evanescent and is untouchable! Writing is permanent, embodies the idea of "hereditary" and ironically, is touchable! The possibility of such reversal clearly illustrates the logic of supplementation.

How exactly does this process of supplementation act to create a community of untouchables as something necessary for the sustenance of the idea of a brahmin? This occurs through the creation of inverting the elements of the experience of touching. The supplementation occurs through the change from "not wanting to be touched" to "refusing to touch". It is interesting that both these imperatives come from the brahmin that is, the untouchable brahmin is one who refuses to let others touch him and refuses to touch others. In the case of the untouchables, neither is the case. Such a shift can happen only in the case of touch because of the touch–touched relation.

These are not just theoretical musings without empirical support! An interesting social phenomenon in Indian societies is the existence of communities who specialise in carrying various burdens of other communities. The professional mourners of Rajasthan are a community of women who do the job of mourning when somebody dies. This is one characterisation: these are women of a lower caste who are "hired as professional mourners upon the death of upper caste males... Their job is to publicly express grief of family members who are not permitted to display emotion due to social status." Quigley mentions the Mahabrahmins whose job is to carry the spirits of the dead. Indian society is filled with such examples of "outsourcing". In another book where he relates kingship and untouchability, Quigley gives the example of brahmins who hug a dying king in order to take the king's sin away. Having absorbed the sins of the dying king, the embodied sinner leaves the kingdom never to return. This practice continues to this day; Quigley cites the example of the royal murders in Nepal a few years back when similar rituals were performed. In the case of the untouchables, the untouchability of the brahmins is *outsourced* to the dalits who then carry that burden. Recognising this move of supplementation is first of all a political recognition and enables specific political action.

References

Deliége, Robert. *The Untouchables of India*. Trans. Nora Scott. Berg, 1999.

Mendelsohn, Oliver, and Marika Vicziany. *The Untouchables: Subordination, Poverty and State in Modern India*. Cambridge University Press, 1998.

Moon, Vasant. *Growing Up Untouchable in India: A Dalit Autobiography*. Roman and Littlefield, 2000.

Narula, Smita. Broken People: Caste Violence Against India's "Untouchables." *Human Rights Watch*, 1999.

Rodrigues, Valerian, ed. *The Essential Writings of B. R. Ambedkar*. Oxford University Press, 2002.

Shah, Ghanshyam, ed. *Dalit Identity and Politics*. Sage Publications, 2001.

5

Practices of Untouchability in Villages

A living caste purana provides a complex of richly contextualized and related stories and contentions, presented by those for whom they are directly significant and to informed and for the most part personally involved audiences. With the evidence hitherto available, episodes at best extracted from such larger narratives, often elicited in response to outsider's puzzles, or even perhaps casually encountered in different contexts and periods. Already familiar episodes often appear, but far more of the essential contextual basis for their interpretation is delivered with them. The task of interpretation is not sampled; on the contrary, the illusion of simplicity that may accompany homogenized notions of "the Untouchable" as the epitome of deprivation is dispelled.

Though it was grounded in ancient ideas and practices of pollution and exclusion which are appropriately termed Untouchability, as a label for a major section of the Indian population as a whole it was constructed only in the twentieth century. It came then—it is important to note that this was from perspectives external to the groups concerned—to override in of social and then academic discourses the diverse individual caste identities of those it embraced. Of these the major kinds were those based on traditions of agricultural labour and service to farming families, of leather trades, and of "sweeping" or sanitary work. The scope of the label, and its force, were largely the product of campaigning, mobilization, and legislating in the twentieth century, establishing key elements of the legal, political, and social order of postcolonial India. Hitherto entirely separate caste clusters and individual castes were consolidated—in aspiration if not in reality—into a single section of society. The classification has always been motivated by liberal and humanitarian intentions and has been of immense value for the lives of many. On it was built the vast apparatus of positive discrimination or affirmative action attached to the of social designation "Scheduled Caste." It has derived its power largely, however, from a characterization that is two-edged. Those so labelled have been identified as victims of an iniquitous social order, exclusively victims with absolutely nothing of which they could be proud. A prime significance of this caste purana, and a basic reason for displaying it here, is in providing a forceful reminder of a previous and here persisting order in which the sheer negativity of the Untouchable category had yet to take hold, in which, in varying degree, the castes so reduced were able to distinguish their identities with pride. What emerges is a worldview which does not seek to explain away the discrimination under which they labour but contextualizes it and focuses on presenting an embraceable identity.

5.1. Practices of Untouchability in Andhra

Today's association of leather-working with chappals, the characteristic Indian form of leather footwear, often obscures the former importance of leather items in irrigation, farming, cattle husbandry, transport, and many manufacturing processes. In a world where technological substitutes had yet to be developed, leather goods were of immensely greater significance. The tanning of animal skin to produce leather transforms a messy, smelly, and rapidly decaying substance into one that can be experienced as sweet and clean and of great utility. It is one of humanity's major historic technological transformations, along with the smelting of metal. In India, complex values related to cattle, the main source of the skin, generated a problem but did not prevent the development of a major industry carried on in almost every village and town across the land. Profitability of leather has at times balanced ideas of religious pollution associated most strongly with its basic production process and made leather-related castes one of the major sections of the population, the most numerous and best known being the Chamars of North India. For the South, the great family of Telugu leather-related castes has been analysed in a small but pioneering volume by T. R.

Singh as one of a number of "constellations" of castes. Madigas, as represented here by Jambava, a first ancestor, are a large central caste in the constellation and they have other small "satellite castes," sometimes regarded as sub-castes, attached to them. Apart from Madigas in villages collecting cattle carcasses, tanning the skins to make leather, and then producing items of everyday local use from it, other castes of the constellation specialized in tanning, in high quality manufacturing of particular articles—with the repair of footwear so familiar in the recent past as a generally available fall back—and in the trading of skins, leather, and finished products. The importance of leather and the secure livelihoods to be obtained from it meant that even leather workers based in villages might support satellite castes operating over wider areas, amongst them the Chindus and other performing castes to be noted.

The caste myth (*kula puranam)* here is focused on Jambava, or often Jambavamuni, the ancestral Madiga, and is generally termed the Jamba Purana. Such myths and their hereditary tellers are well known by and for many castes in Andhra Pradesh. Madigas are distinctive here only in having several different groups owning and telling their own versions of the caste myth in their own ways. There are Nulakachandaiahs, who are caste gurus, keepers of legal records and genealogies, as well as narrators. There are also Dakkalis, Baindlas, Asadis, and Masthis, each with their distinctive—but changing—specialisms. Versions from all these have been recorded but only a Chindu text, to be discussed here, has been published. The Chindus are performers of yakshaganas (*yaksaganam*), an ancient genre of musical theatre with stories drawn from the major epic traditions, *Mahabharata* and *Ramayana*, and the puranas. These have taken oral and, from ancient times, written forms. Puranas were denied as early as the fifth century CE as dealing with five themes: genesis, destruction and regeneration, genealogy, cosmic cycles, and dynastic histories. The list remains usefully indicative of the content of this Jamba Purana. Yakshagana is one of the ways in which the puranic tradition lives on, if now more strongly in some regions of India than in others. In the area in question, Chindus are one of two small castes with performance of this kind as their specialism; there are also numerous amateur troupes of enthusiastic yakshagana performers, Madigas prominent amongst them.

This wealth of explicit, complexly developed, and expertly delivered discourse on caste origins and identity contrasts, as noted above, with the impression hitherto given by the literature on Untouchable caste myths of individual stories, often fragments weakly remembered and casually told. Here they reveal themselves as substantial ideological and artistic resources, surprising if their "Untouchable" owners and tellers are thought of merely as devalued objects of deprivation and discrimination.

The Chindu treatment of the Jamba Purana in yakshagana style is generally known amongst performers and audiences as Gosangi Vesham. Vesham signifies a made-up and costumed role, here in the first place and most obviously Jambava, the Madiga first ancestor. Its performance involves dialogue, song, and dance with accompanying musicians. Amongst the components of the Jambava role that will be noted is, however, the power to pacify the enraged goddess through his dancing. This identifiable and, as it turns out, separable role within a role is Gosangi. In the narrative of the performance it is passed on from Jambava to his Chindu son and hence to the Chindus as a whole. They, as performers by caste, are providing the player for the Jambava role, as well as for the other roles required, Brahman, and whatever supporting characters may appear in the performance known as a whole by this title, Gosangi Vesham. The name Chindu, which here represents the caste, means also the dance steps which are a key part of the Gosangi performance. From this association the caste itself may also be called Gosangis.

Though its style is closely linked to yakshagana, Gosangi Vesham is distinguished from it in several important ways. Chindus are not summoned to perform but follow their own programme of visits to a series of villages in which they have rights (*mirasi*) of support and performance. They stay for several days, at first performing overnight as is usual for most village performances. On the last day or possibly two days of their visit they perform instead in the daytime, first Gosangi Vesham and then Yellamma Vesham.

The central *vesham* or role in the latter is of the living idol of a goddess with whom Madigas have a special but not exclusive relationship. Yellamma herself, a popular goddess to whom animal sacrifice is directed, is vividly described in the Gosangi Vesham but does not appear there. When she does appear subsequently, she is played by a female Chindu performer and becomes the object of worship (*puja*) in a procession from house to house around the Madiga area and beyond. The two performances together become a forceful assertion, directed both to Madigas themselves and to other villagers more generally, of the special significance of Madigas. Through Yellamma, their importance for the religious interests of many other villagers is displayed; through the Gosangi Vesham, they assert Madigas' cosmic significance, practical importance, learning, and piety in the face of everything for which the Brahman tradition, in their perception of it, stands.

5.1.1. Gosangi Vesham

The content of the living purana has now to be outlined, drawing on two main sources, both from Nalgonda District of Telangana, the northeastern region of Andhra Pradesh. One is a village performance observed, recorded and videotaped in March 2003, the other a published Telugu text.

Preparations for the village performance took place at the house of the Madiga leader of a yakshagana troupe in a village of about four thousand people, one hundred and forty kilometres from the state capital Hyderabad. The Jambava himself was the main focus of attention, his costume and make-up heavily laden with explicit symbolic reference. Two subsidiary performers, playing members of high and low status trading castes, Komati and Balija, and the other main protagonist, Brahman, joined him. Four *dappu* drummers arrived, led by one of the two elders of the Madiga community. Their first task was to deliver Komati and Balija to the performance space at a street corner in the neighbouring section of the village belonging to the Goud or Toddy Tapper caste. Once arrived and already attracting an audience, the two played out a short comedy of interactions between themselves and a farmer character in everyday dress. Such supporting caste *veshams*—performances of stereotypical caste roles—are usual, but the particular choice was unexpected and unfamiliar to most: Washerman and Barber had been expected. Though such opening episodes are essentially about gathering an audience in preparation for the arrival of Jambava, they establish the inter-caste context and theme from the beginning.

Meanwhile the final stages of Jambava's own preparation and the ritualization of the event were completed at the gate of the house yard. Turmeric and pink patches representing the smallpox with which Yellamma is associated were applied to his legs, water poured around his feet, a coconut broken and vermillion (*kumkum*) applied to foreheads of the other participants, signalling their participation in worship. Decked in leaves of the neem tree (*Azadirachta indica*), preceded by the drummers, and with a canopy carried along behind him, Jambava then advanced out of the colony brandishing his cutlass and a heavy bamboo stick and dancing fiercely (*raudra*). Brahman, with book, spectacles, an elegant black stick, and his umbrella open against the sun, walked calmly along in the same procession.

5.1.1.1. Themes and Format

The performers distinguished three puranas as making up their Gosangi Vesham. The first is the Adipurana (*adipurana*), dealing with origins, the second, the Shaktipurana, dealing with the feminine principle of force or energy (*šakti*), the Goddess and village goddesses, and the third, the Basavapurana, dealing with the significance of leather. Performance is continuous however. The three sections start in the order suggested but interweave as they are developed. Confrontation as a narrative theme is directly relevant mainly for the last: in the two preceding, Brahmans as such are significantly absent from the stories told. The Trimurthis—Brahma, Vishnu, and Shiva—have their place in the Adipurana but it is, as will be seen, a subordinated one. The form throughout is, however, confrontation moderated by cooperation: Brahman facilitates Jambava's explanations from the beginning, respectfully asking him to explain himself and prompting the next stage of the narrative. Jambava intersperses his dialogue with songs, mostly with responses (*vanta*) from the musicians, and the cindu footwork. The songs are more or less relevant, more or less readily understood, sometimes subsequently explained. Brahman keeps mostly to dialogue and supporting action. In the observed performance but not in the published text, he was the more fluent performer, at times helping Jambava out with his own points and explanations. At the same time he was intermittently provocative. Jambava responded physically, once or twice chasing Brahman escaping from the performance site altogether. His response to the most offensive and outrageous of Jambava's assertions was to cry exaggeratedly, to the amusement of the audience. They also tricked each other on occasion, with acted humour relevant to their role. Brahman offered Jambava his fine scarf if he could catch it; but then threw it bundled into a ball into the air, in the opposite direction. Jambava got Brahman to bend before his seated self, as described below. He interacted with a young boy in a sketch about wanting to buy sweets as another family had done; this had been for their grandfather's death anniversary. "Grandfather, when will you die?" Responded the boy. He enquired of his fellow Chindus about their performing of lady roles, and parodied the way it should be done. The performance ended, in typical yakshagana style, with *mangalam*, auspicious praise for the gods, and for the sponsors of the event performed by Brahman. The performers then returned as they had come, in procession to the Madiga settlement.

5.1.1.2. Adipurana

At the beginning of the text Jambava claims that he was sent to earth one night by Brahma, Vishnu, and Ishwara (*Shiva*). Almost immediately, in a song he proclaims himself as "born six months before the earth itself." Then there is a lotus in the waters and its flowers are producing fruits. Jambava cuts one open and Adishakti emerges, crowing and dancing like a peacock. She delivers three eggs. What follows expands and fills this out with a second and apparently different genesis narrative of the emergence from nothingness of the sound OM with lights flashing colors. Names are acquired and these names are the original god, Adidevudu (*adidevudu*). From it/him the waters formed and the lotus in the waters. And in the lotus, again six months before the birth of the earth, Jambava was born.

In the main development the precedence of Jambava is therefore boldly established. He is present at the origin of everything. Though he is going on to proclaim himself the grandfather (*tata*) of Brahma, Shiva, and Vishnu—the Trimurthis—he has from the beginning a separate identity distinguishing him from the gods.

Though not carried systematically all through, a claim that Madigas recognize eighteen ages (*yugam)*, as compared with Brahmans' four, provides the frame for ordering this and the following narratives. Their names are recited in the first example of the naming and listing which occurs throughout. It is one of the favoured forms of learning—or performance skills—displayed repeatedly by Jambava. It was in the first age that the original god was born. Subsequently he is most often called Parabrahmasvarupam, which may be glossed as "the essential self-created spirit," and he has super-anthropomorphic form: five faces, ten eyes, ten hands, and all the vedas in him. A lotus and other plants in the water were created in the second age. Jambava himself emerged from the water looking like a hairy animal and carrying out austerities (*tapas*), and this marked the end of the fourth age. In the fifth it was the creation of Adishakti who also, like Parabrahmasvarupam, had five faces and ten hands but also an extra eye (*palanetram*) in her forehead, which was capable of burning up whatever it blazed on. She had five names, stars on her tongue and mantras in her mouth, and a jewel granting all wishes (cintamani) in her navel. Again she is in the lotus but otherwise the story is now different and Jambava and Adishakti have not met.

In the form of a bee, however, she searched the lotus looking for someone else and found Jambava sleeping. Growing up, she tried to persuade him to have sex with her but he refused: he was her elder brother, born in the preceding age. Instead she should undertake austerities for the original god. By such means she would summon him to fulfil her desire. This was accomplished and, in the form of peacocks, she and he played in the waters. He impregnated her with three drops of his tears and she laid three eggs. From the eggs Brahma, Vishnu, and Shiva were born. Providing for them in the watery world required an island and the building of a nest on it, and Adishesha, the original serpent, to guard them. From the shells remaining, the rest of the form, furniture, and living beings of the world were created. Their resonant names and vast numbers are impressively listed, arriving finally at Kamadhenu, the cow that provides unlimited milk—or perhaps anything that can be wished for; Kalpavriksham, the tree that is similarly bountiful with fruits; and Palasamudram, the ocean of milk the churning of which was to yield immortality for the gods. They were to provide sustenance for the newly born Trimurthis. At this point the purana of origination can be regarded as completed, with the Shaktipurana already grounded within it.

5.1.1.3. Shaktipurana

Jambava is still the muni, holy sage and adviser of the gods, in this next stage, but the narrative now goes beyond this to link him with his Madiga and other descendants and provide charters for their relationships, privileges, and pains. The three young gods have grown up and Adishakti now wants sex from them. Though she claims to be only the mother of the eggs, hence their grandmother, they regard her as their own mother. They therefore refuse her and she seeks to kill them. They turn to Jambava for protection. His advice is to agree to her request but to ask her to bathe first. She will then remove her dangerous third eye before entering the water—the gods should seize it and use it to burn its owner herself up. They do as instructed and she is reduced to ash. From the ash Parabrahmasvarupam, who now re-enters the story to provide wives for the young gods, creates a new image of Adishakti. He divides it into five parts. From the head, chest, and navel he creates Saraswati, Lakshmi, and Parvati, as wives for Brahma, Vishnu, and Ishwara (*Shiva*) respectively. From the fourth part, two wives are created for Jambava, and from the last part Kali, not as a wife but to help the gods (*devata*) fight the anti-gods (*asura*) and demons (*raksasa*) she would do so in a succession of forms and would be worshipped and receive animal sacrifice under so many names: forty-three are listed in this text, most of them the names of village goddesses. The passage locates the wives of Jambava amongst the goddesses but without being goddesses themselves. Their clearest significance is that they express the relationship between the Madigas and their Chindu performers: the first wife is the ancestress of the former, the second wife of the latter.

Having created wives for the Trimurthis, the task then is to get them married. This necessitates jewellery, requiring the creation of precious metals for it. Vishwabrahma and other craftsmen are required to make it, and Jambava is to provide the leather bellows needed for melting the metal. Leather was however lacking: this is its first appearance in the narrative and it is noted that he did not have cows. Having given his word to provide the bellows nonetheless, a son, Yugamunindrudu, was born from the right side of his own stomach, to be killed by his own father so that his skin would provide the necessary material. Once killed and his skin—indeed his bones too—used for necessary implements, he still came back to life and cursed his father:

"You will forget your austerities and will become a Chandala"—the puranic outcaste. Nobody would touch him. Eventually the curse was limited to five thousand years, but Jambava nevertheless cursed him in return: "You will be called Dakkali. You will beg for food in the houses of my descendants." The episode is completed with the successful making of the jewellery and the creation of a Kummari (potter caste) to make the pots needed for the marriages.

This is a passage of immense significance for Madigas. It establishes the link with skin or leather, only it is not the skin of cattle but almost Jambava's own. It exemplifies the dependence of others on the leather he provides, which is to be the major theme of the last section of the performance. And it fixes another inter-caste relationship, that between Madigas and Dakkalis, another of their satellites. At its centre is the rooting of untouchability, not in working with leather or even in anything to do with the cow, but in a human tragedy. Such generous pledging of help as Jambava displays and its potentially tragic consequences are a well-known spring of action and emotion in the epics and the rendition of stories from them in yakshagana: Lord Krishna, for instance, commits himself to avenge the spat-upon Gayodu in the popular Gayopakyanam. In yakshagana, however, ultimate tragedy is avoided through the powers of gods: here however, it is the outcome in mutual cursing amongst humans which is envisaged as having the direst of consequences for them and their everyday world. Curses are, in the universe of Hindu thought, neither in themselves wicked nor the historic fantasy that they are in contemporary Western thought. It is not a mistake, nor wickedness, nor is it portrayed as entrapment by the gods: it is a tragic consequence of a good man trying in extraordinary circumstances to do what is both necessary and right.

5.1.1.4. Basavapurana

It is the following episode that sets up a dangerous relationship between Jambava and the cow. The story now brings him into relation with the key source of the leather, dead cattle, indeed with the skinning of the dead Kamadhenu. It is framed in a way which avoids any implication that this in itself is other than a valued skill. From this Madiga perspective, the impending problem lies elsewhere, and blame will be firmly attached to a non-Madiga. Parvati and her husband were moving in the forest. Parvati injured herself and blood from the wound became a tree. At its foot a boy, Chennaiah, was born. The implication of his birth is that he is the child of Parvati, and quasi kinship with Jambava is established too. The gods (*devata*) told Chennaiah to address Jambava, "born six months before the birth of the earth," as grandfather (*tata*). Chennaiah is first taken back with Parvati to Kailasam, Shiva's abode, to be the keeper there for Kamadhenu. He, however, forms a desire to taste her meat, at which she dies of sorrow in front of Lord Shiva. The gods are not up to the task of removing and cleaning the body. Chennaiah is therefore sent to fetch Jambava from his own place where he is sitting, high up and engaged in the worship of lingams, the symbol of Shiva. Chennaiah means to call him: "Grandfather, come down!" but instead mispronounces the intention, saying instead "Grandfather Madiga come!"

The portents are bad: the disturbance has caused him to lose his lingams and to be called "Madiga." He descends, interpreting events as the working of the curse of his Dakkali son. He opens his treasures and hands on to his Chindu son, Jihmamuni, a bell which Adishakti had given him. It is a conspicuous ornament worn by the Chindu playing Jambava in Gosangi Vesham. His Chindu son is to come twice a year to the houses of the Madigas to receive his dues. Jambava and Chennaiah return to Kailasam where he and the gods cut up the carcass. Chennaiah is to cook it for eating, but in the course of the cooking a piece falls from the pot. He picks it up, blows on it to clean it and pops it back. This is the offence: he has polluted it with his breath and the gods reject it: "It is for Jambava and his grandson." By implication, the gods are ceasing to eat polluted beef; it is to be for those cursed with untouchability only, but the restriction is linked to the polluting of food, not to the sacredness of the living cow or danger from the dead one. Pollution as a phenomenon is not denied, but any understanding of the cow in its death as intrinsically dangerous is turned aside. Disaster hangs over the whole sequence of events and is expressed in a tirade of blame aimed at the unfortunate Chennaiah. Jambava proclaims him a Mala, the progenitor of the other main "Untouchable" caste of the region.

The impending end of the last age before the present age of ultimate degeneration, Kaliyugam, is signalled. The gods will withdraw, leaving him, says Jambava, helpless in the bad place to which they had summoned him. He begs from them the boon of the provision for his Madigas of paddy and other foods. He lists thirteen kinds of residue from harvesting and threshing, as well as other items that people are to give them annually. Thus the final element in the relationship of untouchability for the present age is set up. In it Madigas will continue to deal with the successors to Kamadhenu as they die; they will continue to have the beef to eat but will be regarded as polluted for doing so; and they will be provided with paddy and other means to life by those growing it. They will have a livelihood but its cost in pollution and status loss is not disguised.

5.1.1.5. Performance and the Goddess

Next we are taken into the world of war between the gods and the anti-gods and demons. Shankara (*Shiva*) is killing them but with the resulting problem that from every drop shed of their blood another opponent springs up. Adishakti reappears to provide a solution: she prevents the blood falling to earth by catching it on her tongue and drinking it. However, this blood drinking enrages her and she turns on the gods themselves. Jambava is recruited to pacify her. To carry out this great service he is presented with thirty-two badges of distinction or "honours" (*birudamu*) by the gods. Vishnu creates for him the distinctive Madiga drum (*dappu*); Shiva presents a tiger skin; Virabhadra the ankle bells (*gajjelu*) that all performers who dance wear; Shanmuka peacock feathers; and so on. These are more or less closely connected with performing and were displayed in the performance observed. Jambava, supported by his sons and his wives, pacifies the fury of Adishakti by his Gosangi Vesham and returns to his home, Jambalagiri.

Only now does Goddess Yellamma enter the narrative for the fist time, in her Brahmanical form as Renuka, wife of the Brahman sage Jamadagni. She is destined to be killed at her husband's behest by her son Parashurama. The focus is now on Chindus rather than Madigas. Renuka/Yellamma is represented as fleeing from her son to Jambalagiri and seeking Jambava's protection. Parashurama, however, comes to the town, manages to find his mother and kills her. She becomes a demon and chases the people to kill them. Jambava therefore needs to protect his people from her but is unable to do it himself. He calls first on his guru, Rudramahamuni. He could not help, but his mention emphasizes yet again Jambava's standing and piety.

Likewise his first wife's Madiga sons and his Dakkali son declared themselves unable to help. The Dakkali parried the request: his father having made him Untouchable, how could he possibly have that strength? Finally Chindu Jihmamuni, the son of his second wife, was asked. He accepted the task but on condition that all his father's thirty-two honours received from the gods should be passed on to him. This was agreed and, so equipped, Jihmamuni and his wife Sridevasalani danced before Renuka and finally she was appeased. Yellamma—as she is now named in the text—blessed the couple and gave Jihmamuni seven gifts of her own ornaments. His wife was to perform Yellamma Vesham and they were to take it round people's houses every year. In return, they would receive offerings from the people.

The text appears then to revert to the perhaps older story which preceded this Renuka episode. Chindu Jihmamuni is again being given performance instructions but now by Parabrahmaswarupa and the other gods. Yellamma is not referred to again until the very end of the performance. Taking up the earlier story, the Chindus are to perform for Jambava's people and to take round with them the honours Jambava had handed on to them. There should be no marriage between Madigas and Chindus. The Dakkali son receives instructions too: he is to beg in the houses of Madigas and to live to the east of them. Five Jetti castes, attached to Madigas, Malas, Toddy Tappers, Weavers, and Washermen—apparently descended from those to whom the falling drops of blood mentioned above gave rise—are also called for instruction. They are to make the people happy with their performances, except perhaps for the Madiga Jettis who are to be guards.

5.2. Caste Schemes and Challenge to Brahmanism

The Shakti purana theme has been completed and the stories of origination (*Adipurana*) are about to be with one short section grounding links with pastoral Gollas. Jambava's claims to superior knowledge of caste and genealogy come to the fore. Only the Basavapurana theme remains to be finally developed. Cattle and leather are emphasized as the source of Madigas' importance for others, simultaneously as the source of problems for themselves. The latter is identified as essentially Brahmanical and is challenged. This is the theme that comes to dominate the last part of the performance.

The first major demonstration of superior knowledge here is the listing of castes in three separate schemes. These start with strong quasi-Brahmanic reference but move into the immediately experienced caste universe of the region, before taking off finally, after immense displays of virtuoso listing, into an imaginative assertion of Madiga superiority. The beginning is a scheme which Jambava represents as set out by Vyasa, the classic "arranger" of Brahmanical lore for the present Kaliyugam. The three "Twice-born" varnas of the well-known Brahmanical scheme of four, or five, lead the listing, but it then continues with eighteen more. They are named with Brahmanic terms first, each then equated with a contemporary and locally familiar name: for example Lingadharaka (those wearing lingams) are Jangams, Gorakshaka (cow protectors) are Gollas, Nartaka (dancers) are Bhogams, Matanga are Madigas, and Chandala are Malas. The orthodox fourth varna term, "Shudra," does not appear; Madigas and Malas are not placed at the end of the list; and there is no division for "Untouchables." The second listing gives striking expression to the caste-constellation concept. Seventeen major divisions are shown as made up of one hundred and forty-two subgroups and, in one case, a sub-sub-group. Brahmans are still put first, with ten kinds distinguished by their specialized activities: performing rituals, working as village heads and accountants, narrating vedas, and so on. Some of the names at each level correspond with the first scheme, but the two lists are very partially consistent. The third scheme leaves Brahmanic categorizations entirely behind, setting out minor or satellite castes which thirty-three major castes have attached to them. Brahmans are now mentioned in third place, with Vipravinodulu, a known performing group, attached to them. All but two are shown with one satellite only. Gollas are shown with three, and when Jambava arrives at his own Madigas he sets off on a fanciful stream of dependants and the dependants of dependants. It starts with the by now familiar Dakkali and continues for ten levels beneath them. As a flight of listing fancy and a flourish of greatness in the published text, it is magnificent; in the observed performance, however, none of this was even attempted.

The theme of caste knowledge and the relationships of Madigas and other castes does not end here. Two further strands are woven together, one concerning puranic relationships of origins and genealogy—another Brahmanical sphere of knowledge to be contested—the other representing the importance of Madigas' leather products for people of all castes. Relationships with Gollas lead the first strand: the idea that Lord Krishna was a Golla rather than—the usual Brahmanic version—only brought up by pastoralists leads into genealogical issues. The Madiga version has Jambava giving his daughter, Jambavathi, to Krishna, making him the Madigas' son-in-law. The son of Jambavathi and Krishna, Sambudu, then married Lakshana, daughter of Dhuryodhana, the Kaurava king in the Mahabharata. The extended and contentious debate refers to inter-caste marriages, mixed descent, and anomalous births. Jambava uses it to ridicule Brahman ideas of proper descent and any radical separation between Brahmans and Madigas.

> Don't say that you are superior and Madigas are inferiors. Oh fool! Do you know who was superior and who was inferior in the past? Don't talk without knowing the past! Oh Brahman, you are the son of a donkey. Brahmans are the slaves of other castes…. To whom was Vyasa born? Was he born to a Madiga or to a king?… Tell me who are bastards, Brahmans or Madigas?
>
> *(Venkateswarlu 1997, 28).*

Brahman bounces back with protests and counter-assertions. The text runs on in sharp banter and mutual abuse. Sexual morals and practices—whether it is Brahmans or Madigas who were born to prostitutes (lanja); who practise abortion to hide sexual irregularities; who refuse remarriage to child widows—these and more are brought into vigorous contention.

Madigas' identification with leather is the last strand running through the final section of the performance. The dependence on them of other castes as leather users is argued, with song and acting, culminating in a final mocking of Brahmanical notions of leather as impure. Even Reddy landlords, Jambava asserts, though they will not touch Madigas, use the footwear made by them. Others depend on their leather for their traditional callings: Gouds use a leather sling made by Madigas to enable them to climb their toddy trees; Bhogams as dancers use it as skins for their drums; Washermen (sakali) as blinkers for their donkeys. Even Brahmans, when they draw water for their daily bath, must come into contact with leather. But not nowadays, responds Brahman: today we press the button on an electric motor. Ah, Jambava answers, but the belt on the motor is prepared by Madigas. "Everything in the world can only work with the help of Madigas". Mingled with this are direct challenges to Untouchability. Brahman: "Hey, you son of a dog, don't touch me!" Jambava: "Hey, I touched you—you are impure!" He rebukes Brahman for calling him "Untouchable" and educates him in the work of Sri Virabrahman, a popular seventeenth-century saint who denounced ideas of pollution and Untouchability.

The published text ends with the acting out of a scene between Jambava as a contemporary village Madiga and Brahman as a would-be customer for his chappal repair services. Brahman asked him to mend his chappal; Jambava denied that Madigas do such work any more. Brahman tried to remind him that he wanted him to fix the propitious time for his son's marriage. Jambava denied it: they are knowledgeable too and can fix it for themselves. Brahman appealed to his good nature and kicked the chappal to be mended over to him. In the performance this was a symbolic chappal, a stick with a thread tied round it: his own potentially polluting leather chappals remained firmly on his feet. Though the represented insult was supposed to anger Jambava, it also cued a wordplay song proclaiming the central importance of footwear for life and for Goddess Yellamma herself. He then distracted Brahman with talk of Madiga marriage customs and his son's wedding before asking him to try the repaired chappal. This necessitated his bending, only to be teased for bending before a Madiga. "Yes, yes! That is how you pay the respect that everyone offers to Madigas. Bend down again and repair your own footwear". This was too much: Brahman announced that he was going to Kashi, otherwise Varanasi, the holy city of Hindu pilgrimage and death on the Ganges. He enacted his going, finally overtly complicit in the undermining of Brahman ideas, values, and even dignity. He comes to a river; his chappals will be soaked; the water is rising; he will carry them in his hands; the water has reached to his shoulders, to his head. So finally Brahman is carrying his leather footwear on his head. He demonstrates where the real priority lies, not in issues of purity and pollution but in keeping one's chappals dry. In the performance, though the action was over with this final discomfiture of Brahman, it was he who led the final singing of praise to the gods and gave a concluding speech. In the past they used to perform Jamba Purana for the Madigas, he said. In return they would receive donations. But now these people from Hyderabad had come to watch their performance. God had sent these people from the city to help them. All Gods are the same: Adam, Eve, Allah, Rama, Krishna, all are the same. People from different places worship the God with different names. Finally, everyone set off back whence they had come, to the Madiga settlement for the working out of the "help" which was to be provided.

5.3. Untouchability in Kerala

As per historians untouchability started in Kerala with the advent of Nambudiris. In Kerala, anyone who was not a Namboothiri, was treated by the Namboothiris as an untouchable. The Namboothiris had different rules regarding the degrees of pollution for the different classes. If a Namboothiri happens to touch or comes in physical contact with an Embraanthiri, he gets the Embraan Sudham, which is supposed to be one step lower in rank among various types of purity of Namboothiris. But it is not compulsory that an adult male Namboothiri should bathe before performing "sandhyaavandanam" if he is polluted due to "Embraan sudham". Also Namboothiris will get Eda Sudham if they are polluted by the touch of Iyers. Namboothiri women (and not men) are not permitted to eat if they become Eda Sudham. For doing Sandhyaavandanam, Namboothiris should take bath if they are polluted with Eda Sudham. Asudhams are practised not only by Namboothiris, but also people of other communities in Kerala, such as the royal families, temple employees, Nairs, etc., who are closely associated with Namboothiris. Other South Indian Brahmanans also follow this custom. Clothes of Namboothiris, washed by Veluthedans, if touched by other Nairs, are not impure. But if touched by a person below the rank in the hierarchies of caste system, it becomes impure. Other classes had different distances after which they could be considered polluting. For example, if an Ezhava got within 24 feet of a Namboothiri, the Namboothiri was considered to be polluted. Untouchability was not isolated to Hindus in Kerala, amongst Christians the original Syrian Malabar Nasranis considered newly converted Latin Christians (usually fishermen) to be untouchables.

· The most extreme form of untouchability in all of India was practised in Kerala.

A Nair was expected to instantly cut down a Mucua, thiyya who presumed to defile him by touching his person; and a similar fate awaited a slave, who did not turn out of the road as a Nair passed" According to Kerala tradition the Dalits were forced to maintain a distance of 64 feet from Savarnas as they were thought to pollute them. Other castes like Nayadis, Kanisans and Mukkuvans were forbidden within 72 feet, 32 feet and 24 feet respectively from Savarnas.

When British banned the right of the Nairs to carry swords with them, caste related violence steeply decreased. The observance of untouchability vanished consequent to the movements of social reforms, especially the one initiated by Sree Narayana zGuru. Temple Entry Proclamation of the Raja of Travancore effective by put a end to the system of untouchability in South Kerala.

5.3.1. Mannappedi/Pulappedi

Mannappedi or Pulappedi was a custom which existed until 17th century. An upper caste woman could lose her caste if any male from the castes like Pulayan, Parayan or Mannan happened to see her or touch her by any means. Then she would be expelled from the caste or had to move with the "low caste" person or will be under discretion of the elders to decide. This would apply especially on the night of a specific day that fell in the month of Karkatakam (roughly corresponding to the dates 15 July to 15 August) in the Gregorian calendar. Given the social and economic status of lower caste people of that era, it is believed that this practice could not be perpetuated without social sanction, and definitely not without the connivance and/ or tacit support of the men of upper castes. Thus, the men folk used this in the garb of a custom to stifle the freedom or rights of women belonging to upper castes. Another view of the practice is that it was a route provided by tradition to the oppressed Pulayan class for registering their intentions of revenge as a symbolic act . The practice was abolished by the then Kerala Varma in 1696 after which he had to face the ire of the royal servants.

5.4. Untouchability in Other Regions

When the constitution of India outlawed untouchability in 1950 many national leaders believed that a centuries old practice had been brought to an end. But now nearly 60 years later there is no total success of the statutory measure. Millions of Dalits across the country who account for roughly 1/5th of the population continue to suffer birth-based discrimination and humiliation. In states like Tamil Nadu which boasts a long history of reformist movements is no exception.Infact untouchability has not only survived the constitutional ban but taken new avatars in many parts of the state. Caste-based discrimination has often led to violence, leaving hundreds of the disadvantaged people in distress particularly in the 1990s.

Over 80 forms of untouchability have been identified, many of which are apparently free India's additions to the list. From time immemorial Dalits have been deprived of their right to education and the right to possess land and other forms of property. Left with nothing but their physical labor to earn their livelihood they have all along been forced to do the toughest and most menial jobs for survival.

Apart from the denial of access to public roads,tanks,temples and burial/cremation grounds there are other forms of untouchability.Segregation of Dalits is seen almost everywhere in Tamil Nadu's villages. But nothing can perhaps beat the high wall 500 meters long that has been built at Uthapuram in Madurai district as a barrier between Dalits and caste Hindus.

While untouchability is still rampant and is taking new forms particularly in villages, the constitutional ban and compulsions of modernity and development have to some extent blunted its rigor. Rail transport has been unifying forces in society. Yet the Railways have been among the worst offenders in respect of the law against manual scavenging.Dalits constitute a significant portion of its workforce of manual scavengers along railway lines.

Although all state governments claim that they have abolished manual scavenging reports reveal that this practice is very much alive in many places. Postmen have also been found to practice untouchability.A study conducted in Tamil Nadu noted that in two villages in Madurai district postmen did not deliver postal articles to

Dalit addressees.Dalits were required to collect the articles at the post office. There are also road transport related violations of the law against untouchability.Among them is the unwritten rule that gives caste Hindus priority over Dalits in boarding buses in many areas, buses not stopping in Dalit areas, transport employees picking quarrels with Dalit passengers without provocation and Dalits not being allowed to use bus shelters. State government still follows a traditional procedure of making announcements in villages by beating a drum and for that they deploy Dalits.

Worse still are the roles of schools and teachers in perpetuating untouchability and sowing the seeds of caste-related discrimination in young minds. The Dalit children are often discouraged by teachers and fellow students belonging to caste Hindu social groups. In many schools Dalit pupils were not allowed to share water with caste Hindus. To punish an erring or naughty Dalit boy teachers scold him by calling him by his caste name. If the teacher decides that the boy needed a beating as punishment the task was assigned to another Dalit boy. There is also systematic refusal of admission to Dalits in certain schools particularly at the plus two levels.

In some villages during the temple festivals Dalits are supposed to stay hidden from caste Hindus. The two-tumbler system under which Dalits and non-Dalits are served tea in different vessels is still prevalent in some teashops. In some eateries they are compelled to sit on the floor.

References

Anandan, T.R. "The Failure of Anti-Caste Movements." The Hindu, 24 July, 2001. Reg. ed.: OB-1.

Das, Ashol. "Untouchability not an issue in Telengana." Hindustan Times 9 July, 2001 Reg. ed.: 9.

Forster, E.M. *A Passage To India*. San Diego, A Harvest Book/Harcourt, 1924.

Hazari. *Untouchable: The Autobiography of The Indian Outcaste*. New York: Fredrick A. Praeger, 1951.

Sidney, Bashiruddin Ahmed, and Anil Bhatt. *Caste, Race, and Politics: A Comparative Study of India And The United States*. Beverly Hills: Sage Publications, Inc., 1971.

6

Caste Inequalities among Muslims and Christians

A large and varied body of social scientific literature establishes a fact that is now largely taken for granted, namely that like other religious communities, Muslims and Christians in India are heterogenous rather than monolithically homogenous communities. The most prominent divisions and differences have to do with the presence of multiple sects and denominations among both Muslims and Christians, with the Shia-Sunni or the Catholic- Protestant divide being the best known. However, caste refers to an institution of adifferent sort, one which would generally be expected to reproduce itself across and within denominational or sectarian boundaries. The specific notion of caste involved here is that of *jati* rather than *varna*. While scholars differ on the exact relationship between these two categories, it is generally agreed that the latter refers to an overarching pan-Indian division between the four major groupings of castes (the so called *chatur-varna:* brahman, kshatriya, vaishya and shudra), whereas jati is a more local category indicating an endogamous group with a strong network of social and kinship ties.

Common social-anthropological definitions of caste include the following features:

1. A caste is a *closed, ascriptive group* whose membership is decided by birth and is hereditary (i.e., one inherits the caste of one's parents); mandatory (i.e., it is not a matter of choice); and unalterable (i.e. caste identity cannot be changed).

2. Castes impose *rules of conduct* on their members, the most prominent being those on marriage (endogamy, or marriage within the caste group, is a common requirement); social interaction (including specially the sharing of food and water); and occupation (castes were traditionally restricted to particular occupations, though these restrictions are much weaker now than they used to be).
3. Castes are part of a *system* in which they are both strictly separated and closely integrated in a hierarchy determined, in the original Hindu case, by notions of graded ritual purity or pollution. This hierarchy is supposed to be authorized by Hindu religious scriptures, though the precise nature and extent of this authority are matters of debate. Thus, taken as components of a system, castes are non-competing, interdependent but strictly hierarchized groups.

Before we ask whether caste in this definitional sense exists among Muslims and Christians in India, it should be noted that the above definition is an ideal typical construct that rarely exists in reality. Even among Hindus, there is considerable regional and temporal variation in the concrete, living forms of caste, which correspond only roughly to the theoretical model. The effective question therefore is not whether some classic definition of caste can be found on the ground, but whether caste-like groups, or social divisions displaying a significant proportion of these features (albeit in modified form) are present in Muslim and Christian society today.

When asked in this form, there is an overwhelming consensus on the answer – scholars are almost unanimous in their opinion that caste-like divisions exist among Muslims and Christians in India. But while this fact itself is beyond debate, there is some variation ofopinion on the issues of the origins and the precise nature of caste among Muslims and Christians. On the whole, there seems to be more of a debate with regard to Muslim society than Christian society. In the latter, it is generally agreed that caste tends to survive the process of conversion, so that Christian communities reproduce the caste structure prevalent in Hindu society, at least in its broad features if not in exact detail. In the case of Muslims, scholars have differing interpretations of the degree to which caste is:

a) a purely Hindu 'survival' in post-conversion communities;

b) a 'learnt' or newly reproduced institution due to the influence of surrounding Hindu society; and

c) the product and expression of tendencies internal to Islam.

What precisely is caste-like about the caste-analogues found in Muslim and Christian society? The answer to this question is more complicated because of considerable variation in the relative importance of different aspects and features of caste in different communities and regions. While there will always be exceptions in particular cases, it is possible to arrive at the following general order of caste features, beginning with the most universal aspects found everywhere, to the most differentiated aspects on which there is too much variation to permit easy generalisation:

1. Hereditary membership conferred by birth.
2. Endogamy, usually strictly observed, but with 'hard' and 'soft' divisions.
3. Social segregation, i.e., the exclusion of lower by higher all along the hierarchy.
4. Occupational segregation and economic differentiation.
5. Specific practices of untouchability and other forms of exclusion against Dalits.
6. Belief in notions of ritual purity and pollution as the basis for caste divisions.

Of these six broad features of caste, the first two may be safely said to be universally present in Muslim and Christian society in India. The simplest way of stating this fact is to say that in India, one is never 'just' a Muslim or a Christian.

The Muslim and Christian communities – like other religious communities in India – are always further subdivided into caste-like social groups to which individuals belong. Membership in these groups is determined by birth and is taken to be hereditary, so that one's parentage is always a salient feature of one's community identity. Further, the pattern of marriage relations usually follows these caste-like divisions strictly, though the degree to which this is enforced tends to vary. In general, the strictest taboos are invariably directed at the

Dalitcommunities or those identified as such. The Dalit castes cannot marry outside their boundaries because none of the other caste groups will consent to such relations. Violations of this prohibition usually invite severe social sanctions, including in most cases the ex-communication of the erring family of the higher caste.

Apart from the Dalit—Non-Dalit divide which is always a 'hard' boundary, other boundaries are 'softer' to a greater or lesser degree. This means that prohibitions on inter-marriage across non-Dalit caste groups may or may not invite severe social sanction. Although such marriages are discouraged, they tend to be tolerated, particularly if they occur within the same broad class or economic status grouping.

Thus, it can be said that there is hardly any variation in these two features of caste grouping, so that they may be considered to be a routinely present aspect of Indian Muslim or Christian identity as it exists in practice.

The next two features, namely social segregation along caste lines, and hierarchization in economic and occupational terms, are also universally present, but with significant variations in the nature and extent of such hierarchical segregation. The social scientific literature of the last four decades shows that caste-like identities among Muslims and Christians are generally closely aligned with larger social, economic and political hierarchies despite local differences. Social segregation and economic hierarchies *always* follow the caste hierarchy – i.e., the 'lowest' castes are always the most excluded and most resource-poor; there is never an instance where the hierarchies are reversed or even disturbed substantially.

What can and does vary greatly, however, the distance that separates different caste groups – in some contexts the distance separating the lowest from the highest may be relatively small, in other cases quite large. It is also possible for some sections or small portions of a particular caste grouping to be at roughly the same level as lower or higher groups, but this rarely happens for the group as a whole or even for a substantial portion of the group. Thus, for example, while it is possible for some sections of the upper castes to be quite poor, or for a few families or clans among the lower castes to be quite wealthy, these remain exceptions to the general rule.

The most common segregation practices, apart from endogamy, are those involving differential access to community resources, including specifically religion-related areas. Thus, access to collective worship may be actively denied to the lowest castes, or may only be granted on differential terms. Dalit Christians generally tend to have separate churches and are served by different priests. In the case of Muslim Dalits, actual exclusion is unusual (though not unknown), but is at the cost of an unambiguously inferior status expressed through such practices as having to sit in the back, not being allowed to sit in front of (or to precede) the upper castes, and so on.

Not surprisingly, social segregation maps quite directly on to economic status hierarchies. The lower and specially the lowest caste groups among both Christians and specially Muslims find themselves left out of the networks that provide social capital, which in turn can yield opportunities for accumulating economic capital.Once again the patterning of difference is very stable and follows caste hierarchy, though the extent of difference between high and low may vary.

The fifth aspect of caste, specific practices of untouchability, are subject to great variation. In some instances, as with Christian communities in south India and specially Kerala, these practices seem to be virtually identical with Hindu practice. In other instances, the specific belief in or practice of untouchability may be absent, although the Dalit castes are marked out in every other way.

It is not useful to ask only whether untouchability of a particular sort is practiced or not – it is much more important to ask about the concrete nature of inter-caste relations. So, although there is a lot of variation with regard to the practice of untouchability, and many Muslim and Christian communities in many regions do not seem to have this institution, it is still true nevertheless that Dalits in these communities are at the receiving end of a variety of discriminatory and derogatory practices, as well as being at the bottom of the material status hierarchy.

Finally, beliefs about ritual purity and pollution are the most variable. They are present in some communities, but not in most; even where they are present, they are subject to change like all other aspects of society. However, whether these beliefs are present or absent, they do not seem to make very much difference to the material and social condition of Dalits vis-à-vis non-Dalits.

6.1. Implications of Caste for Dalit Muslims and Dalit Christians

If caste is a reality for Indian Muslims and Christians, then does caste impose the same disabilities on Dalit Christians and Dalit Muslims as are known to be imposed on Dalits of other religions? Before one proceeds to answer this question in detail, one unmistakable conclusion needs to be stressed. Regardless of whether and to what extent the caste disabilities of Dalit Muslims and Dalit Christians resemble those of Hindu or other Dalits, this survey of social scientific literature establishes beyond doubt that, compared to other castes, Dalits suffer the most from their caste identity. Thus, whatever the nature and extent of the disabilities imposed by caste on Muslims and Christians, it is beyond debate that such disabilities are imposed most severely on Dalit Muslims and Dalit Christians. In short, if Muslims and Christians in India 'have' caste, then it is clear that Dalit Muslims and Dalit Christians have it the most.

To begin a detailed consideration of this question it is necessary to go back to the earliest attempts to identify the 'depressed classes' as they were known in the early twentieth century. The most significant such effort is no doubt that of the 1931 Census.

This effort is all the more important since it became, in effect, the basis for the inclusion of particular Tribes and Castes in the Schedules drawn up as part of the Government of India Act of 1935 which inaugurated the 'reservations' policy in India. The list of questions created by the then Census Commissioner (and later professor of anthropology at Cambridge) Sir J.H. Hutton are not necessarily the best or the most decisive. As scholars including Lelah Dushkin and Marc Galanter have shown, some of these questions don't have clear answers, and some others which can be easily answered are not very helpful. If this were to be used a standard for identifying Dalits today, there would be considerable variation even among Hindu castes long recognised as Dalits, leave alone among other religious communities. But the basic feature of this list, namely various forms of religious and social exclusion and discrimination, would certainly be found among Muslims and Christians.

Despite the presence of larger groupings like 'Ashraf' and 'Ajlaf', what really matters in everyday social life and in interaction with other groups, both within the Muslim community as well as with members of other communities, is the caste-analogue. In terms of social significance, therefore, the caste-analogue matters more than other identities which may also be used.

Compared to Muslims, there is much less ambiguity about caste practices amongs Indian Christians.

6.2. Caste-Analogues in Indian Muslim Society

Recent empirical sociological literature suggests that the conception of Muslim society as divided into two broad categories, 'ashraf' and 'ajlaf', is a gross over-simplification of the existing reality.

Social stratification among Muslims in any local area or community presents a highly complex picture. In any local area or community the Muslim population is divided into a number of social groups which are analogous to castes among Hindus. These caste-analogues are small, and they are named groups of persons characterised by endogamy, hereditary membership, and a specific style of life, which sometimes includes the pursuit by tradition of a particular occupation and is usually associated with a more or less distinct ritual status in a hierarchical system.

Persons belonging to different caste-analogues are to some extent expected to behave differently and to have different values and ideals. The 'ashraf-ajlaf' dichotomy presents a convenient set of values to people, and people do fit themselves into this frame. But the real units of social stratification are the caste-analogues, and the day-to-day relationships between different individuals in any local community are determined by their membership of the caste-analogue rather than by the broad categories. In the study of Muslim social stratification, therefore, it is the caste-analogue which constitutes a more significant analytical unit.

6.3. Caste-based Inequalities

This section discusses the available macro-statistical data on caste inequalities among Muslims and Christians in India. The basic questions around which the data are organised remain the same: how do Dalit Muslims and Christians compare with (a) their own community members of different castes; and (b) Dalits of other religious communities? The main source of the data used here is the National Sample Survey Organisation's most recent five-yearly survey from its 61st Round, canvassed in 2004-05. These data are the latest available at the national level, and are widely used by social scientists and policy makers in a variety of contexts.

For obvious reasons state institutions are the most important sources of social statistics all around the world. Given this fact, it follows that social groups which are not recognized by the state tend to become statistically 'invisible', for the state organs that routinely collect data – the Census, other government departments and official survey organisations – do not record information on such groups. This is in fact the most discouraging aspect of studying groups like Dalit Muslims and Christians. The legal definition of 'Scheduled Castes' was originally restricted to those professing the Hindu faith, and though it was later extended to those professing Sikhism (in 1956) and Buddhism (in 1990), Muslims and Christians continue to be excluded and cannot be classified as Scheduled Castes regardless of their caste status.

However, despite receiving no official recognition at the central level, Dalit (and backward caste) Muslims and Christians have been recognised to varying degrees and in different ways by many state governments. In fact, as many as 12 major states accord recognition to sections of their Muslim and Christian populations within the Other Backward Classes (OBC) category.

Ironically, this recognition creates further problems in the context of national level surveys where information on DMs and DCs may be available. DMs and DCs may return themselves as OBCs because they are recognised as such in their state and region. This makes it virtually certain that the numbers of DMs and DCs as revealed by caste-religion crosstabulations of NSSO data are significantly understated, without any reliable method of being able to estimate the extent of such underestimation. This problem seems to be particularly acute in the case of DCs, as discussed below.

Apart from this, DMs and DCs also run into purely statistical problems associated with sample surveys. Because they are such a small proportion of the population, they are naturally a small proportion of the sample as well, even of a large one such as that of the NSSO's big five-yearly surveys. This means that it is virtually impossible to do any disaggregated analyses on DMs and DCs due to the sample size being unacceptably small and thus statistically unstable. Hence this chapter is restricted to national level analyses, though the usual division into the rural and urban sectors is maintained throughout. For this reason no regional, gender- or occupation-specific analyses has been attempted.

Tables 6.1 and 6.2 show the distribution of the NSSO 61st Round sample for the rural and urban sectors respectively. These are the unweighted or 'raw' sample sizes – they represent the actual number of households surveyed. Due the fact that the sample involves several stages (including administrative and other regions of dissimilar size) and strata (again not of uniform size), each 'raw' sample household stands for or 'represents' differing numbers of households in the population.

To take care of this variation, each household (and individual) is associated with a sampling 'weight' which adjusts the statistical 'contribution' of the household to its proper representative extent. The actual (raw) number of Muslim sample households that claimed to belong to the SC category (presumably on caste grounds, since they are not officially recognized as such) are 93 and 59 respectively. Similarly, 155 rural and 123 urban Christian households also claimed SC status. The bulk of the analysis in this chapter is based, ultimately, on data from these households where DMs and DCs are concerned, and more generally, on the 79,235 rural and 45,352 urban households for whom both caste and religion data are available.

Just how many DMs and DCs are there in India? There are no authoritative estimates available for the reasons mentioned above. But if some rough estimates are to be constructed, they must begin with the NSSO data. The general procedure that is followed here is to ascertain the NSSO shares or *proportions* and to apply these proportions to the *population totals* obtained from the Census.

The NSSO's estimate of the population shares of the SCs for both rural and urban India exceeds the Census figures by well over three percentage points. This is broadly in keeping with the past trend as the NSSO estimates have generally tended to be higher than the Census, specially for this category.

Table 6.1. Number of Sample Households by Caste and Religion NSSO 61st Round, Rural India, 2004-05

Caste / Religion	Scheduled Tribes	Scheduled Castes	Other Backward Classes	Upper Castes	All Castes Values	Missing	Grand Total
Hindu	6,845	12,704	26,011	15,149	60,709	32	60,741
Muslim	115	93	3,011	5,261	8,480	6	8,486
Christian	4,203	155	494	787	5,639	16	5,655
Sikh	17	634	493	1,076	2,220	1	2,221
Buddhist	533	336	27	105	1,001	1	1,002
Others	978	7	78	123	1,186	6	1,192
All Religions	12,691	13,929	30,114	22,501	79,235	—	—
Missing Values	3	0	2	1	—	3	9
Grand Total	12,694	13,929	30,116	22,502	—	65	79,306

Table 6.2. Number of Sample Households by Caste and Religion NSSO 61st Round, Urban India, 2004-05

Caste Religion	Scheduled Tribes	Scheduled Castes	Other Backward Classes	Upper Castes	All Castes Values	Missing	Grand Total
Hindu	1,314	5,735	13,172	14,092	*34,313*	12	34,325
Muslim	161	59	2,395	3,683	*6,298*	1	6,299
Christian	1,788	123	419	586	*2,916*	4	2,920
Sikh	4	139	177	496	*816*	0	816
Buddhist	66	292	3	16	*377*	0	377
Others	176	7	66	383	*632*	4	636
All Religions	*3,509*	*6,355*	*16,232*	*19,256*	*45,352*	—	—
Missing Values	0	0	0	1	—	0	1
Grand Total	3,509	6,355	16,232	19,257	—	21	45,374

While the scholarly debate on this continues, it is reasonable to point out that this discrepancy could be due as much to conservatism on the part of the Census as to sampling errors in the NSSO survey, or non-sampling errors induced by misreporting due to confusion about the official category of the Scheduled Castes.

In passing that Muslims on the whole tend to be underestimated the most – by almost half a percentage point in rural and a little less than one point in urban India. Christians are also marginally underestimated, more so in urban India, by about one-third of one percent. So all in all, the apparent overestimation –relative to the Census figures – of Dalits is the most significant point to be kept in mind.

Moving on to the next step in estimating the population of DMs and DCs, Tables 6.3 and Table 6.4 show the NSSO estimates of the caste composition of different religious communities in rural and urban India. It can be seen right away that DMs are a very tiny proportion of the Muslim population, being just over half of one percent in both rural and urban India.

DMs are thus by far the least numerous Dalits of any religious community, specially if one sets aside the anomalous "Others" category (consisting of Jains, Zoroastrians, other religions and persons with no religion). Muslims also seem to have by far the largest proportion of 'Upper' castes. (as in the many others to follow, the term 'Upper' caste (also abbreviated as UC) refers to those who do not belong to the ST, SC or OBC categories; they are thus identified residually, not positively through caste identification. However, it is less misleading to refer to them as 'Upper' caste than to use the term 'Other' castes that is used in the official documents.) Compared to Muslims, Christians seem to have a much larger proportion of Dalits – around 10%, with a little less in rural and a little more in urban India.

These figures are almost universally believed to be gross underestimates of the true proportion of Dalits among Indian Christians. Most scholars and activists put the proportion at between 50 and 75% percent of all Indian Christians, although it is not possible to corroborate these claims in any decisive manner due to the difficulty of the category being officially unrecognized. Since the lower bound of such 'guesstimates' seems to be 50%, it should be kept in mind that the proportion (and therefore also the number) of DCs could be at least five times what the NSSO estimates show it to be.

Table 6.3. Estimated Caste Composition of Religions, Rural India, 2004-05

Religious Communities	Scheduled Tribes	Scheduled Castes	Other Backward Classes	Upper Castes	All Castes
Hindu	11.2	23.4	44.6	20.9	100.0
Muslim	0.5	0.6	39.7	59.2	100.0
Christian	38.9	9.4	20.9	30.8	100.0
Sikh	1.2	34.8	24.3	39.8	100.0
Buddhist	11.4	85.0	0.6	3.1	100.0
Others	72.9	2.0	4.2	20.9	100.0
All Religions	10.6	20.9	42.8	25.7	100.0

Table 6.4. Estimated Caste Composition of Religions, Urban India, 2004-05

Religious Communities	Scheduled Tribes	Scheduled Castes	Other Backward Classes	Upper Castes	All Castes
Hindu	3.0	18.2	36.4	42.4	100.0
Muslim	0.3	0.6	38.4	60.7	100.0
Christian	17.5	10.5	31.8	40.3	100.0
Sikh	0.1	15.2	18.6	66.2	100.0
Buddhist	1.7	97.0	0.3	1.0	100.0
Others	10.1	1.4	1.8	86.7	100.0
All Religions	2.9	15.7	35.6	45.8	100.0

Tables 6.5 and 6.6 show the shares of the major caste groups in the population of the main religions of India. They show that Dalits are overwhelmingly Hindu – more than 93% in rural and 90% in urban India. In fact, Dalits are the caste category with the highest proportion of Hindus, and the other religions contribute very small proportions. Within these the share of Muslim and Christian Dalits amounts to a miniscule 1.2% in rural and 2.3% in urban India. However, the share of DCs is about three times that of DMs in rural more than double in urban India.

Table 6.5. Estimated Religious Composition of Castes Rural India, 2004-05

Religious Communities	Scheduled Tribes	Scheduled Castes	Other Backward Classes	Upper Castes	All Castes
Hindu	88.3	93.4	87.3	68.0	83.7
Muslim	0.6	0.3	10.6	26.2	11.4
Christian	7.3	0.9	1.0	2.4	2.0
Sikh	0.2	3.2	1.1	3.0	2.0
Buddhist	0.6	2.2	0.0	0.1	0.5
Others	3.0	0.0	0.0	0.4	0.4
All Religions	100.0	100.0	100.0	100.0	100.0

Table 6.6. Estimated Religious Composition of Castes Urban India, 2004-05

Religious Communities	Scheduled Tribes	Scheduled Castes	Other Backward Classes	Upper Castes	All Castes
Hindu	79.9	90.3	79.3	71.9	77.6
Muslim	1.8	0.7	17.7	21.7	16.4
Christian	14.3	1.6	2.1	2.1	2.4
Sikh	0.1	1.6	0.9	2.4	1.7
Buddhist	0.5	5.7	0.0	0.0	0.9
Others	3.4	0.1	0.1	1.9	1.0
All Religions	100.0	100.0	100.0	100.0	100.0

DMs appear to be only about 8 lakhs in all, 5 in rural and 3 in urban India. DCs are almost four times the number of DMs at 23.5 lakhs, almost 15 lakhs in rural India and a little less than 9 lakhs in urban India. The figures for DCs are very likely to be substantial underestimates. Nevertheless, it should be noted that DMs and DCs are a very small part of the Indian Dalit population. Quite apart from the huge numbers of Hindu Dalits – over 18 crores – DMs and DCs are considerably smaller than even the Buddhists (over 71 lakhs) and Sikhs (almost 57 lakhs).

6.4. Material Status of Dalit Muslims and Christians

In keeping with the objectives set, the comparative analysis employs two main reference groups: a) the non-Dalit co-religionists of DMs and DCs; and b) Dalits of other religions, namely Hindus, Sikhs and Buddhists. How does the condition of the DMs and DCs compare with that of non-Dalit Muslims and Christians, and with non-Muslim and non-Christian Dalits? These are the basic questions addressed. Four main types of evidence are considered:

1) *Poverty profiles* of the different socio-religious groups with the main focus on DMs and DCs. Evidence of this sort mainly involves looking at the *distribution of the population of a group across the economic spectrum*. What proportion of each group is very poor, and what proportion is affluent? How do these proportions compare with the group's share in the total population – i.e., is the community over-represented or underrepresented among the rich or the poor? Clearly, a group that has larger proportions in poverty and lower proportions among the affluent is considered to be worse off and vice versa. The main data on which this kind of evidence relies is the monthly percapita consumption expenditure data collected by the NSSO. This is the principal source for determining poverty levels and is extensively utilised in scholarly literature and in designing and evaluating developmental policies.

2) *Average Consumption Levels* are the second set of criteria considered. Here the focus is not so much on the proportion of population falling in particular class segments, but on the *absolute levels of average consumption*. This involves looking at the levels of monthly percapita consumption expenditure (henceforth MPCE), whether in terms of averages like the median, or a broader view profiling the entire distribution via selected percentiles of MPCE.

3) *Occupational Structure* is the third dimension of comparison. This provides a rough sense of the economic condition of a social group. In both the rural and urban sectors, there are some occupational categories that indicate relatively higher economic status than others; so comparing the proportions of population of each group that fall in these categories tells us about their relative

condition. For rural India, the NSSO provides a broad classification of households into the following types: a) self-employed in agriculture; b) agricultural labour; c) other labour; d) self-employed in non-agricultural activities; and e) others, which is obviously a residual category. For urban India, the categories provided are: a) self-employed; b) regular wage or salaried employment; c) casual labour; and d) others.

All other things being equal, it is generally true that households in the 'self-employed in agriculture' category are much better off than households in the 'agricultural labour category. The former usually implies landownership or at least some sort of stable access to land, while the latter usually indicates landless labour. Similarly, in the urban sector, the category 'regular wage or salaried employment' is clearly a better place to be than 'casual labour'. Comparing the proportions of households in different social groups that are in these 'better' or 'worse' occupational groupings gives us some sense of their relative status.

4) *Educational Status* is the final criterion for comparison. This requires little explanation. The NSSO provides data on the levels of general education ranging from 'not literate' to 'diploma holder, graduate, or above', with primary, secondary and higher secondary school levels in between. Unlike the occupational category criterion, which has the household as its unit, the unit for education is the person. This data is available from the Employment and Unemployment survey (Schedule 10.0) of the NSSO survey. Comparisons of proportions of population at different educational levels provides one more way of assessing the relative status of different social groups.

6.4.1. Comparative Poverty Profiles

This section considers relative proportions of the population that are in different economic classes as defined by MPCE. The focus is on the bottom and the top ends of the economic spectrum. The bottom is defined by the official Poverty Line, which represents the minimum level of consumption expenditure needed to meet basic nutritional norms. As is well known, the PL is a very conservative and strict measure of poverty since it specifies what is almost a biological minimum for survival The top of the economic spectrum is defined by the level of MPCE that represents the top five percent (or roughly the 95th percentile) of the national population (including all castes and religions for each sector).

The top 5% level may seem rather a high level to take, but this is done to offset the fact that consumption expenditure severely underestimates inequality. Because MPCE does not take account of savings, investments or accumulated wealth, it tends to understate the actual income of the rich (who spend a relatively small fraction of what they actually earn) and overstate the income of the poor (who may actually be forced to spend more than they earn by incurring debt).

The MPCE levels of the top are thus relatively low levels and they seem to include a much larger proportion of the population than the category intuitively suggests. Thus, for example, Rs. 2500 is the 'top 5%' level of MPCE for urban India. This implies a household of 5 with a monthly expenditure of about Rs. 12,500 at 2004-05 prices! It is difficult to think of such a household as being really rich – but the NSSO data suggest that it belongs in the top 5% of the class spectrum of urban India. That is why taking the top 5% may not be as restrictive as it appears at first.

Tables 6.7 and 6.8 provide data on the proportion of population of Dalits belonging to different religions that falls in different economic classes along the spectrum of MPCE. Five size classes of MPCE are shown, ranging from the Below Poverty Line or BPL category right up to an MPCE of Rs.1200 for rural and Rs. 2,500 for urban India.

Table 6.7. Estimated Class Composition of Dalits by Religion Rural India, 2004-05

Religious	MONTHLY PERCAPITA CONSUMPTION EXPENDITURE CLASSES					All
Community	Below PL	Rs.357–450	451–650	651–1200	Rs.1200 +	Classes
Hindu	37.7	23.6	25.0	11.7	2.0	100.0
Muslim	39.6	15.8	37.1	4.9	2.6	100.0
Christian	30.1	33.5	14.0	16.4	6.1	100.0
Sikh	7.6	19.1	41.2	28.5	3.6	100.0
Buddhist	45.9	21.4	23.7	6.6	2.5	100.0
All Dalits	36.8	23.5	25.4	12.2	2.1	'00.0

Table 6.8. Estimated Class Composition of Dalits by Religion Urban India, 2004-05

Religious Community	MONTHLY PERCAPITA CONSUMPTION EXPENDITURE CLASSES Below PL	Rs.357–450	451–650	651–1200	Rs.1200 +	All Classes
Hindu	40.9	28.3	21.2	8.1	1.6	100.0
Muslim	46.8	33.1	9.8	10.3	0.0	100.0
Christian	32.3	30.9	22.0	12.7	2.1	100.0
Sikh	24.8	39.6	20.1	12.3	3.2	100.0
Buddhist	28.9	28.1	28.4	13.1	1.6	100.0
All Dalits	39.8	28.5	21.5	8.6	1.6	100.0

In rural India, the Dalit Sikhs are the only group that is significantly better off than other Dalits. Less than 8% of Dalit Sikhs are in the BPL category compared to at least 30% of more for all others. Buddhists are the worst off, followed by DMs at nearly 40%. After Sikhs, DCs are the next best though they have a BPL rate of over 30%. At the other end of the spectrum, it is the DCs that are best off with about 6% in the Rs.1200 & above category. DMs do slightly better than Hindu dalits, but the difference is not significant. Thus, DCs in rural India have substantial numbers of poor, but they also have a small proportion in the affluent category. DMs have more in the poor and less in the affluent category than DCs, but they are broadly comparable to all other dalits except Sikhs.

DMs are by far the worst off among urban dalits. About 47% of them are in the BPL category – significantly more than Hindu dalits who are the next at about 41%. But the really striking fact is that there seem to be almost no DMs at all in the affluent category, so much so that they don't register as a significant proportion of population. DCs are better off than DMs and all other groups except the Sikhs, who are once again the best off among urban dalits.

6.5. Judicial Perspectives on the Status of Muslims and Christian Dalits

Judicial perspectives on the status of DMs and DCs have been shaped by three main considerations:

1) the Presidential Order of 1950 (and its subsequent amendments);
2) the caste status of converts from Hinduism;
3) the specific grounds on which social groups may be included in the SC list, including questions about the nature and quantum of the admissible evidence in this regard.

6.5.1. Evolution of Judicial Perspectives

In the year 1950, the president of India issued the "Constitution (Scheduled Castes) Order, 1950" specifying the castes to be recognised as the Scheduled Castes by exercising the authority conferred on him under the article 341(1) of the Constitution India. The third paragraph of the order however qualifies that "notwithstanding anything contained in para 2, no person who professes a religion different from Hinduism shall be deemed to be a member of the Scheduled Castes".

Subsequent amendments to the 1950 Presidential Order in 1956 and 1990 provided for the inclusion of Sikhs and Buddhists respectively within the Scheduled Caste category to avail the benefits of reservation. The Constitution, however, does not recognise SC converts to Islam and Christianity as eligible for benefits of affirmative action and this has been the site of struggle for Dalit Muslims and Christians who have challenged the constitutional validity of para 3 of the 1950 order. The main plank of this argument is that denial of SC status to DMs and DCs constitutes a violation of Articles 14 (equality before the law); 15 (prohibition of discrimination on grounds of religion); and 25 (freedom to profess and practice any religion) of the Constitution.

6.5.2. The Caste Status of Converts

The original rationale for including only Hindu castes in the SC list (as per the first such list prepared in 1936 by J.H. Hutton, the Census Commissioner for the 1931 Census) was directly linked to the practice of untouchability and other caste sanctions against the lowest castes. Since caste as an institution was said to be native to Hinduism, not beingpart of the scripture or core beliefs of any other religion, only Hindu Dalits qualified to be designated as SCs. However, the later extension of this designation to Sikhs and then to Neo-Buddhists seems to have been justified on the grounds that these groups were recent converts, and their caste was still the predominant aspect of their social identity. In fact, a few Sikh castes (Mazhabis, Ramdasias, Kabirpanthis and Sikligars) had been included even in the first post-Independence version of the SC lists in the 1950 Presidential Order. The remaining Dalit Sikh castes were added in 1956.

The Courts seem to have been quite willing to concede the point that caste survives conversion, and that despite professing faith in a religion which has no scriptural sanction for caste distinctions, may continue to be identified and treated as a member of the original caste. While they have rejected the claim that caste may be acquired by marriage, they have allowed that it is retained despite conversion and re-conversion. So the caste status of persons who have converted to other religions and are no longer practising Hindus, and even of those who were born as non-Hindus and never professed the Hindu faith, is not at issue in the courts.

6.5.3. Criteria and Standards of Evidence

These remain the most contentious issues. The extension of SC status to DMs and DCs appears to hinge on the question of evidence according to the crucial *Soosai* case. As Justice Pathak says in his judgement in this case, 'it is not sufficient to show that the same caste continues after conversion. It is necessary to establish further that the disabilities and handicaps suffered from such caste membership in the social order of its origin –Hinduism – continue in their oppressive severity in the new environment of a different religious community.' This distinction is related to the one that is analysed with admirable clarity by Marc Galanter, namely the distinction between caste as a unit designating a portion of the population (that which is to be measured) and as an indicator of status (measuring rod).

Justice Pathak here appears to be assenting to the use of caste as a community unit (continuance of same identity after conversion) but questioning its use as a status marker. The contention here is that while castes (in the sense of distinct communities) may exist, this fact, which identifies a group as belonging to a particularl caste, does not by itself allow us to come to any conclusion regarding the status of this caste relative to others. Relative status needs to be established independently of (or in addition to) the mere fact of belonging to a particular community. The same judgement complains about the 'cursory' evidence placed before it, and about the absence of any 'authoritative and detailed' study on the condition of the DCs. It is also reiterated that in such cases the onus of proof is on the party that is alleging arbitrariness, not on the state. However, there are two separate issues involved here that need to be carefully considered, both individually and together.

First, there is the question of how precisely caste disability is to be established. The response to this seems to be (though it is not explicitly spelt out as such) that the claimant group (in this case DMs and DCs) needs to establish, in addition to the fact of their caste identity, two further facts:

1) that they are worse off than their non-Dalit co-religionists, and that this is due to their caste status; and
2) that they are comparable in status to the Hindu, Sikh and Buddhist Dalits who are already recognised by the state as being in need of special consideration.

Whether both these criteria are to be explicitly invoked; and if so, the relative weight that is to be attached to each (if it is not equal) are questions that need to be settled at some point if the legal debate is to make any progress. The second issue concerns the standards of evidence on whatever set of criteria that is adopted. Here again there seem to be two issues involved. One is that of the quality of the evidence, that is, the standards of competence and levels of expertise that it demonstrates.

The second issue is that of the extent (or 'quantity') of the evidence and the related consideration of arriving at an overall judgement on a body of material that is bound to present a complex and heterogenous picture. Further clarity on these issues is perhaps only possible after the fact – that is, after a body of material is presented to the courts and they come to some judgement as to their worth on the above counts. It is certainly true that in the two decades since the *Soosai* case (the judgement for which was delivered in 1985) a lot more ethnographic and other empirical evidence has been accumulated on this issue.

Courts have been willing (specially in the earlier period rather than in more recent judgements) to rely on available social scientific studies, and have in fact done so without on their own whenever they have felt this material to be helpful. This is something that needs to be explicitly noted and addressed. It is encouraging to see that what has mattered for the courts is the actual empirical practices associated with caste rather than a simplistic references to belief systems or rigid rules of formal evidence. This willingness to consider competent evidence provides ample opportunities for further action on this front.

6.5.4. Legal Rationale for Special Treatment

The state may provide special treatment for the advancement of socially and educationally backward classes of citizens or for Scheduled castes and Scheduled tribes. The state to promote the educational and economic interests of the weaker sections of the people, and in particular SC's and ST's and protect them from social injustice and all forms of exploitation.

The object of Ar. 341(1) is to provide additional protection to the members of the scheduled castes, recognising the educational and economic backwardness from which they suffer.

Criteria for inclusion of any community in the list of scheduled castes is that such a community should suffer from extreme social, educational and economic backwardness arising out of traditional practices of Untouchability

6.5.5. Constitutional Issues

The range of constitutional issues arising from the demand of Dalit Christians and Muslims for inclusion with the Scheduled Caste category may be broadly summarisedunder two categories: (a) Position of those claiming SC status; and (b) Perspectives of the State on the issue concerned.

6.5.6. Demand for SC status

Social and educational backwardness persists even after conversion. State denies recognition of SC status only on the grounds that the concerned groups profess Islam and Christianity. In refusing SC status to Dalit Muslims and Christians the State violates ar. 14, 15 and 25 of the constitution that guarantees equality before the law and prohibits discrimination on grounds of religion.

Such benefits have been extended to converts from Hinduism to Sikhism and Buddhism even though both these religions, like Christianity and Islam, do not recognise the caste system. Therefore, the state discriminates on grounds of religion which is violative of the fundamental rights enshrined under the constitution.

6.5.7. Perspectives of the State

The criteria adopted for determining whether a community is eligible for inclusion in the list of SC's is extreme social, educational and economic backwardness arising out of traditional practices of Untouchability. Since caste system and practices of Untouchability are a feature of Hindu society, historically the system of special representations for SC's was evolved specifically in relation to the position of these castes in Hindu society who were affected by the practice of Untouchability. In conception Christianity is an egalitarian religion which does not recognise caste and is therefore antithetical to practices of Untouchability.

Lack of authoritative and detailed study on the nature and extent of social disabilities, including Untouchability prevalent in the Christian community in India. Studies available at the time the Supreme or other Courts dealt with this issue did not, in the opinion of the Court, constitute adequate evidence. Similarly, studies based on subjective responses of small sample of SC Christian converts do not conclusively show that their social and economic position is the result of persistence of Untouchability practices.

In case SC converts to Christianity are accorded the status of SCs, administrative difficulties would arise at the time of issuing caste certificates because of the difficulty, in many cases, of determining their pre-conversion caste standing. Thedifficulties in precise and objective determination of pre-conversion caste origin would open the floodgates for issuance of bogus SC certificates which is a cause for concern. In contrast, the nature of conversion to Buddhism has been different. Neo-Buddhists embraced Buddhism voluntarily at the call of

Dr Ambedkar in 1956 on account of social political imperatives. The original caste/community of such converts can be clearly determined.

6.5.8. Major Cases and the Judicial Reasoning Involved

1. *State of Kerala and another vs. Chandra Mohan (2004) 3 SCC 429:*

   Issue involved: The question before the Supreme Court was whether a person on conversion to another religion (here Christianity) continues to remain a member of his tribe.

   Judgement/Reasoning: The court rules that upon conversion a person may be governed by a different law but that does not in itself result in his loss of membership of the tribe, given that it is established that a person who has embraced another religion is still suffering from social disability and following the customs and traditions of the community to which he earlier belonged.

2. *Valsamma Paul (Mrs); v. Cochin University and Others, Kerala Public Service Commission v Dr. Kanjamma Alex and Another (1996) SC 3950. (Judgement was followed in 31 cases)*

   Issue Involved: Two posts of lecturers in Law Department of Cochin University were notified for recruitment, one of which was reserved for Latin Catholics (Backward Class Fishermen). The appellant, a Syrian Catholic (a Forward Class), having married a Latin Catholic, had applied for selection as a reserved candidate. The University selected her on that basis and accordingly appointed her against the reserved post. Her appointment was questioned by one Rani George by filing a writ petition, viz., OP No. 9450 of 1991 praying for a direction to the University to appoint her in place of the appellant to the said post.

   Judgement/Reasoning: The Full Bench in the judgment held that though the appellant was married according to the Canon law, the appellant, being a Syrian Catholic by birth, by marriage with a Latin Catholic (Backward Class), is not a member of that class nor canshe claim the status as a Backward Class by marriage. The special provisions under Articles 15(4) and 16(4) of the Constitution intended for the advancement of socially and educationally backward classes of citizens cannot be defeated by including candidates by alliance or by any other mode of joining the community. It would tantamount to making a mockery of the constitutional exercise of identification of socially and educationally backward classes of citizens. The appellant, having had the advantage of starting life as Syrian Catholic being born in a forward class, though she voluntarily married a Backward Class citizen, cannot claim the status as a Backward Class to avail of protective discrimination unless she further pleads and establishes that candidates like her suffered all the handicaps and disadvantages having been born as Backward Class citizens or Scheduled Castes or Scheduled Tribes. Mere recognition of and acceptance by the community after her marriage is not relevant for the purpose of availing of the benefit of Articles 16(4) and 15(4). Acceptance may be only for recognition as a legally wedded wife of a Backward Class citizen and nothing more.

3. *Soosai Vs Union of India and others (1985) (supp) SCC 590:*

Issue Involved: The Government of India set up a Special Central Assistance Scheme for the welfare of Scheduled Castes. Consequent to a proposal under this Scheme, allotment of bunk free of cost were to be made to cobblers by profession who worked on the roadside, by the State Government of Tamil Nadu. This Order specifically stated that persons belonging to the Scheduled Castes and who converted to Christianity were not eligible for assistance under the scheme. The petitioner, who was a Hindu belonging to the Adi-Dravida caste and on conversion to Christianity, continued as a member of that caste,-contended in his writ petition to the court that he had been denied the benefit of the welfare assistance intended for Scheduled Castes on the ground that he professes the Christian religion, and that such discrimination had been affected pursuant to the provision contained in paragraph 3 of the Constitution (Scheduled Castes) Order, 1950 and that the provision was constitutionally invalid as being violative of Articles 14 to 17.

Judgement/ Reasoning: The court held the following: "...it cannot be disputed that the caste system is a feature of the Hindu social structure. The division of the Hindu social order by reference at one time to professional or vocational occupation was moulded into a structural hierarchy which over the centuries crystallized into a stratificationwhere the place of the individual was determined by birth. Those who occupied the lowest rung of the social ladder were treated as existing beyond the periphery of civilised society, and were indeed not even "touchable". This social attitude committed those castes to severe social and economic disabilities and cultural and educational backwardness. Both history and latter day practice in Hindu society are heavy with evidence of this oppressive tyranny.

...The demand of the Sikhs that some of their backward sections, the Mazhabis, Ramdasias, Kabirpanthis and Sikligars, should be included in the list of Scheduled Castes was accepted on the basis that these sects were originally Scheduled Caste Hindus who had only recently been converted to the Sikh faith and had the same disabilities as Hindu SCs. It is quite evident that the President had before him all this material indicating that the depressed classes of the Hindu and the Sikh communities suffered from economic and social disabilities and cultural and educational backwardness so gross in character and degree that the members of those castes in the two communities called for the protection of the Constitutional provisions relating to the Scheduled Castes... To establish that paragraph 3 of the Constitution (Scheduled Castes) Order, 1950 discriminates against Christian members of the enumerated castes it must be shown that they suffer from a comparable depth of social and economic disabilities and cultural and educational backwardness and similar levels of degradation within the Christian community necessitating intervention by the State under the provisions of the Constitution. It is not sufficient to show that the same caste continues after conversion. It is necessary to establish further that the disabilities and handicaps suffered from such caste membership in the social order of its origin – Hinduism – continue in their oppressive severity in the new environment of a different religions community. References have been made in the material before us in the most cursory manner to the character and incidents of the castes within the Christian fold, but no authoritative and detailed study dealing with the present conditions of Christian society have been placed on the record in this case. It is, therefore, not possible to say that the President acted arbitrarily in the exercise of his judgment in enacting paragraph 3 of the Constitution (Scheduled Castes) order, 1950. It is now well established that when a violation of Article 14 or any of its related provisions is alleged, the burden rests on the petitioner to establish by clear and cogent evidence that the State has been guilty of arbitrary discrimination. *Issue Involved:* The following is not a judgement. However, opinion of the law court is sought on reservations with respect to two issues (a) How to identify backward classes for the purpose of reservation? (b) What should be the permissible extent of reservation? (A bench of 5 Judges have separately responded to the above questions) *Reasoning:* In this context, one such judge Chinnappa Reddy J. made a case for caste as the primary index for social backwardness. He argues that "…one must recognise the omnipresence of caste in the Indian society. So sadly and oppressively deep rooted is caste in our country that it has cut across even the barriers of religion. The caste system has penetrated other religious and dissentient Hindu sects to whom the practice of caste should be anathema and today we find that practitioners of other religious faiths are sometimes as rigid adherents to the systems of caste as the conservative Hindus. We find Christian Harijans, Christian Madars, Christian Reddys, Christian Kammas, Mujbi Sikhs etc."

5. *S. Anbalagan Vs B. Devarajan and others (1984) AIR SC 411 (Judgement followed in 7 cases)*

Issue Involved: The first respondent was elected to the Lok Sabha from a constituency which was reserved for the Scheduled Castes. The appellant challenged the election of the first respondent on the ground that he was not a member of the Scheduled Castes. The appellant urged that the parents and the sisters of the respondent were shown to be Christians and the respondent was born a Christian and there was no way he could acquire a caste and become an Adi Dravida on conversion to Hinduism.

Judgement/ Reasoning: The judge ruled in the above cases that precedents, particularly those from South India, clearly establish that no particular ceremony is prescribed for reconversion to Hinduism of a person who had earlier embraced another religion.

Unless the practice of the caste makes it necessary, no expiatory rites need to be performed and, ordinarily, he regains his caste unless the community does not accept him. In fact, it may not be accurate to say that he regains his caste; it may be more accurate to say that he never lost his caste in the first instance when he embraced another religion. The practice of caste however irrational it may appear to our reason and however repugnant it may appear to our moral and social sense is so deep-rooted in the Indian people that its mark does not seem to disappear on conversion to a differentreligion. If it disappears, it disappears only to reappear on reconversion. The mark of caste does not seem to really disappear even after some generations after conversion. In Andhra Pradesh and in Tamil Nadu, there are several thousands of Christian families whose forefathers became Christians and who, though they profess the Christian religion, nonetheless observe the practice of caste. There are Christian Reddies, Christian Kammas, Christian Nadars, Christian Adi Andhras, Christian Adi Dravidas and so on. The practice of their caste is so rigorous that there are intermarriages with Hindus of the same caste but not with Christians of another caste. Now, if such a Christian becomes a Hindu, surely he will revert to his original caste, if he had lost it at all. In fact this process goes on continuously in India and generation by generation lost sheep appear to return to the caste-fold and are once again assimilated in that fold. This appears to be particularly so in the case of members of the Scheduled Castes, who embrace other religions in their quest for liberation, but return to their old religion on finding that their disabilities have clung to them with great tenacity. We do not think that any different principle will apply to the case of conversion to Hinduism of a person whose forefathers had abandoned Hinduism and embraced another religion from the principle applicable to the case of reconversion to Hinduism of a person who himself had abandoned Hinduism and embraced another religion. ... Assuming that the parents and sisters of the first respondent had become Christians and that the first respondent himself had been baptised when he was seven months old, we see no difficulty in holding on the evidence in the case that the first respondent had long since reverted to Hinduism and to the Adi Dravida caste.

6. *Kailash Sonkar vs. Smt Maya Devi (1983) SC 295 (Judgement was followed in 16 cases)*

   Issue Involved: What happens if a member of a scheduled caste or tribe leaves his present fold (Hinduism) and embraces Christianity or Islam or any other religion – (a) does this amount to a complete loss of the original caste to which he belonged, and (b) if so, if he or his children choose to abjure the new religion and get reconverted to the old religion after performing the necessary rites and ceremonies, could the original caste revive?

   The question posed here arose and has formed the subject-matter of a large catena of decisions starting from the year 1861, traversing a period of about a century and a half,and culminating in a decision of this Court in the case of G. M. Arumugham v. S. Rajagopal.

   Judgement/Reasoning: The court held that on reconversion caste automatically revives.

   Even if a person was born of Christian parents, on voluntary reconversion caste revives. The court also ruled that the views of the community are not all that important and one cannot insist upon the acceptance of the community as a pre requisite for membership within the caste. The main test rather is the expression of a genuine intention of the reconvert to abjure his new religion and completely disassociate himself from it. He must express a genuine intention to adopt the customs and practices of the old fold.

7. *C.M Arumugam vs. S. Rajgopal (1976) 1 SCC 863*

   Issue Involved: The appellant and the first respondent have been opponents in the electoral battle since a long time. The constituency from which they have been standing as candidates is 68 KGF constituency for election to the Mysore Legislative Assembly. They opposed each other as candidates from this constituency in 1967 General Election to the Mysore Legislative Assembly. Now, the seat from this constituency was a seat reserved for scheduled castes and, therefore, only members of SCs could stand as candidates from this constituency. The appellant there upon filed Election Petition challenging the election of the first respondent on the ground that the first respondent was not an Adi Dravida professing Hindu religion at the date when he filed his nomination and was, therefore, not qualified to stand as a candidate for the reserved seat from 68 KGF constituency. The issue before the court was whether a person belonging to adi dravida caste before his conversion to Christianity, could on reconversion to Hinduism, once again become a member of his caste.

Judgement/ Reasoning: In this judgement the court shifts the burden of decision to the community itself. It argues that conversion from Hinduism to another religion may not result in loss of caste. However, ultimately it must depend on the structure of caste and its rules and regulations, whether a person would cease to belong to a caste on abjuring Hinduism. It cannot, therefore, be laid down as an absolute rule uniformly applicable in all cases that whenever a member of a caste is converted from Hinduism to Christianity, he loses his membership of the caste. It is true that ordinarily on conversion to Christianity, he would cease to be a member of the caste, but that is not an invariable rule. It would depend on the structure of the caste and its rules andregulations. There are castes, particularly in South India, where this consequence does not follow on conversion, since such castes comprise both Hindus and Christians. Whether Adi Dravida is a caste which falls within this category or not is question which would have to be determined on the evidence in this case. There is on the record evidence of Kakkan (PW 13), J. C. Adimoolam (RW 1) and K. P. Arumugam (RW 8), the last two being witnesses examined on behalf of the appellant, which shows that amongst Adi Dravidas, there are both Hindus and Christians and there are intermarriages between them. It would, therefore, prima facie seem that, on conversion to Christianity, the first respondent did not cease to belong to Adi Dravida caste. ...Further, the court held that having regard to its structure, as it has evolved over the years, a caste may consist not only of persons professing Hindu religion but also person professing some other religion as well, conversion from Hinduism to that other religion may not involve loss of caste, because even persons professing such other religion can be members of the caste. This might happen where caste is based on economic or occupational characteristics and not on religious identity or the cohesion of the caste as a social group is so strong that conversion into another religion does not operate to snap the bond between the convert and the social group. This is indeed not an infrequent phenomenon in South India where, in some of the castes, even after conversion to Christianity, a person is regarded as continuing to belong to the caste.

References

Gopalkrishnan, V.S. 2006. *Is it Time to Recognise Dalit Muslims and Dalit Christians*? www.chowk.com (Dec 30)

Soares-Prabhu, George S. J. 1992. 'The Table Fellowship of Jesus: It's Significance for Dalit Christians in India Today'. *Jeevadhara 22, 140-59.*

Syeda, Saiyidain Hameed. 2000. *Voice of the Voiceless: Status of Muslim Women in India*. New Delhi: National Commission for Women

Tharamangalam, J.1996. 'Caste among Christians in India' in M.N Srinivas (ed) *Caste: Its Twentieth Century Avatar*. 263-91, Delhi, Viking: Penguin India.

Thattumakal, John. 1983. *Caste and the Catholic Church in India*. Rome. Pontificia Universita Lateranense

Webster, John C.B. 1990. *The Dalit Christians: A History*. New Delhi: Indian Society for the Promotion of Christian Knowledge.

Wilfred, Felix. (1995). From the Dusty Soil: Contextual Reinterpretation of Christianity. Department of Christain Studies, University of Madras

Wilson, K. 1982. *The Twice Alienated: Culture of Dalit Christians*. Hyderabad: Booklinks Corporation.

7

Caste-based Violence

Organised violence directed against members of identified groups/communities has been a distinct feature of the Indian society for quite sometime. Though violence does take place in the process of change in many societies, and particularly so when radical alterations take place in the existing social and power relations, it usually does not choose its victims on the basis of birth in a given social entity. In India, however, this is precisely what has defined the character of violence in relation to certain groups. The country has witnessed increase in both caste and communal violence since independence which the processes of modernization have not abated. Rather, in some respects, it has been intensified by them.

While communal violence is a relatively recent phenomenon rooted in the events leading to partition, caste violence has a much longer history and a firmer anchorage. It also has the distinctiveness of being embedded in the social structure of the dominant community itself which lays down the norms of conduct between its more privileged groups and the subdued and subordinated segment. It is this age old caste relationship in Hindu Society which is getting disturbed by pressure of forces both from above and below. The frequency and intensity of violence is an offshoot of desperate attempts by the upper caste groups to protect their entrenched status against the process of disengagement and upward mobility among lower castes resulting from affirmative action of State Policy. The violence takes brutal forms and turns into acts of atrocities against a whole group of people, such as massacre, rape, burning of houses and through more subtle methods like social boycott, which are intended to block their access to basic necessities and services. This phenomenon has to be positioned in the larger perspective of State-Society dynamics in order to understand why it happens and how it can be checked.

7.1. Target of Caste Violence

The target of caste violence is largely the people belonging to the lowest rung in the hierarchy of Hindu social order, who are known as the 'untouchables', or Scheduled Castes bound to the rest of the caste society in immutable relationship of rights and obligations. The practice of "untouchability" characterises this relationship. The emergence of untouchability in the caste based social order has a complex history with little consensus or clarity on its origin. While some have attributed it to the growth of agricultural civilization in the country and the emergence of agricultural castes, who needed assured access to manual labour for agricultural operations, others have traced its genesis to expansionist phase of Indian civilization which led to the conquest of indigenous inhabitants and their consequent enslavement by the Aryans.

The 'shudras' in the social hierarchy towards the end of the Rig Vedic period represent these enslaved persons who were assigned inferior status, which was related to their birth in that community. Whatever be the explanation of its origin, the institutional structures which governed social conduct in the society are subsumed under the nomenclature of 'Caste System', which broadly represents a vertical arrangement of social division of the Hindu population into four major groups, known as 'Varnas'. At the top of this arrangement are the Brahmana, followed by 'Kshatriya' and 'Vaishya' 'Shudra' stood at the bottom of hierarchy. The 'untouchables' were not a part of this Scheme. However, over a period of time, the exigencies of situation led to the addition of a Fifth group to this classification which was not given any 'caste status' as such, but nonetheless integrally linked to the social order and is referred to as 'untouchables' or 'outcasts'. The membership of this group was determined by birth and could not be changed by individual effort or social acceptance. These four 'Varnas' subsequently transformed/got divided into hundreds of sub-castes, known as 'jati', each 'jati' having its own norms of social conduct. The caste structure is characterised by six important features:

— Segmented division of Society,
— Hierarchy,
— Restrictions on feeding and social intercourse,
— Lack of unrestricted choice of occupation,
— Civil and religious disabilities and privileges of different sections, and
— Restrictions on marriage

The segmentation of society into four groups represents a tightly divided arrangement, of both status and occupation which is linked to each other in a hierarchical relationship. Brahmins occupy the top slot in the hierarchical ladder and 'untouchables' the bottom. As the caste hierarchy operates around the concepts of 'purity' and 'pollution', 'untouchables' are considered as the most degraded because they perform polluting tasks. The restrictions on feeding and social intercourse incorporates code of conduct for each caste on what one can see and cannot see, what one can and cannot touch and what can or cannot be accepted by a person of one caste from a person of another caste. Restrictions on occupation are intended to prevent any destabilization of hierarchy.

Civil and religious disabilities mandate 'untouchables' to live at a distance from the main village, not to draw water from village well, enter the village temple, wear the sacred thread, acquire education or recite the religious texts. Untouchables are required to undertake the most polluting and degrading occupations, such as cleaning filth, including human excreta, flaying dead animals, digging graves, etc. The absolute restriction on marriages outside the caste and, in fact, even sub-castes ensures that there is no mobility from one group to another. Thus, the untouchables face total segregation in all matters, subjected to acute discrimination, do the most menial and degrading jobs and have no right to change their status. The transition from caste disabilities to commission of atrocities, has been traced to 3rd and 4th Century A.D. when varna system faced crisis of deviations from the prescribed social conduct and the need was felt for coercive measures to enforce caste discipline and boundaries. The King emerged as the Upholder of the system. Those who violated the system were subjected to secular punishment as well as performance of various rituals. This is how physical violence by higher castes on the lower castes was sanctified. This situation continued for centuries. The persons of suppressed communities acquiesced in this arrangement, as there was no option for them to escape from it. Perhaps they may have been made to believe that life in the next birth may be better if discipline imposed by existing status is adhered to.

During the medieval period some saints, Kabir, Nanak, Ravidas were critical of existing social order and preached a religion of love, compassion and consideration and a more tolerant social arrangement. But there was no protest against the caste system and its social ramifications as such. The prevailing laws continued to support the caste system and the rulers upheld them.

During the Muslim Rule in India, some people from the suppressed communities might have converted to Islam as a way out of their degraded status, but there is no evidence that the Muslim rulers ever tried to interfere with the Hindu caste system or reform it. Their strategy of governance may have prevented them from doing so. The British established the rule of law which was based on a concept of equality. The law applied to all persons irrespective of their position. This was a major departure from the pre-British judicial system where caste distinctions were not only recognized but also enforced and differential punishment was awarded, for the same offence, depending on the caste status of the offender. In any case, the suppressed castes neither had the courage nor resources to seek any relief under the new system. But even in the British period caste distinctions remained relevant in matters relating to Hindu Law.

The general features of the legal system did not change the status of lower castes, as the overall British policy remained one of non-interference. In matters such as entry to temples, ritual pollution and rights to exclusiveness, the Courts supported the customary laws of Hindus and their view was upheld even at the level of Privy Council. There was, however, some difference in the attitude of Courts towards secular public facilities such as streets and roads where such disabilities were not enforced. However, the Courts did not provide any support for removing caste disability in matters which came up before their consideration.

On a social plane, the period witnessed many reform movements in Hindu Society, such as Brahmo Samaj, Prarthana Samaj, Arya Samaj, Ramakrishna Mission, Theosophical Society, the Social Conference which attacked the caste system and some other features of Hindu social order. These movements, while supporting the four varnas, condemned the inhuman practice of untouchability. Later, during the freedom movement, Gandhiji contributed a great deal towards abolition of untouchability and later founded the All India Harijan Sangh for this purpose. In south, self-respect movement was launched against Brahminical tyranny. It was Dr. Ambedkar, who took up the fight against caste oppression more vigorously through the All India Depressed Classes Federation. Around 1909, the issue of untouchability acquired political significance when proposals were made for special legislative representation for untouchables. In 1917 the Congress passed anti-disabilities resolution. In the 1930s anti-disabilities bills were introduced in Central Legislative Assembly, Madras and Bombay Legislatures.

In 1938, Madras Legislature passed the first comprehensive law to remove social disabilities making it an offence to discriminate against the untouchables. In fact, in the publicly supported facilities, such as roads, wells, transport vehicles, etc. as also in other secular institutions, such as restaurants, hotels, shops, the law also prohibited judicial enforcement of any customary right or disability. This was followed by similar legislations in other provinces. Later, initiative was also taken by Madras to facilitate temple entry for Scheduled Castes by making it a criminal offence for any person to prevent any Hindu from entering or worshipping at any temple. Similar Acts were passed in other provinces later.

However, the British Government never took positive action to improve the condition of shudras and untouchables and to remove their disabilities. Apparently, the larger consideration of consolidating their rule prevented them from interfering with the customary practice associated with indigenous religions. Thus, at the time of independence, the traditional status of untouchables and caste disabilities, which prevented them from leading a life of dignity and self-respect continued to prevail. It was, therefore, left to the Constitution of India after independence to make the first comprehensive break with the past and to pronounce the policy of abolition of untouchability and declare total equality for the shudras and untouchables in Indian society. The Constitution also laid down means to achieve these objectives.

7.2. Commitment to Equality

The Scheme of the Constitution reflects a three-pronged strategy for changing the status of Scheduled Castes [and the Scheduled Tribes] based on the traditional social order.

This consists of:

— *Protection:* Legal/Regulatory measures for enforcing equality and removing disabilities; Providing strong punitive action against physical violence inflicted on them; Eliminating customary arrangements which deeply hurt their dignity and person; Preventing control over fruits of their labour and striking at concentration of economic assets and resources and setting up autonomous watchdog institutions to safeguard interests, rights and benefits guaranteed to them.

— *Compensatory discrimination:* Enforcement of reservation provisions in public services, representative bodies and educational institutions.

— *Development:* measures to bridge the wide gap between the Scheduled Castes and other communities in their economic conditions and social status, covering allocation of resources and distribution of benefits.

This strategy was subsequently operationalised in the State policy and the commitment to this policy has been a feature of Indian State ever since. The policy has been strengthened and revised and its ambit made wider from time to time.

As regards the protective arrangements, to begin with, the Constitution itself has provided an elaborate framework for eliminating those customs, practices, or institutional arrangements, including provisions in laws, if any, which tended to sanctify and reinforce untouchability practices and other discriminatory and degrading conditions imposed on these communities. Laws were made to operationalise these provisions. For example, The Untouchability Practices Act, 1955 was enacted in pursuance of Article 17 of the

Constitution. This was subsequently strengthened and amended in 1976 and rechristened as Protection of Civil Rights Act to make it more effective. Later, as a result of implementation of State policies, when there was spurt in physical violence against members of Scheduled Castes and Scheduled Tribes, leading to brutalities such as mass murder, rape, arson, grievous injuries, etc. enactment of a special law for their protection was resorted to known as Scheduled Castes and Scheduled Tribes (Prevention of Atrocities) Act, 1989 to provide for strong punitive measures which could serve as a deterrence.

Additional laws were enacted from time to time to protect Scheduled Castes and Scheduled Tribes from sanctions of any customary laws and enforcement of degrading and humiliating practices imposed on them. The Employment of Manual scavengers and Construction of Dry Latrines (Prohibition) Act, 1993, which eliminates the most degrading practice of manual scavenging of human excreta by members of Scheduled Castes, is the most important among them. The other practice sought to be stopped related to sexual exploitation of SC girls. Andhra Pradesh and Karnataka enacted laws to eliminate practice of Devdasi system which sanctified a customary practice of dedicating a young girl from the SC community to the local deity which virtually resulted in her sexual enslavement. Maharashtra already had a law enacted in 1934 on the subject.

Laws were also enacted to prevent employers from appropriating fruits of labour, denying freedom of choice and resorting to other forms of exploitation of persons employed by them, though their focus was not confined to members of these communities but extended to all those who came within their ambit irrespective of their caste or social background. These labour laws, in any case, have impact on Scheduled Castes more than any other group in society by virtue of their poor economic conditions and low social status. Prominent among them were the Bonded Labour System (Abolition) Act, 1976, Minimum Wages Act, 1948, Equal Remuneration Act, 1976, Child Labour (Prohibition and Regulation) Act, 1986, Inter-State Migrant Workmen (Regulation of Employment and Conditions of Services) Act, 1979.

Laws were also enacted and arrangements made to strike at concentration of productive assets and economic resources in caste Hindus. In this category were included Land Reforms laws aimed at redistribution of land to SCs/STs and other rural poor and debt relief legislations for regulating credit transactions and checking usurious money lending.

The second part of this strategy relating to compensatory discrimination is reflected in making provisions for reservation of posts in public services through recruitment and promotion, reservation of seats in Legislative bodies at the Central, State and Panchayat Raj institutions and Municipal bodies, reservation of seats in admission to Educational and Professional Institutions, including relaxation of eligibility qualifications. This was done with a view to ensuring that members of these communities have their share in positions of power and decision making as also access to opportunities for higher education. It was felt that in open competition they may not be able to obtain their legitimate share because of their accumulated disabilities over centuries. These provisions had the intended objective of bridging the vast gap that existed between these groups and the rest of the society in these areas.

The third part of the strategy related to focused and comprehensive development of Scheduled Castes/Scheduled Tribes which was operationalised through allocation of funds and earmarking of benefits under various development programmes for members of these communities in order that they improve their economic conditions as a route to upward mobility. This was sought to be achieved by creating a mechanism within the planning process through which a specified percentage of budgetary resources could be earmarked for the benefit of these communities. In respect of Scheduled Castes, this is known as the Special Component Plan, which laid down that the concerned agencies should prepare a separate plan for development of Scheduled Castes by allocating a percentage of resources, which is at least equivalent to the percentage of their population in the State and the Centre, as the case may be. These resources would be exclusively devoted to taking up programmes and activities which directly improved their economic conditions. This provision was further strengthened by allocation of certain resources directly by the Central Government known as Special Central Assistance to be used for this purpose in addition to the earmarked funds under the Special Component Plan. As a corollary to this arrangement, the State policy also mandated that in various development programmes which have a beneficiary orientation, it should be ensured that the number of beneficiaries belonging to Scheduled Castes (as also Scheduled Tribes) should at least be equivalent to the percentage of their population so that implementing agencies do not produce any alibis or resort to manipulation to deprive these communities of their share of benefit. In certain programmes where the gaps between Scheduled Castes (the same applied to Scheduled Tribes) and the rest of the community is excessively large, special arrangements are made to bridge this gap by way of additional resources allocation and through special institutional arrangements. Some of the areas qualifying for this dispensation are extension of literacy, poverty alleviation, land allotment for housing and cultivation, etc.

With the elaborate arrangements to protect SCs, it was necessary to monitor whether benefits were reaching the targeted communities and safeguards were getting enforced. Therefore, laws were made to set up watchdog institutions to look after this task. Four such institutions have been set up. While the National Commission for SCs and STs has been set up under the Constitution itself, National Human Rights Commission, National Commission for Women and National Commission for Safai Karamcharis were creation of separate Acts, i.e. Protection of Human Rights Act, 1993, National Commission for Women Act, 1990 and National Commission for Safai Karamcharis Act, 1993 respectively.

State clearly recognized that the violence, overt and covert, inflicted on the Scheduled Castes was rooted in the social structure and relations, which condemned them permanently to a life of indignity and social subordination. The three-pronged strategy referred to above would gradually help to eliminate conditions which lead to this violence and over a period of time promote equality in society. Thus, the elaborate constitutional framework and the meticulously crafted state policy flowing from it, refined over a period of time as experience was gathered, was a conscious attempt at social engineering. It also emerges unequivocally that in this process of altering social relations, State had a very crucial, rather decisive, role to play. This role, without doubt, had to be exercised through a conscious and positive tilt in favour of these marginalized and disadvantaged communities whenever pitted against formidable high caste groups, since the former would be too powerless to take on the fight on their own for a long period of time. It was, therefore, hoped that institutions of the State-the Executive, the Legislature and the Judiciary would positively respond to the letter and spirit of the constitutional scheme as well as the State policy. Lest the Government apparatus acts in an indifferent or biased manner, special watchdog bodies were also created to ensure that commitment to this policy and institutional arrangements created for this purpose are not deviated from. Embedded in this strategy was also the cherished hope and idealistic vision that the larger Hindu society would also get transformed under the thrust of a liberal and humanistic polity and democratic process which would characterise its operations. In this manner, support base for this effort at social engineering would get widened leading to a positive change in the attitudinal and behavioural response of other communities towards these oppressed groups and their consequent mainstreaming of the latter as equal members of society.

7.3. Legal Instruments against Caste Violence

The Constituent Assembly debate recognized that a section of people in Indian Society had been denied certain basic rights since ancient times and had therefore remained economically, socially and educationally backward. As a result, this had created widespread disparities between them and the rest of the society and a situation had emerged which underlined the need for special measures to uplift their status. This understanding is clearly reflected in the Constitution itself where a chapter under the title "Special provisions relating to certain classes" in Part-XVI has been incorporated. Special provisions have also been made for the Scheduled Castes and Scheduled Tribes in Part-X of the Constitution. The Constitution provides for protection and promotion of their social, economic, educational, cultural and political interests to remove the disparities and to bring them on par with other sections of the society. In addition, many articles in Parts III, IV, IX, IX- A, Fifth and Sixth Schedule of the Constitution reinforce these arrangements.

Article 14 provide that States shall not deny any person equality before law or the equal protection of laws within the territory of India. Article 15 operationalises the concept of equality in a manner which specifically touches upon the conditions of the Scheduled Castes and Scheduled Tribes. It says:

— The State shall not discriminate against any citizen on grounds only of religion, race, caste, sex, place of birth or any of them.

— No citizen shall, on grounds only of religion, race, caste, sex, place of birth or any of them, be subjected to any disability, liability, restriction or condition with regard to:

1. Access to shops, public restaurants, hotels and places of public entertainment; or
2. The use of wells, tanks, bathing ghats, roads and places of public resort maintained wholly or partly out of State funds or dedicated to the use of the general public.

— Nothing in this article shall prevent the State from making any special provision for women and children.

— Nothing in this article or in clause (2) of article 29 shall prevent the State from making any special provision for the advancement of any socially and educationally backward classes of citizens or for the Scheduled Castes and the Scheduled Tribes.

The Constitution also contains provisions which guarantee certain minimum rights for all its citizens and also specifies duties which the State should discharge for social and economic development of backward classes, specially Scheduled Castes and Scheduled Tribes. The rights of the citizens are guaranteed under the Chapter on Fundamental Rights contained in Part-III of the Constitution. The duties of the State are included in the Chapter on Directive Principles of the State Policy.

Article 46 under the Directive Principles of State Policy provides that "The State shall promote with special care, the educational and economic interest of weaker sections of the people and in particular of Scheduled Castes and Scheduled Tribes and shall protect them from social injustice and all forms of exploitation".

Article 366 (24) defines Scheduled Castes and Article 341 identifies the process through which such groups will be identified. Similar provisions have been made for Scheduled Tribes in Article 366(25) and Article 342 respectively.

The Constitution provides various safeguards to implement objectives enshrined in the preamble to the Constitution. These safeguards include social, economic, educational, cultural, political and service.

Social safeguards are contained in Article 17, 23, 24 and 25(2)(b) of the constitution. As per Article 17, untouchability is abolished and its practice in any form is forbidden. The enforcement of any disability arising out of "untouchability has been made an offence punishable in accordance with the law." Two important legislations have been enacted to give effect to contents of this article. The Protection of Civil Rights Act, 1955 has been enacted with the objective of providing punishment for preaching and practice of untouchability, in the enforcement of any disability arising there from and for matters connected therewith. Article 25(2)(b) provides that Hindu religious Institutions of a public character shall be open to all classes and sections of Hindus. The term "Hindu" includes persons professing Sikh, Jain, and Buddhist religions. This provision strikes against the opinion held by some sects of Hindus that members belonging to Scheduled Castes / Scheduled Tribes have no right to enter the temples. Scheduled Castes and Scheduled Tribes (Prevention of Atrocities) Act 1989 seeks to prevent the commission of offences against the members of Scheduled Castes and Scheduled Tribes.

Article 23 prohibits traffic in human beings and 'begar' and forced labour in any form and contravention of this provision has been made an offence punishable in accordance with law. In pursuance of this Article, Bonded Labour System (Abolition) Act, 1976 has been enacted and a special programme for identification of bonded labourers, their liberation and rehabilitation has been in existence to operationalise its provisions. While this Act does not specifically mention Scheduled Castes and Scheduled Tribes, it is of special significance for them because majority of the bonded labour belongs to Scheduled Castes and Scheduled Tribes.

Article 24 provides that no child below the age of 14 years shall be employed to work in any factory or mine or engaged in any hazardous employment. There are Central and State Laws to prevent child labour practices and providing relief to those engaged as child labour. The Central law is The Child Labour (Prohibition and Regulation) Act, 1986. A large number of child labourers engaged in hazardous employment belong to Scheduled Castes and Scheduled Tribes.

7.3.1. Economic Safeguards

The provisions of Articles 23, 24 [referred to above] and 46 form part of economic safeguards for Scheduled Castes and the Scheduled Tribes. Article 46 provides that State shall promote with special care the educational and economic interests of weaker sections of the people and, in particular, Scheduled Castes/Scheduled Tribes and shall protect them from social injustice and all forms of exploitation. It is in pursuance of this Article that special programmes for extending educational opportunities to Scheduled Castes and Scheduled Tribes have been taken up. Institutional arrangements for their development, including earmarking of specific percentage of funds from the budget for various development activities in the form of a Special Component Plan for Scheduled Castes and Tribal Sub-plan for Scheduled Tribes have also been in operation for a long time.

7.3.2. Educational and Cultural Safeguards

Article 15(4) empowers the State to make special provisions for advancement of any socially and economically backward classes or citizens and for Scheduled Castes/ Scheduled Tribes. This provision has enabled the State to reserve seats for Scheduled Castes/Scheduled Tribes in educational institutions including technical, engineering and medical colleges.

Article 29(1) provides that "Any section of the citizens residing in the territory of India or any part thereof, having a distinct language, script or culture of its own shall have the right to conserve the same".

Article 350(a) provides for adequate facilities for instructions in the mother tongue at the primary stage of education for children belonging to linguistic minority groups. The above Articles have relevance for Scheduled Tribes as some of them have a distinct language/dialect.

7.3.3. Political Safeguards

Article 164(1) provides that in the specific States there shall be a Minister in charge of tribal welfare who may, in addition be in charge of welfare of Scheduled Castes, Backward Classes or any other work.

Article 330 provides for reservation of seats for Scheduled Castes/Scheduled Tribes in Lok Sabha.

Article 332 provides for reservation of seats for Scheduled Castes/Scheduled Tribes in State Vidhan Sabhas. Under Article 243(D), reservation of seats in Village Panchayats, Zila Parishads has been made for Scheduled Castes / Scheduled Tribes in proportion to their population at respective level in direct election. It has also been provided that the reserved seats for Scheduled Castes/Scheduled Tribes shall be allotted by rotation to different constituencies in Panchayat at each level.

Under Article 243-T, reservation of seats for Scheduled Castes / Scheduled Tribes in proportion to their population has been made in municipal bodies at each level. Out of these reserved seats for Scheduled Castes/Scheduled Tribes, at least l/3rd has been reserved for SC/ST women.

Articles 371, 37l(b), 371(c), 371(f),371(g) and 371(h) deal with special provisions in respect of North Eastern States.

7.3.4. Service Safeguards

Article 16, which provides equality of opportunity for all citizens in matters relating to employment or appointment to any office under the State and prohibits any discrimination on grounds of religion, race, caste, sex, descent, place of birth, residence or any or all of them, has made a very special provision which permits Parliament to make any provision for reservation of appointments or posts in favour of any backward class of citizens which, in the opinion of the State, is not adequately represented in the services under the State. It is through this provision that reservations in appointments and promotions for Scheduled Castes and Scheduled Tribe and for OBCs in the matter of recruitment have been made.

Under Article 16(4)(a), this benefit of reservation in the matter of promotion has been extended to Scheduled Castes and Scheduled Tribes to overrule the judgment of the Supreme Court.

Article 16(4)(b) has further made provisions to permit backlog vacancies as a separate category in any year for determining the ceiling of 50% reservation on total number of vacancies that year.

Article 335 provides that the reservation provisions shall be made taking into consideration efficiency of administration. Through a specific amendment to the Constitution, the State has been empowered to make any relaxation for qualifying mark in any examination or lowering the standards of evaluation for enforcing reservation in matters of promotion to any class or classes of service or posts in connection with the affairs of the Union or of the State.

In addition to the protections referred to above, which deal with both Scheduled Castes and Scheduled Tribes, special safeguards have also been made for Scheduled Tribes.

Article 244 provides for legislation for special problems for Scheduled areas and lays down provisions of the 5th Schedule in respect of administration and control of such areas. Provisions have also been made for administration of tribal areas in the 6th Schedule.

5th Schedule to the Constitution, under Article 244(1) authorizes the Governor to direct that a particular law or notification passed by Parliament or Legislative Assembly shall not apply to the scheduled area or any part thereof or shall apply subject to certain exceptions and modifications. Governor is also authorized to make regulation for peace and good government in the scheduled areas of the State.

Article 275(1) provides that specific allocations may be made from the Consolidated Funds of India to give as grant-in aid for each such area for meeting the cost of schemes of development and for promoting the welfare of Scheduled Tribes in the State. Similar provision exists for such special grants for the 6th scheduled area.

Article 338 of the Constitution provides for a National Commission for Scheduled Castes and Scheduled Tribes and specifies the functions it would discharge and the report it is required to present to the President.

7.3.4.1. For Removing Inequlities

Untouchability Offences Act, 1955

Through Article 17 of the Constitution, untouchability was abolished and its practice in any form had been abolished. Untouchability means the practices evolved as social restrictions in sharing food, access to public places, offering prayers and performing religious services, entry in temple and other public places and denial of access to drinking water sources, etc. Within 5 years of adoption of Constitution of India, the Untouchability (Offences) Act, 1955 was enacted by the Parliament. The Act contained a significant provision that where any of the forbidden practices "is committed in relation to a member of a Scheduled Caste" the Court shall presume, unless the contrary is proved, that such act was committed on the ground of "Untouchability". This implied that the burden of the proof lies on the accused and not on the prosecution.

Soon after that Act came into force there was a general feeling of dissatisfaction with its impact as the legislation failed to serve the purpose for which it was enacted. The punishments awarded under the Act were also not adequate. Government of India, therefore, appointed a Committee in April 1965 under the Chairmanship of Shri Ilaya Perumal to study, inter-alia, problems of Untouchability vis-a-vis the working of the Untouchability (Offences) Act 1955 and to suggest changes therein. The Committee's report was submitted in 1969.

Protection of Civil Rights Act, 1955

Based on the recommendations of the Committee, this Act was comprehensively amended in 1976 and its name was changed to "The Protection of Civil Rights Act, 1955". The amended Act came into force from 19th November 1976. Under this Act, the preaching and practice of 'Untouchability' or the enforcement of any disability arising there from and for matters connected therewith, was made cognizable and non-compoundable offence and the terms of imprisonment were enhanced. The State Governments have been empowered to impose collective fines on the inhabitants of any area found committing and abetting the commission of untouchability offences. This Act, along with the Rules framed thereunder, lays down elaborate procedure for ensuring protection of the victims of such practices by providing for special courts, special prosecution, fixing period for investigation, etc.

7.3.4.2. For Creating Deterrence against Physical Violence

Scheduled Castes/Scheduled Tribes (Prevention of Atrocities) Act, 1989

The enforcement of Protection of Civil Rights Act, 1955 also brought to the fore limitations both of the law as well as its implementation in eliminating the practice of untouchability in view of its entrenched position in the psyche and behaviour of the caste Hindus and their resistance to change. Society as a whole never accepted the Protection of Civil Rights Act. Meanwhile various atrocities against scheduled castes and scheduled tribes continued to be committed in different parts of the country. It was realized that even the amended Protection of Civil Rights Act, 1955 and normal provisions of IPC did not provide deterrence in preventing violence on scheduled castes and scheduled tribes especially offences committed on caste grounds. Accordingly, Parliament passed another law called "Scheduled Castes and Scheduled Tribes (Prevention of Atrocities) Act, 1989". The Rules under the Act were framed in 1995 to prevent commission of atrocities against members of the Schedules Castes and Tribes, to provide for special courts for the trial of such offences and for the relief and rehabilitation of the victims of such offences and for matters connected there with or incidental thereto.

In the 'Statement of Objects and Reasons' appended to the Bill when it was moved in the Parliament, it was observed that despite various measures to improve the socioeconomic conditions of Scheduled Castes and Scheduled Tribes, they still remained vulnerable. They are denied a number of civil rights and are subjected to various offences, indignities, humiliation and harassment. They have been, in several brutal instances, deprived of their life and property. Serious atrocities are committed against them for various historical, social and economic reasons. The Act, for the first time, lays down the contours of 'atrocity' so as to cover all multiple ways through which members of scheduled castes and scheduled tribes have been for centuries humiliated, brutally oppressed, degraded, denied their economic and social rights and relegated to perform the most menial jobs.

The objectives of the Act very clearly emphasise the intention of the Government to deliver justice to these communities through affirmative action to enable them to live in society with dignity and self-esteem and without fear or violence or suppression from the dominant castes. The Act provides for strong punishment and compensation to victims and also lays down preventive measures.

7.3.4.3. For Elimination of Degrading Customary Practices

Employment of Manual Scavengers and Construction of Dry Latrines (Prohibition) Act, 1993

The most degrading of all occupations and forms of labour thrust upon untouchables by the caste based social order is that of manual scavenging. Members of communities who are engaged in manual scavenging are made to clear faeces from public and private latrines, using broom, tin plate and a basket and carry them to dumping grounds or disposal sites. Those working in private establishments and households are paid very low wages. In cities, scavengers are lowered into filthy gutters in order to unclog them and are fully immersed in human waste without any protective gear. A number of them die as a result of carbon monoxide poisoning.

The practice of manual scavenging has been prohibited by law under the Employment of Manual Scavengers and Construction of Dry Latrines (Prohibition) Act, 1993. The Act bars any person to engage in or employ or promote to be engaged in or employed any other person for manually carrying human excreta or construction of a dry latrine. The Act also empowers the State Governments to make one or more schemes for regulating conversion of dry latrines into water sealed latrines and rehabilitation of persons who were engaged in or employed for manual scavenging. The Act mandates a time bound phased programme for conversion of dry latrines into water sealed latrines, provision of technical or financial assistance for alternate low cost sanitation, construction and maintenance of community latrines, registration of manual scavengers and their rehabilitation. The Act makes violation of the law an offence punishable with imprisonment for a term which may extend to one year or with fine or with both.

In pursuance of the Act, Ministry of Urban Development operates a scheme for conversion of dry latrines into water sealed latrines, in which some element of subsidy is provided by the Central Government. Ministry of Rural Development administers Rural Sanitation Programme for construction of sanitary latrines in rural areas for conversion of dry latrines into wet latrines and construction of village complex for women. Ministry of Social Justice & Empowerment has a centrally sponsored scheme, called the National

Scheme for liberation and rehabilitation of scavengers. This Ministry, through another scheme, provides pre-matric scholarship to children of those engaged in unclean occupations, which is intended to benefit children of scavengers primarily. Government of India has also set up a National Commission for Safai Karamcharis under an Act of Parliament to monitor progress of the programme on elimination of manual scavenging and the rehabilitation of liberated scavengers.

Devdasi System Abolition Acts

Devdasi means a female servant of God. This ancient system entails the ceremonial or ritual dedication or marriage of a girl, traditionally from Scheduled Caste community, who is yet to attain the age of puberty, to a deity or to a temple. Devdasis originally had only religious functions, but the practice subsequently degenerated into sexual abuse of these women by high priests and royal patrons and, later, by landed gentry and other powerful persons. Once dedicated, the Devdasi girl cannot marry and is forced to become a prostitute for caste Hindus and eventually auctioned to a brother. The practice is prevalent largely in Karnataka, Andhra Pradesh, Maharashtra and Orissa. There is no national legislation outlawing the practice of Devdasi system. However, Andhra Pradesh has enacted a law called "Andhra Pradesh Devdasi (Prohibition of Dedication) Act, 1988 which provides for rehabilitation of such women, Karnataka Government has also enacted the Karnataka Devdasi (Prohibition of Dedication) Act, 1992.

7.3.4.4. For Preventing Control over Fruits of Labour

Bonded Labour System (Abolition) Act, 1976

Bonded Labour system refers to work in slave like conditions in order to repay a debt. The poor people largely belonging to Scheduled Castes and Scheduled Tribes incur debt for survival and meeting certain urgent and basic necessities of life for which they are charged exorbitant interest. Due to their illiteracy, lack of bargaining power and extremely low wages, creditors manage to create a situation where the debt is never liquidated and consequently the debtor has to render labour in lieu thereof. The Bonded Labour System (Abolition) Act, 1976 abolished all agreements and obligations, including customary sanctions which permit bonded labour system in various forms. The

Act also released all such labourers from these obligations, cancelled their outstanding debts and prohibited creation of any new bondage agreement. The Act also mandatorily provided for economic rehabilitation of freed bonded labour by the State. Keeping a bonded labour is a violation of law and is punishable with sentence of 3 years imprisonment and a fine of Rs. 2,000/-. Ministry of Labour operates a centrally sponsored scheme for rehabilitation of released bonded labourers.

The Minimum Wages Act, 1948

This Act provides for fixing of minimum rates of wages in different employments and appointment of Committees or Subcommittees for this purpose. The act also fixes the norms of hours of work, rest and overtime rates. The machinery for enforcement of the Act has also been provided for.

Equal Remuneration Act, 1976

The Act mandates that there shall be no discrimination in the payment of wages to women workers performing same or similar nature of work as men.

Child Labour (Prohibition and Regulation) Act, 1986

The Act prohibits the engagement of children in certain employment and regulates the conditions of work of children in certain others. It outlines severe penalties for those violating its provisions. The Act also provides for a Child Labour Technical Advisory Committee to advise the Central Government on which occupations and industrial processes the employment of child labour should be prohibited.

Various other laws which prohibit the employment of child labour on grounds of safety, etc. include The Children (Pledging of Labour) Act, 1933, The Employment of Children Act, 1938, Factories Act, 1948, Plantation Labour Act, 1951, The Mines Act, 1952, The Merchant Shipping Act, 1958, The Motor Transport Workers Act, 1961, The Bidi Cigar Workers (Conditions of Employment) Act, 1966, The Shops and Commercial Establishment Acts, etc.

Inter-State Migrant Workmen (Regulation of Employment and Conditions of Service) Act, 1979

The Act, as the title suggests, lays down the conditions of employment of migrant labour to protect them from exploitation by contractors, middlemen and employers. It applies to establishments employing five or more than five migrant workmen and provides for issuance of license to contractors who supply migrant labour. It also fixes the responsibility of Principal Employer with regard to fulfilment of conditions pertaining to payment of wages and welfare measures by the contractor. Violation of the provisions of the Act has been made punishable.

7.3.4.5. For Curbing Unequal Distribution of Economic Assets

Land Reform Laws

The Agrarian structure in the country prior to independence was characterised by high degree of concentration of land by a small section of society and the actual cultivators of land were acutely exploited by them. Land Reforms Policy, introduced in the country after independence, introduced a five fold programme to check this concentration of economic power. The policy abolished intermediaries from ownership of land and conferred this right on the tillers of the soil. It also abolished tenancy as a form of cultivation and mandated that the actual tiller of the soil should be its owner. A radical redistribution programme of land among the landless agricultural labour was undertaken by introducing ceiling on land holding and acquisition of surplus land for this purpose. Through the programme of consolidation of land holdings, arrangements were made under which small parcels of land could be exchanged for a compact contiguous plot through mutual adjustment in the village. Land records were also sought to be updated so that rights and interests of cultivators were safeguarded against manipulation. Land reforms laws were enacted and other regulatory arrangements were made giving effect to this policy by all States.

Debt Relief Legislations

Indebtedness is a chronic problem of all poor persons but it affects SCs/

STs more severely. Indebtedness arises because of their poverty and therefore need to borrow for subsistence and to meet other emergent social expenditure like illness, marriage, etc. Since no such credit is available from institutional sources, money is borrowed from private money lenders who charge exorbitant rates of interest. Due to their inability to pay back, the borrowers are enmeshed in a vicious cycle of debt-bondage.

Several States have enacted legislation to regulate money lending activity, impose limit on gross rate of interest and nullifying loans given by unlicensed money lenders, discharging debt incurred before a specified date, etc. Special features have been inserted in these legislations for the benefit of SCs and STs. These laws were enacted in the late 70's and early 80's. The provisions of these legislations have considerable relevance for SCs (also STs) as their enforcement can help them disengage from exploitative money transaction on this account relationship and use their meager income for their benefit.

7.3.4.6. For Positioning Watchdog Arrangements

National Commission for SCs and STs

In view of their weak social position, it had been realized at the time of framing the Constitution itself, that safeguards provided for SCs/STs in its provisions and also other laws, regulatory arrangements and policy measures, may not get implemented due to apathy or bias of the implementing agencies or pressures mounted by vested interests in the civil society who stood to lose from them. Accordingly, the need was felt to have a standing body as a watchdog institution to continuously monitor whether the activities of the Government are in consonance with the declared intentions, designed legal & institutional arrangements and policy statements. A permanent institutional arrangement called the Special Officer for SCs and STs incorporated under Article 338 of the Constitution served this purpose. Later, this arrangement was strengthened and in 1990 the Constitution was amended providing for a multi-member National Commission for SCs and STs with enhanced powers. The Commission is required to submit report annually to the Parliament. The first Constitutional Commission became operational on 12th March 1992.

National Human Rights Commission

The Human Rights Act, 1993 seeks to provide regulatory framework for protection of rights related to life, liberty, equality, dignity of individuals guaranteed by the Constitution or embodied in the International Covenants and enforceable by courts in India. Section 3 of the Act provides for constitution of National Human Rights Commission and Section 21 provides for constitution of State Human Rights Commission. In pursuance of Section 3, a National Human Rights Commission is already in existence since 12th October, 1993. It takes up the cases regarding human rights violations addressed to it and through its own initiative. As atrocities on SCs are violation of Human Rights, it intervenes in complaints relating to them also. The Commission is also required to submit a report annually which is laid on the table of both Houses of Parliament.

National Commission for Women

Section 3 of National Commission for Women Act, 1990 provides for the constitution of National Commission for Women to investigate and examine all matters relating to safeguards provided for the women under the Constitution and various other laws.

The First National Commission was constituted on 31st January, 1992. It takes up complaints of women referred to it for redressal irrespective of caste. Accordingly, problems of SC women including those of physical violence against them are also dealt with by it. As other statutory Commissions, the Commission has to submit a report annually which is laid on the table of both the Houses of Parliament.

National Commission for Safai Karamcharis

This Commission was set up under the National Commission for Safai Karamcharis Act, 1993 on 12th August, 1994 for a period of three years. But its tenure has been extended from time to time. Unlike the other three Commissions, this Commission does not have a permanent status perhaps because it was set up to look after a specific programme of liberation and rehabilitation of scavengers and may be wound up after this programme is completed. This Commission also submits a report every year which is laid on the table of both Houses of Parliament.

7.3.5. International Standards Applicable to India

Various International Human Rights covenants and conventions applicable to India, include:

— Universal Declaration of Human Rights 1948,

— International Covenant on Civil and Political Rights 1966,

— International Covenant on Economic, Social and Cultural Rights 1966,

— International Convention on Elimination of all forms of Racial Discrimination 1965,

— Convention on Elimination of all forms of Discrimination against Women 1979,

— Convention on Rights of the Child 1989,

— ILO Convention No. 29-Forced Labour Convention 1930,

— ILO Convention No. 111-Discrimination (Employment and Occupation) Convention 1958,

— ILO Convention No. 107-Indigenous Peoples Convention 1957.

All the above have been signed and ratified by the Government of India. In addition, the Convention against torture and other cruel, inhuman or degrading treatment or punishment (1984) has also been signed but not yet ratified. There is pressure on Government of India to ratify it since mechanisms have been provided against the practice of torture and Courts and National Human Rights Commission have also issued directions in this matter. These international instruments lay down norms and standards for treatment of individuals and groups and protection of their rights. As a result of these conventions, Government of India is required to submit periodical reports to the concerned international organizations monitoring their enforcement. The concerned Committees of these organizations make observations or furnish comments on the reports submitted.

References

Human Rights Watch, *Broken People: Caste Violence Against India's "Untouchables"*. New York: Human Rights Watch. 1999.

Jaffrelot, Christophe. *India's Silent Revolution: The Rise of the Lower Castes*. C. Hurst & Co. 2003.

Kothari, Rajni. *Caste in Indian Politics*. Orient Longman.2004.

Michael, S.M., (ed.) *Untouchable: Dalits in Modern India*. Boulder. Lynne Rienner Publishers. 1999.

Pauline Kolenda. *Caste in Contemporary India: Beyond Organic Solidarity* Menlo Park. Benjamin/Cumming Publishing Co. 1978.

8

Discrimination against Dalit Women

Even as we are in the 21st millennium, caste discrimination, an age-old practice that dehumanizes and perpetuates a cruel form of discrimination continues to be practised. India where the practice is rampant despite the existence of a legislation to stop this, 160 million Dalits of which 49.96% are women continue to suffer discrimination. The discrimination that Dalit women are subjected to is similar to racial discrimination, where the former is discriminated and treated as untouchable due to descent, for being born into a particular community, while, the latter face discrimination due to colour. The caste system declares Dalit women as 'impure' and therefore untouchable and hence socially excluded. This is a complete negation and violation of women's human rights.

Dalit women are thrice discriminated, treated as untouchables and as outcastes, due to their caste, face gender discrimination being women and finally economic impoverishment due to unequal wage disparity, with low or underpaid labour. According to the Hindu caste hierarchy, there are four castes namely the Brahmins (priestly caste), the Kshatriya (warriors), the Vaishyas (traders and the Shudras (menial task workers). Below this four tier caste ladder is another rung, who are called the untouchables(Panchamas). Among the untouchables, the status of women is further eroded and closely linked to the concept of purity. This is what the rigid, fundamentalist Hindu promotes through continuation of caste system, imposing the Brahminical values to maintain the caste system'

The creation of a number of Hindu religious books including the *Manusmriti, Atharva Vedas, Vishnu smriti*, and many others like these and their strict compliance by the Brahmans (upper priestly hindu caste), led to a society in which equality between men and women was far from existent. Dr. B.R. Ambedkar, an architect of the Indian constitution, also makes it very clear in his article titled "The rise and fall of Hindu woman" that the root cause of suffering for women in India are these so called Hindu religious books. Books like the Manusmriti divide people into a stratified caste system and promotes inequality between men and women. According to the *Manusmriti*, women have no right to education, independence, or wealth (n.pag). It not only justifies the treatment of dalit women as a sex object and promotes child marriage, but also justifies a number of violent atrocities on women as can be seen in the following verses:

Even the killing of a dalit woman is explicitly justified as a minor offence for the Brahmins: equal to the killing of an animal (*Manusmitri*). If the killing of an untouchable was justified as a minor offence, you can imagine the treatment they received throughout their lives.

In a male dominated society, Dalit women suffered unimaginable oppression, not only through caste, but gender too, from which there was no escape. The laws in the *Manusmriti* and other Vedic scriptures close all economic, political, social, educational, and personal channels through which Dalit women could be uplifted (Thind n.pag). The horrendous Laws in the *Manusmriti* were incorporated into Hinduism because they were favourable only to the Upper castes, which form the majority of India. Even today, in modern times, we see the severe oppression and exploitation of Dalit women. The Laws of the *Manusmriti* have a devastating effect on the level of education reached by Dalit women.

The caste discrimination inherited by birth results in Dalit women facing multiple oppression that violates their economic, political, social and cultural rights. The most deprived section of the society comprises of dalit women who are the poorest, illiterate and easy targets for sexual harassment. The women face not just caste violence inflicted on them by the dominant castes, but also state violence.

Of the total population, Dalit women constitute 16.3% of which 18% women live in rural areas. The women perform hard domestic labour which is unpaid and as agricultural labourers or casual labourers they continue to toil under the burning sun, with no protection or benefits that labour laws should provide, since majority of these women are in the unorganized sector. They do not even get the minimum wages that the state/country has specified, since they are unable to organize and demand for decent wage. Dalit women undertake manual, low paying, tedious, time consuming work. They earn less than one U.S. Dollar.

The women have to walk miles to fetch drinking water and often the water is not safe and potable. Dalit hamlets are usually at the end of the main village or in the village outskirts. They live in small huts and even the few who may have slightly better housing are devoid of basic amenities such as sanitation, light and safe and clean drinking water. The women work on construction sites, carrying heavy loads of construction material. They also work in brick kilns for long hours, as casual labourers to lay roads with hot tar in the burning sun, without sandals and any other protective gear. The women have to walk miles not just for collecting water but also fuel and fodder for their domestic chores. Dalit women are victims of bonded labour, they are abused, sexually exploited by other caste, humiliated and are easy targets of insult.

A study conducted come up with some shocking facts about the work of dalit women. What is horrifying is that Dalit women work more than bullocks and men. Bullocks and men work in a hectare in a year for 1064 hours and 1202, respectively, while women work for more than 3485 hours. The caste and patriarchal norms legitimise the poor economic conditions of Dalit women. She has to work to survive. She is powerless and has neither access nor control over resources. Manual scavenging continues as an occupation in India and most of the manual scavengers are Dalit women. The women are subjected to do this humiliating and degrading work, which further results in discrimination and social exclusion.

8.1. Impact of Globalisation

The process of globalisation has affected Dalit women considerably.

With the introduction of new farming techniques such as, mechanization for harvesting and transplanting, women have lost their traditional work in the agricultural sector. Food crops have been replaced by Cash crops. Horticulture has been introduced by, big agrobusiness corporations for export purposes. This has deprived Dalit women of their land and the common resources in the village. Formerly women used to collect greens, fish, and shells from fields free for their food requirements. This is no longer available to them. The abject poverty condition has driven large numbers of Dalit women into sex trade to earn for their families. The Globalisation process has increased the feminisation of poverty and this has affected Dalit women in every sphere of their lives. There is also large scale migration from rural areas to the urban centres in search of better livelihood options. Women are left behind to bear the responsibility of the family. This further adds to the existing burden that Dalit women are trying to cope with. More and more female headed households emerge and most of them are Dalit women. Such situations push the women into further situations of impoverishment, making them more and more vulnerable to all forms of discriminations and violations.

8.2. Health Condition

The health condition of Dalit women is alarming with high incidence of maternal mortality and infant mortality. This is due to the fact that Dalit women are unable to access health care services. Due to denial and sub standard healthcare services the life expectancy of Dalit women is as low as 50 years. The infant mortality rate is 90 / 1.000. The sex ratio of Dalit women is 922 / 1000 compared to 927 / 1000 for rest of the population in India. Due to poverty, Dalit women are malnourished and anemic. Early marriage and multiple child births causes the women to suffer from prolapsed uterus. Continuous bending and working while sowing and harvesting in agricultural causes acute back pain. They also develop skin irritation and allergy due to excessive use of pesticides. As they work barefoot and the soil is damp and wet, the women develop soars between their toes. Due to lack of awareness and medical care, many of them suffer from reproductive health complications, including STDs and cervical cancer with white discharges.

Dalit women are easy target for the Government Birth Control Schemes. Women face forced sterilization, are tested for the use of new invasive hormonal contraception like guinea pigs. They are forced to use long-acting, hormonally dangerous contraceptives. They do not get basic medical facilities. Pregnant Dalit women receive discriminatory treatment in hospitals and there are instances where doctors have refused to conduct the delivery of Dalit women.

8.3. Educational Status

A large majority of the illiterate population comprise of Dalit women with 76.24% of Dalit women being illiterate. The girl drop out rate among Dalit families is increasing with girl-children are forced to work as child laborers, More and more girl children from Dalit communities are school dropouts and working as child labourers. Dalit women are illiterate because they have less access to education which is an inherent part of the caste system. There are not enough secure facilities for education, taking care of small children and they join the adults to add to the income of the family. Dalit girl children are involved mostly in hazardous work like Beedi making, working in match factories and in the fireworks industry.

Traditionally dowry, which is not a practice of the Dalits has now became a bane. Due to Sanskritisation by the caste Hindus, the Dalits have begun to emulate the customs and rituals of the hindus. Dowry is one such custom. The Dalit families have succumbed to the societal pressures, added to this the fear of sending the girls to schools which are usually located in distant places deprive them of education.

Girl children are deprived of access to education as belonging to economically weak families, they are unable to pursue their education. They do not get uniforms, school books, special fees, and have to walk long distances to reach their school. This is a limiting factor for dalit children.

8.4. Political Power

Dalit women are excluded from decision making. They are not in a position to exercise their power. Wherever dalit women have contested, they have faced stiff opposition and even been brutally attacked. The 73rd amendment provides for mandatory reservation for Dalit women to be elected to the local governing bodies. They are elected but not able to exercise their power. Menaka (a Dalit women and a village Panchayat President was killed in broad day light.

Ranganayaki was deposed for solemnising an inter-caste marriage. Banwari was gang raped when she objected and reported to the authorities against child marriage in her village. Gowri was made to parade naked for hoisting a flag on Independence Day. Dalit women are militant and powerful. They are now fighting for political power within this caste system.

There are instances where Dalit women have been elected into local governance and through the reservation policy nominated as the President of the local governing unit called Panchayat. But when these women have endeavoured to exercise their role, it has met with resistance even to the extend of physical violence. A Dalit woman President is not allowed to sit on a chair if the other caste members do not allow this. She is forced to be a mere figure head, while the functioning of the Panchayat is taken over by other upper caste members.

There are several traditional practices and customs that violate human rights. The practice of dedicating girl-children to become Devadasis, Basavis and Mathammas. This practice is a violation of Dalit Women's Rights. Dalit women are discriminated and treated as untouchables. The shoemakers, Arunthathiar, practice Mathamma, dedicating Dalit girl children to their goddess Mathamma.

Superstition coupled with poverty and illiteracy is responsible for such practices. It is also using religion to sanction prostitution through the interpretation of mythology by the upper caste so that they can both economically and sexually exploit dalit women. It also is a form of upper caste manipulation to control the lives of Dalits. Further the lack of medical services, allows for such practices to flourish. There is a strong belief that the goddess has healing powers. So when a Dalit girl is sick. She is taken to the temple and left there till she is cured of her sickness. As already mentioned the economic situation is another reason that Dalits are unable to spend money to buy good health service. Once the child is cured, the child is named after Mathamma and married to the goddess with the "Pottu Thali" (wedlock). After she becomes a dancer she belongs to the temple. During temple festivals she dances and earns her livelihood. She is not treated with respect and publicly humiliated by men who harass her sexually.

The team which plays music with her exploits her by having a share in what she earns. Once the girl is dedicated to Mathamma, she cannot marry and lead a family life, as she is wedded to the Goddess. Therefore, she is sexually exploited by her partner who leaves her, to fend for herself and her child. Other men also tend to sexually exploit these Dalit women. Mathammas have no family, no security and left all alone with a child, so she has to struggle life long to maintain herself and the child.

Dalit women who are dedicated to Mathammas end up in the sex trade and become vulnerable to sexually transmitted diseases including HIV/AIDS.

Dalits facing Human Rights violations is a legion. A random sampling of headlines in mainstream Indian newspapers tells their story: "Dalit boy beaten to death for plucking flowers"; "Dalit tortured by cops for three days"; "Dalit 'witch' paraded naked in Bihar"; "Dalit killed in lockup at Kurnool"; "7 Dalits burnt alive in caste clash"; "5 Dalits lynched in Haryana"; "Dalit woman gang-raped, paraded naked"; "Police egged on mob to lynch Dalits".

India's Untouchables are relegated to the lowest jobs, and live in constant fear of being publicly humiliated, paraded naked, beaten, and raped with impunity by upper-caste Hindus seeking to keep them in their place. Merely walking through an upper-caste neighbourhood is a life-threatening offence.

8.5. Non-implementation of Existing Safeguards

Despite the existence of constitutional, administrative and legal provisions to protect women from all communities, and specific provisions for women in the Scheduled Caste and Scheduled Tribes (Prevention of Atrocities) Act (1989), women of disadvantaged groups are vulnerable to gender-specific abuses such as rape, stripping and being paraded naked. AI found non-implementation of the provisions set up to protect these very women against such abuses and to enable them to take advantage of the criminal justice system. Impunity for perpetrators remains one of the main obstacles to stopping violence/torture of women both in the community and by employees of the state. This pattern of non-implementation leads AI to believe that the government of India is failing to exercise due diligence in preventing these abuses.

Caste, class and gender discrimination prevents Dalit women from enjoying their basic human rights, particularly to dignity, equality and development. Atrocities and violence against Dalit women are both a means of sustaining systemic discrimination, as well as a reaction when particularly untouchability practices and caste norms are challenged or not adhered to. Impunity for this discrimination and violence is then used as a means to preserve the existing caste and gender disparities. Before Dalit women can enjoy their human rights, and before the Millennium Development Goals can be achieved, discrimination, violence and impunity must stop.

8.6. Cases of Atrocities committed on Dalit Women

8.6.1. Dalit Social Worker Gangraped–January 24th,2006

In a chilling reminder of the Bhanwari Devi case, a Rajasthan anganwadi worker was allegedly gangraped by her supervisors during a state sponsored training session. Instead of helping the 25 year old Dalit woman, the police tried to hush up the incident, declaring her mentally unstable and packing her off to a psychiatric clinic. According to the FIR the woman, an anganwadi sahyogini, was raped by three of her supervisors after her female supervisor took her to a room at the training center in Karauli, some 150 km from Jaipur. The incident took place on the night of December 30th,2005. Her husband was told three days later that she had been admitted to a hospital after a 'mental breakdown'. We brought her back to Karauli but the police refused to file our case. When they finally lodged an FIR on January 20, the SP again sent her with a constable to Jaipur to get her admitted to the SMS Hospital's psychiatric center. Her husband Ram Niwas Meena said that SP B K Pande denied the charge: 'We did not send her to the psychiatric center. We have arrested two accused and are hunting for the other two'. Home Minister Gulab Chand Kataria, who visited her in hospital today, said a probe will be held.

8.6.2. Dalit Women Tortured in Jail–Punjab

Three Dalit women from Muktsar district in Punjab have accused the police of torturing them, including administering electric shock to their "private parts" and confining them illegally. Talking to reporters at the BJP headquarters in Chandigarh on Friday, Amarjit Karur, Virpal Kaur and Rarni alleged they were picked up by the police after they rejected the overtures of two drug traffickers to join the flesh trade. Amarjit alleged she and Virpal were detained for five days at the police station. "We were tortured in the presence of the SHO. We were stripped and electric shock administered to our private parts," she said, adding that she suffered a miscarriage due to this. Virpal said their families were silenced with threats. Both claimed they were let off without registration of any complaint or FIR after five days. They alleged the SHO was acting at the behest of the drug traffickers. Rani's claims were similar. The district BJP unit arent't buying the DSP's claim that the women were picket up for trafficking poppy husk and plan to approach the Punjab Human Rights Commission, National Women's Commission and SC/ST Commission.

(Hindustan Times 18.2.06)

8.6.3. Dalit Women Denied Passport

Girija Devi, a Dalit woman who was scheduled to attend a UN seminar in the US, failed to get her passport. Opposition parties in the state have threatened to take up the issue in the assembly, Girija Devi, a 59 year old mother of four from the Musahar community, was scheduled to address a seminar on 'Women Environment and Development Organisation' in Bhojpuri. "It was the state government's fault. This was done to stop her from attending the UN convention to present her views" said RJD leader Shayam Rajak. Musahar Vikas Manch leader Amar Kumar Majhi said red-tapism was to blame. "The old Dalit woman was forced to run from one office to another. She would had done Bihar proud by speaking at an international convention" he said. Chief Minister Nitish Kumar said, "I will take action. Let me collect the facts".

(Hindustan Times 28.2.06)

8.6.4. Death in Police Station, Probe Sought , *Jaipur*

The National Campaign for Dalit Human Rights has demanded a CBI enquiry into the death of a Dalit woman in Chomu police station of Jaipur district on Thursday. The woman, Kamla, who was brought to the police station to meet her son who was in police custody on a charge of murder, had died of mental shock and agony due to police misbehaviour, an enquiry report by NCDHR and Centre for Dalit Rights said. The main opposition in the State, the Congress party had made a similar demand. Pradesh Congress Committee president B.D. Kalla in a statement on Friday demanded a judicial enquiry into the case. The party has alleged that the death had taken place at the police station following the ill treatment of the victim. The Chomu police last week had arrested Kammla's son Sumit on a charge of murdering a history sheeter Sikandar Khan. Kamla, a schoolteacher was taken to the police station on Thursday last by five constables, including two women constables to meet her son in the lock up. The police version is that the woman, apparently depressed over the act of her son had consumed poison at home before leaving for the police station. She gave a dying declaration to this effect but her family members had challenge this. The NCDHR team, which visited the spot, found the role of the police and administration "doubtful".

(The Hindu 5.6.06)

8.6.5. Upper Castes ill-treates Dalits

Dalits in Cidiyas village, in Rajasthan's Bhilwara district, say they were ill treated when they worked as labourers engaged in famine relief. "The upper caste Hindus treated us as untouchables when they served drinking water," said Prema Meghwal. The village falls under the constituency of Rajasthan rural development minister Kalular Gujar and has a small Dalit population. The upper caste Hindus employed three upper caste women–Madhu, Chandi and Pushpa Suthar to serve water to the Dalits at the relief work site Badri Meghwal told this correspondent. Last week, they decided to clean up the temple to Devra, a local deity, and asked the relief workers to volunteer. "They employed Dalit women to clean the premises. When the work was finished, they collected Rs.5 from each worker, barring Dalits, saying their contribution would not be accepted by the deity," claimed Bhanwar Meghwanshi, a Dalit activist in Cidiyas. "It is shocking for us as the deity accepted our voluntary work, but not offerings," said Mr. Meghwanshi, well known among Rajasthan's Dalits as he publishes a magazine title Diamond India from his village Cidiyas. His wife Prema, who feeds her family by working as a relief worker, said there were 50 people employed at a government relief work of which 13 were Dalits. "You can see 23 workers are from a single powerful caste. Their males will not work, but they get a share in the earnings because the payment is taskbased," Said Prema, adding, "We were not allowed to touch the pitcher and water served by upper caste women when we requested them," She said. The Dalits raised the issue in the village, but the upper caste Hindus said it was a tradition and no one had the right to oppose it "I have asked the sub-divisional officer to look into the matter and send a report," said Bhilwara additional district magistrate M.L. Yadav Reeling under severe drought conditions, Cidiyas has 300 Dalits and is dominated by caste Hindus. "Many times we quench our thirst with polluted water served by caste Hindus, "said Mr. Meghwanshi. "It is painful for as it happens during government-run relief work," he added.

(Asian Age 21/6/06)

8.6.6. Dalit Woman beaten up and Paraded Naked

A 50-year-old Dalit woman in a Jharkhand village was beaten up and paraded naked for allegedly "selling" a 12 year old boy in Uttar Pradesh two years ago. Balchand has been traceless ever since Sukri took him to UP with the assurance of a job. After the family of Balchand Oraon failed to trace the boy, they approached Sukri, a resident of Saram village. When Balchand's father Mangra Oraon inquired about his son, Sukri said he had run away at Mugalsarai station and she had no clue about his whereabouts. Some people who had accompanied Mangra Oraon started beating up Sukri. Her husband Indru Nayak was also beaten up when he tried to intervene. Sukri was then forcefully taken to Balchand's village and stripped. She was forced to roam around the village and was later tied to a tree. The villagers then started beating her with sticks. The boy's family believes Sukri sold Balchand and that he was still in the captivity of the owner of a brick kiln. After seven hours of trauma, the village elders decided that the Dalit woman should be burnt alive so that no other person would dare to so such a thing. Just when kerosene was being poured on her, some local journalists and the Chanho police reached and rescued her. Mangra has been arrested.

(Asian Age 24/6/06)

8.6.7. SC Body backs Woman Sarpanch

The National Commission of Scheduled Castes has asked the Superintendent of Police of Jhajjar district (Haryana) to furnish the details in the alleged implication of a "Dalit woman sarpanch", Sheela Devi, in a murder case. Her family members have approached the National Commission for Scheduled Castes which had earlier sent notice to the SP of Jhajjar that if the reply was not filed within the stipulated time, the commission may exercise the powers of civil courts conferred on it by the Constitution. On February 24, 2006. Youth Congress leader Bachu Pehlwan was shot dead in broad daylight by three men, near local MLA's office in Bahadurgarh. Immediately, the police arrested nine people for his murder including a Dalit woman sarpanch of Mandothi. Sheela Devi had won the village Panchayat election in 2000 from a reserved seat. Currently Sheela is under police arrest. But her family members are crying foul. According to them the village is notorious for group politics that has resulted in several gang wars. They allege that murder of Bachu Pehlwan is the result of a gang war. To vindicate their stand they sighted the 26 murders that have taken place in the village after the gang war was ensued between the two groups of Jats in 1994. The family members of Sheela Devi also allege that the village Panchayat was about to receive Rs. 4 crores as land compensation and one group was eyeing this amount. The group with the support of local MLA Rajendar Joon has falsely implicated Sheela and her husband. MLA Rajendra Joon was quick to refute the charges. He said, "The matter has not occurred because of the money, instead it is because of the rivalry that Bachu was murdered." "In the war of the two groups, the Dalits are suffering as the poor people have to do what the groups of the goon are saying. They used to ask the sarpanch to use scandalous methods to siphon off the allocated money," he said. Mr. Joon further countered the charges by saying, "It was me who used to stop them and this has made me an eyesore for them."

(Asian Age 28/6/06)

8.6.8. Dalit Women in UP Protection Force

In a move that will lead to empowerment of Dalit women in Uttar Pradesh, the Mulayam Singh government has decided to enroll Dalit women in the Prantia Rakshak Dal. The Prantiya Rakshak Dal (PRD) is a state level protection force that is usually deployed to maintain law and other in villages, in large congregations like the Kumbh Mela and during elections. The strength of the PRD force in UP is 24,000 and PRD jawans are sent for refresher training every three years. This will be the first time that women will get a chance to be a part of the PRD which, till now, is an all male force. The state government has now cleared the way for enrolment of more than 500 Dalit women in the PRD and recruitment will begin shortly from the district to the block level. Talking to this newspaper on Saturday, a senior official of the PRD department said,

> "This is being done for the first time to empower Dalit women in the age group of 20 to 30. Under the gender budgeting programme, nearly 30 per cent of the PRD force will comprise of women. In the coming assembly elections, people will see Dalit women dressed in khaki PRD uniforms deployed at polling booths".

The state government believes that this decision will not only instill confidence in Dalit women but will also take them away from traditional menial jobs. "Once the PRD enrolment begins, we see Dalit women moving away from menial jobs and becoming increasingly aware of the need for education", the official said. According to sources, the state government has decided to encourage women to seek enrolment through a massive publicity campaign next month. "We will convince the women in the SC/ST categorize to step out of their homes and join the PRD which will give them financial independence, dignity and status in society," the official added.

(Asian Age 24.9.06)

8.6.9. Dalit Paraded half-naked for 'not toeing' Panchayat line

Bhopal: A women was allegedly beaten up, stripped and paraded by women in Dedgaon village of Harda district because a young girl from the village had been found in her house in a compromising position with an upper-caste boy. Fulvatibai of Korku tribe alleged she was paraded naked in public. Four female relatives of the girl, of Gond tribe, and two upper-caste women allegedly also strung a garland of shoes around her neck. According to Fulvatibai, she was tortured because she refused to give a false statement to the police that she invited had the girl to her house and locked her in. She claimed the girl had an affair with the boy and the two had entered the house in her absence. However, the girl's family in a counter complaint alleged Fulvatibai of inviting the 17-years-old to her house where Madan was already present and he molested her. SP (SC/ST) M.L. Solanki told. The Indian Express of shoes. Four women have been arrested and the poiice are looking for Madan, an OBC, who is at large. The police have also booked Fulvatibai for abetment to molestation on a complaint from the girl's father. The girl told the police Fulvatibai had invited her home when she was returning after immersing a Durga idol at night. A team of state women's commissions has left for the village to investigate the matter. The commission said it saw no reason to disbelieve the girl's statement but felt the women should not have taken law into their own hands. A police official said the village Panchayat met after the incident and wanted Fulvatibai to give a statement to the police that would save the girl's honour. When she refused to toe the majority line, the women decided to teach her a lesson, he said. Ramesh, the girl's brother, has also been identified as an accused.

(Indian Express 5/10/06)

8.6.10. Dalit gets Rs. 4.5 lakhs for Deaths

Nagpur: Over 12 days after the merciless lynching of four members of the Bhotmange family of village Khairlanji in Bhandara district, the Maharastra government has woken up and paid compensation of Rs.4.5 lakhs to the victims' kin. The Maharashtra government on Thursda paid compensation of Rs. 4.5 lakhs to Mr. Bhaiyyalal

Bhotmange, whose wife Surekha (44), daughter Prinyanka (18), and sons Roshan (23) and Sudhir (21) were killed in mob frenzy on September 29. The cheque was handed over by Maharashtra minister for social justice Chandrakant Handore. Speaking to reporters in Nagpur later, Mr. Handore said the incident was clearly a case of atrocity against Dalits and hence compensation was paid as per the Atrocity Act. Under the provisions of the Act, a compensation of Rs. 2 lakhs is paid for the death of each earning member of a family and Rs. 1 laky for the death of each non-earning member. The compensation payable to Mr. Bhotmange was Rs. 6 lakhs for the death of two earning members and two non-earning members of the family, Mr. Handore said. However, only 75 per cent of the total amount due is paid to the next of kin pending the disposal of the case, hence the cheque for Rs. 4.5 lakhs, the minister explained. Mr. Handore said Mr. Bhotmange owned five acres of land in the village. The owner of the adjacent field wanted to have a passage through the middle of the field, and would not make do with the passage provided by Mr. Bhotmange along one edge. The dispute was deliberately allowed to aggravate and ultimately assumed the form of mob frenzy against a particular section of society to which the Bhotmange family belonged, Mr. Handore said. The police had arrested 32 persons in this connection, and two or three other suspects were absconding, he said. All the suspects were from the same village, he said.

(Asian Age 13/10/06).

8.6.11. Up Govt. Orders Fresh Probe into Rape by SDM Father

New Delhi: The Uttar Pradesh government has ordered a fresh inquiry into the sensational case of a 25 year old Dalit woman who has accused her SDM (Sub-Divisional Magistrate) father of raping her and unleashing a reign of terror against her husband's family to avenge her escape. Pratima, a science graduate, had approached the National Commission for Woman (NCW) nearly a month ago. Although the authorities in Lucknow are yet to respond to NCW letters, Pratima was called by the Director General of Police Bua Singh and Chief Secretary Navin Chandra Bajpai to Lucknow recently. "They gave me a patient hearing and have promised a fair inquiry into the false cases lodged against my husband's family and also my personal exploitation by my father," She told The Indian Express. An officer of the rank of Senior Superintendent of Police has been given the charge of the inquiry. Pratima has alleged that her father Birendra Kumar, SDM of Derapur in Banda district of Kanpur, had repeatedly raped her for one year and the police authorities did not pay heed to her several complaints. Buckling under SDM's influence, inquiry officers would inform her father about it and eventually she would be made to deny having made such a complaint. Finally, she had escaped and married a distant relative's son. Pratima's petition with the NCW said her "powerful father used his influence to allegedly kill her brother in law and got several false cases lodged against her in-laws." In between, she was allegedly abducted and raped by her father again and only a habeas corpus petition filed by her husband set her free. Pratima, who is seven month pregnant, has been offered a job by the DGP. "They arranged a job for me for Rs.15,000 per month in a sugar mill and assured full security to the family. "Fearing attacks, Pratima and her husband have taken refuge in Delhi. However, maintaining her skepticism, Pratima said: "I want the false legal cases against my husband;s family withdrawn to feel secure." The NCW has decided to send a special team to Lucknow to conduct an independent probe.

(Indian Express 24/10/06)

8.6.12. Village quiet after it Ganged up to hack Dalit Mother, 3 Children

Khairlanji (Bhandara): A day after mobs ran riot in Nagpur, protesting the killing of four of a Dalit family, an eerie silence has descended on Khairlanji, the village in Bhandara district where the family was hacked to death. No one here's willing to talk, not anymore: "We haven't seen anything. So what can we say?" Policemen, who weren't there when they were needed, simply wave you on. In eastern Vidarbha's paddy belt, Khairlanji has never been the same ever since the Bhotmanges, one of the three Mahar families in the village who became Buddhists, objected to people cutting across their field to get to their own. The Bhotmanges, who had land in Khairlanji, had moved in from neighbouring Ambagadh. This simple assertion of their right annoyed others in the village. Cutting across castes, they all ganged up against the Bhotmanges. Surekha Bhotmange, a mother of three, sought the help of Siddharth Gajbhiye, a cousin from neighbouring

Dhusala, in the matter and this annoyed the villagers even more because Gajbhiye had already had a fight with one of them over a money transaction. Some villagers chased and beat up Gajbhiye. The Bhotmanges, especially Surekha, stood up for Gajbhiye and testified against the villagers, leading to their arrest. On September 29, Surekha, her sons Sudhir and Roshan and daughter Priyanka were hacked to death and their bodies thrown in a nullah. Priyanka and Roshan were stripped before they were killed. The attackers showed no mercy to even Sudhir who was visually impaired. Bhaiyyalal, Surekha's husband, was the only one to survive. "I was in the field when I heard people shout. When I rushed to my hut, I saw some 50-60 people attacking my family. "Realising he couldn't take on the mob, Bhaiyyalal fled, seeking shelter with relatives in nearby Warthi. "The local police should have gauged the seriousness of the development that led to the incident and acted to prevent it. They are at fault," says a police officer.

(Indian Express 8/11/06)

8.6.13. Khairlanji Protests: Cops Look for the Invisible Hands

Nagpur: Two front activists of ultra-left is groups taken over the protests against the Khairlanji killings? This is the question nagging the Nagpur police though. In a flare-up in the city yesterday, protests in Dalit majority areas against the killing of four members of a Dalit family turned violent. The police resorted to lathi charge to disperse the rioting mob. The protests shifted to the satellite town of Kamptee around 11 p.m. The situation became so tense that the police had to call in a State Reserve Police company and impose curfew, which is still in force. Today, similar protests were staged in Yavatmal city leading to imposition of curfew in Patinagar and Ambikanagar. Bhandara district also witnessed minor incidents of violence. "These kinds of protests are generally organized by leaders wanting to take credit for the same. We do not know any such leaders here. So who are the people who instigated the mobs yesterday is what we trying to find out, said commissioner of police SPS Yadav here today. It was an entirely new kind of protest organization. Handbills were distributed first through back doors and suddenly there was a crowd of some 3000 people in Indora,' Yadav said. The Handbills categorically declared that henceforth the agitation won't be allowed to be led by any politician and it called upon the Dalits to exact justice for themselves. "The Hindus will rape and kill our daughters and sons. Shall we remain mute? it asked. Response to the appeal was instant. Protesters stoned the house of north Nagpur Congress MLA Nitin Raut, himself a Dalit, who was the first one to visit Khairlanji and raise the issue. Throughout the day, protesters allegedly made abusive calls to a Hindi channel correspondent asking him to cover the protests and threatening to kill him he did not do so. When asked if the instigators were non-politiical, Yadav said, "I can't say everything now. We hope to catch them soon". A lot of misinformation was also being spread.

(Indian Express 8.11.06)

8.6.14. Safai Karmacharis Demand Alternative Livelihood

Manual scavenging, despite an Act banning it during the tenure of late Biju Patnaik, continues to be very much an obnoxious reality in most parts of the State. The disgusting practice is very much a reality even 13 years after the legal ban, even after the Centre asked all States to draw a list of manual scavengers engaged in the shameful practice of lifting human excreta with their hands and carrying it on their heads.

Cleaning of dry latrines and transporting human excreta have been banned since 1993. Under the Employment of Manual Scavengers and Construction of Dry Latrines (Prohibition) Act, 1993, the employment of scavengers or the construction of dry latrines (latrines that are not connected to a drainage system) could result in imprisonment of up to one year and/or a fine of Rs 2,000. Offenders are also liable to prosecution under the Scheduled Castes and Scheduled Tribes (Prevention of Atrocities) Act, 1989. Estimates say there are more than 13 lakh manual scavengers in the country while State figure reached at more than one lakh comprising districts of Cuttack, Kendrapara, Phulabani, Nayagarh, Titilagarh, Sonepur, Kalahandi, Nuapada, Rayagada, Balesore and Puri.

Interestingly, in its latest effort to eradicate manual scavenging, the Centre has set up a deadline of 2008 and asked all States to address the issue on a priority basis and prepare a comprehensive list of manual scavengers along with family details and addresses but ground reality is far to match with what the Union Social Justice and Empowerment Ministry is doing in this regard. Scavengers while speaking at a seminar here on Thursday organised by the Safai Karmachari Andolan demanded the State Government should provide alternative livelihood to them and rehabilitate them.

They demanded the Government should finalise new schemes in which identified scavengers would be provided subsidy and loan for undertaking self-employment ventures, besides the scavengers should also be provided training.

"Poverty has compelled us to this profession, if we stop, we should be given proper rehabilitation and alternative livelihood," said Sabita Das, 65-year old Safai worker of Bapuji Nagar. There are many like Sabita who, despite concerted efforts, cannot shake off the curse of being a lower caste and are forced into scavenging. Refusal to perform such tasks leads to physical abuse and social boycott In yet another case of police excesses which has come to light, a poor Dalit woman allegedly bore the brunt of the Balinga Outpost in-charge's high-handedness on Saturday afternoon.

She was admitted to the District Headquarters Hospital (DHH) here only after the intervention of the locals.

The severely injured woman was reportedly denied even first-aid and the DHH staff, instead, sent her back to report the matter to the woman SP S Shyni.

Some residents of the Hospital Chowk area helped her into a rickshaw and took her to the nearby residence of the SP, according to sources.

Since the SP was not available at her office or residence as she was at the police reserve line on the outskirts of the town, the Dalit woman was brought back to the Chowk.

The irate locals phoned a TV channel's Sundargarh correspondent who recorded her complaints in the DHH premises. This compelled the DHH staff to respond to the woman's plight.

As per reports, the Dalit woman Dashmanti Rohidas (40) had been employed for over a decade as a sweeper at Balinga Outpost under Hemgir police limits since the inception of Basundhara Area MCLowned coalmines at Gopalpur.

When the new in-charge of the Outpost, ASI Kashinath Kujur, took over, he allegedly divested Dashmanti of her job two months back.

When Dashmanti approached Kujur on Saturday at around 3 pm, Kujur allegedly hit her hard, which led to her bleeding.

Kujur, on his part, stated that Dashmanti was habitually drunk and used to hurl abuses at his wife residing in the Outpost premises, following which he had recommended to the local MCL authorities to sack her.

On Saturday afternoon, she once again threw her drunken tantrums, as a result of which he lost his temper and gave her a thorough dressing down. Dalit Murasu, March 2005

8.6.15. Raja Nagar, Kancheepuram District

Dalit women and Dalit community were neglected during the tsunami rehabilitation process. Government and other supporting bodies are only concern with the fisher folk. They didn't even turn to the Dalit community. Caste is playing a violence even in the disasters. 106 Dalit families are starving in Raja Nagar.

8.6.16. Chinnamanickampangu, Nagapattinam

Vanamazhi a Dalit woman, aged 52 years has got few rehabilitation materials. She was directly attacked by the fisher community people and named her that she is taking the materials of fisher communities.

8.6.17. Untouchability practices in Pudukottai District

A survey was conducted in 104 villages of Pudukottai district. In this area, untouchable practices are in various ways.

— *Tea Shop:* Three tumbler system

— *Temple:* Dalit communities are deprived to the temple worship.

— *Saloon Shop:* Dalit people are neglected to cut their hair in the saloon shops.

— *Public Resources:* Village public resources were deprived, no rights to have a bath in the temple ponds, no graveyard for the Dalits.

— *Marriage:* Inter-caste marriage was not allowed in the Dalit community. If they get inter caste marriage they will get punishment, they treat as bonded ages.

8.6.18. Dalit Women key to Land Rights Fight

New Delhi: Dalit women have been at the forefront of Dalit land rights movements and whenever they have participated in these campaigns they have been much more successful, advised Mr. Nicholas, the convenor of the National Federation for Dalit Land Rights Movement, at a seminar at the India Social Forum in New Delhi on Friday. He said at the seminar, which discussed " caste and class attacks on Dalit Land Rights,'that Dalit women must always be involved in land rights movements. Manas Tena, also a convenor of same federation, said there are two areas where the federation is fighting for land rights of Dalit sand these include cases were Dalits hold possession of the land, but do not have right of the land and the other where the land belongs to them on paper, meaning they have rights, but they do not have possession of the land. "We are working at three levels first is the local level, second is the national level and finally at the South Asian level where Dalits from Pakista, Nepal, Bangladesh and Bhutan also face the same problems in their countries." Elaborating on Dalit Land rights movements, Mr. Nicholas said the Dalits are about 162 million strong in India and of these about 70 percent do not own any land. So, we are agitating for land to be given to the Dalits for their upliftment. He said it has been observed that Dalit women retain their land much better than their male counterparts and added that this was also historically true.

(Asian Age 11.11.06)

8.6.19. Dalit Girl refused to Drop Rape Charge, Burnt

Sahalwada, November 23: A 15 year old Dalit girl, who refused to drop a rape charge against an upper caste youth, was burnt alive by the alleged rapist when she was sleeping at her home late Tuesday. Asha katiya told the police before she died of her burns at a hospital in Pipariya on Wednesday that Chhote Singh Rajput had threatened to kill her if she did not change her statement in court. " I will burn you set your house afire and cut your father into pieces,' her mother. Shashibai, quoted the 22 year old as warning them when she was with her daughter in the field on Tuesday afternoon. Late in the afternoon, riding the only horse in the village, Chhote Singh sped past the girl's house and around 9.00 p.m doused the victim with kerosene from an opening in the roof of a room where she was sleeping and threw a burning matchstick. Anita, the Victim's aunt, told the Indian Express on Thursday. Anita claimed she saw Chhote Singh escape into in the fields. Unlike the Dalit family which is very poor, the Rajput family owns two acres of land. The horse belongs to some one else but Chhote Singh rode it occasionally. Asha had been allegedly raped in July and the court proceedings were on in Hoshangabad, the district headquarters about 90 km away. She was to appear in the court in a month. The family had a tough time arranging for a vehicle to take Asha to the hospital as she lay outside her house. The family members alleged that though there are many vehicles in the upper caste dominated village, no one came to their rescue and they had to call one from Sandia, about 8 km away. "They though if Asha dies the rape case will have no meaning".

Asha's grandmother Narbadi alleged. The victim's mother said the family was all prepared to leave the village the next morning but Chhote Singh struck before that. The family, however, did not inform the police or the villagers about the threat to their life. The upper caste villagers deny the charges levelled by the Dalit family. "He was with us when the incident happened, there are many eye witnesses, "Chhote Singh's parents Laxaman Singh and Jeerabai claimed. He wanted to douse the fire but returned when he learnt that the girl's father named him, Govind Sharma, a neighbour claimed. "The police are simply not recording our statements, they are going by what the girl said before dying, they should investigate the case properly," Harish Sharma, a villager said, suggesting that the girl committed suicide. "It was a mistake all of us commit in our youth" he said of the rape charge. According to him, the family was getting frustrated because they could not find a match for her. SP Ved Prakash Sharma and DSP JS Jaggi said the police are going by the dying declaration where the victim clearly named Chhote Singh. The alleged killer was arrested on Wednesday afternoon from his home, a proof the villagers say proves his innocence. "He would have fled the village had he committed the crime," sarpanch Govind Singh Rajput said.

(Indian Express 24.11.06)

8.7. Effects of Violence

Violence against Dalit women causes social, physical and mental trauma to women, much of which is long-term suffering. Where violence is committed with impunity, aided by the failure of the police to effect arrests and prosecutions, the fact of the perpetrators and their colluders in the violence freely moving about the village and often intimidating the woman and her family has a deep psychological impact. Significant are feelings of the futility of legal justice and fatalism about positive changes to address such violence. In total, 71.2% of Dalit women in the study expressed their feelings of helplessness to stop the violence, while 60.4% indicated the atmosphere of constant fear in which they carry on their daily lives. Feelings of depression or low-self esteem and shame also marked out the lives of around 60% of women, while 24 women had tried to commit suicide because of the violence they endured.

At the level of physical effects, among other effects of violence, 92 Dalit women experienced long-term physical health complications arising out of the violence, and a further nine women now live with a permanent physical disfigurement or disability. Twenty-three women endured long-term sexual health complications, while seven women miscarried as a result of violence meted out to them. Sexual violence resulted in 40 women becoming pregnant, though 18 women either opted for or were forced to undertake abortions, and one woman's family killed her child at birth. Social effects of violence include economic punishment in terms of the destruction of Dalit women's livelihood or loss of employment (11 women), or social boycotts (four women). Around 8% of Dalit women (39 women) expressed their inability to get married or to get their child married where especially sexual violence had occurred. Violence also restricted many Dalit women's freedom of movement, while eight girls quit their education due to violence. Otherwise, Dalit women were ostracised from their families (57 women), or their community (16 women), or deserted by their husbands (17 women), or forced to leave their homes (80 women) because of violence in either or both the general community and the family. Finally, 9.6% of women (48 women) experienced contempt or ridicule in the villages following the violence perpetrated against them, often reinforcing the idea that somehow the women were to be blamed for the violence meted out to them. Thus, the harm caused to Dalit women by violence does not stop at the act itself; it has long-term and multiplying social, psychological and physical effects that are not being addressed. Outside of the social movements and organisations working with the community, little supportive or counselling mechanisms exist in India today to deal with caste-and-gender based violence meted out to Dalit women. The result is that the lives of many Dalit women are underwritten by layers of trauma, hindering their rights to live with dignity and reach their full potential.

8.8. Resilience of Dalit Women

Despite all these experiences of violence that leave grave marks on Dalit women's lives and dominant caste perpetrators constantly reiterating gender-based caste norms and Dalit gender subordination, the narratives of the Dalit women also evidence their courage, strength and resilience to assert their right to live a life with dignity. Apart from the courage that Dalit women have shown during violence, their resilience in the post-violence phase is manifested in two respects: first, their determination to pursue a course of action, whatever may be the expected or unexpected outcome, to set right the harm done by the violence; secondly, the tenacity they have shown in their various attempts to sustain their lives against all odds, refusing to let their lives disintegrate further as a result of the violence they have experienced. Whether this was done with success or otherwise in terms of achieving a legal remedy for the injustice they had faced or improving their living conditions, what is significant are their efforts to survive and sustain their lives in some form or another. It is ironic that instead of the Indian State being the custodian of constitutional rights, it is Dalit women themselves who often dare to uphold the rule of law in the face of the "rule of caste". This is evident from cases where Dalit women assert their rights to equality and fundamental freedoms of life, and also where they approach established legal justice mechanisms instead of taking the law into their own hands as the perpetrators have done. And yet, in only a few cases does the state rise up to meet Dalit women's expectations of justice. Therefore, what Dalit women look to is not a paternal way of providing them remedial justice, but support mechanisms that clearly establish and uphold their rights, and bring them into mainstream society with dignity. Failure by the Indian state and civil society to respond to Dalit women's legitimate expectations results in these women experiencing greater marginalisation, to the detriment of a healthy and vibrant democratic polity. There also lies a possibility of increased questioning of the rule of law as the appropriate means to securing justice. What Dr B.R. Ambedkar said in 1949 on the occasion of the Third Reading of the Indian Constitution is well worth noting in this regard:

> "On [enacting the Constitution], we are going to enter into a life of contradictions. In politics we will have equality and in social and economic life we will have inequality. In politics we will be recognising the principle of one [wo]man one vote and one vote one value. In our social and economic life, we shall, by reason of our social and economic structure, continue to deny the principle of one man one value. How long shall we continue to live this life of contradictions? How long shall we continue to deny equality in our social and economic life? If we continue to deny it for long, we will do so only by putting our political democracy in peril. We must remove this contradiction at the earliest possible moment or else those who suffer from inequality will blow up the structure of political democracy which this Assembly has so laboriously built up."

In contravention of both national laws and international human rights standards that prohibit any physical, sexual or psychological violence against women, varying forms of violent acts specifically targeting Dalit women are occurring on a large scale across India today. That physical (affecting bodily integrity), verbal (affecting the psyche), and sexual (affecting bodily/sexual integrity) violence are the most common, and often combined, forms of violence suggests that at every level Dalit women's personae is being attacked. Moreover, given that most of this violence is occurring in public spaces, the additional humiliation of being violated in public drives home a message not only to each Dalit woman, but also to her family and community, that she is not considered worthy of being treated with honour, respect or human dignity. As Dalit women also experience violence in the family, they are effectively left with no safe spaces in which to freely express themselves and reach their full potential.

Dalit women would appear to be extremely vulnerable to aggression primarily by dominant caste persons in their villages and towns. Dominant caste status, often combined with patriarchal status and reinforced by a dominant class position (for example, being a landlord), effectively legitimises many dominant caste men's exercise of power, authority and force over Dalit women. Moreover, reading through the 500 Dalit women's narratives reveals the pan-religious element in that perpetrators of violence come from all major Indian religions – Hindus, Muslims, Christians and Sikhs, indicating that even in non-Hindu traditions the caste hierarchy trumps religious ideals of equality and respect for all human beings.

The range of causal factors for violence in the general community is directly attributable to systemic caste-class-gender factors that ascribe Dalit women's low status in society and consequent disempowerment and exploitation. At the core is patriarchy, which is gender-based and gender-biased against women. Male exercise of patriarchal power to subjugate women is overtly manifested in their attacks on Dalit women's sexual and bodily integrity, as well as their rights in inter-personal relationships with men. At the same time, patriarchy in India is influenced by the caste system and its inherent inequalities arising from hierarchal structuring of the system. Dalit women become specifically targeted for violence as an outcome of their positioning at the bottom of both gender and caste hierarchies, which condone violence against those Dalit women who contravene caste and untouchability norms by asserting their right to equality, or criminalises Dalit women's actions, or deems it socio-culturally acceptable to perpetrate sexual violence on Dalit women.

Moreover, reinforcement of Dalit women's lack of or denial of access to land and other economic resources through violence points to their effective class subordination in order to retain them as an exploitable labour force for their mainly dominant caste employers. There are also interconnections between denial of Dalit women's socio-economic rights or right to livelihood, and the denial of their civil rights; that is, their ability to protest and protect themselves depends to a great extent on their having a sound economic base. Finally, the lack of civil and political freedoms, including the right to justice and protection of the law in the event of violence taking place, reinforce the disempowerment of Dalit women at all levels. Such violence is crucial to the maintenance of caste structures and unequal power relations in society, which serves to highlight key areas requiring urgent intervention to safeguard Dalit women's fundamental rights. Similarly, the multiplicity of causal factors for violence in the family suggests the reproduction of the larger patriarchal caste system's norms in Dalit women's personal lives and interactions in their community. Finally, the culture of impunity built into the caste system has wide-ranging implications as far as violence against Dalit women is concerned. Impunity for violence reinforces that caste-based notions of (in)justice prevail over democratic rights and the rule of law in the country. Justice itself becomes defined in terms of caste-and-gender privileges, with violence serving to reinforce caste law and order at the heavy expense of Dalit women's rights. Violence against Dalit women thus presents one of the greatest challenges to the social justice system in the country, calling for immediate and holistic remedial action at all levels of the government, law and order agents, the judiciary and civil society.

The Indian Government has identified in its 10th Five-Year Plan 2002-2007 the empowerment of socially disadvantaged groups such as Dalits and women as priority strategies for development of the nation. Complementing this development priority is the elimination of discrimination and all forms of violence against women and the girl child, which is a central objective of the National Policy for the Empowerment of Women 2001 in attempting to bridge the gap between de jure equal status and de facto pervasive gender inequality. As the National Policy states, All form of violence against women, physical and mental, whether at domestic or societal levels, including those arising from customs, traditions or accepted practices, shall be dealt with effectively with a view to eliminate its incidence. Institutions and mechanisms/schemes for assistance will be created and strengthened for prevention of such violence, including sexual harassment at workplace and customs like dowry; for the rehabilitation of the victims of violence and for taking effective action against the perpetrators of such violence. A special emphasis will also be laid on programmes and measures to deal with trafficking in women and girls.

Similarly, the National Human Rights Commission has summed up recommendations from the National Commission for Scheduled Castes and Scheduled Tribes, national conferences and various non-state organisations such as the National Campaign on Dalit Human Rightsx vis-à-vis protection of Dalits' rights to life and security of life:

sincere and effective implementation of the law to protect Dalits against "untouchability" practices and atrocities; capacity building within government to protect and promote Dalit human rights; capacity building of statutory watchdog bodies; strict enforcement of Supreme Court guidelines on treatment of persons in custody; convergence of regulatory and development programmes; information for social change in civil society; code of conduct for state agencies; overcoming procedural handicaps to Special Courts taking cognisance of atrocity cases without prior committal by Magistrates; right of separate settlement for Dalits; enhanced central share in schemes for Dalits; and the setting up of independent, non-official monitoring agencies to review cases of atrocities against Dalits. Attacking systemic violence against women demands that patriarchal structures and attitudes in India be contextualised by caste, the eradication of caste inequality being intrinsic to the solution of gender equality.xii It is the institutionalised inequality of the caste system that underpins and reinforces gender inequality in India, rendering marginalised Dalit women particularly vulnerable to violence with impunity. Therefore, an understanding of the intersection of gender and caste discrimination incorporated into government policies is vital to ensuring that Dalit women's rights to life and security of life are respected and protected. This also throws open the challenge to Dalit and women's movements, as for other social movements across the country, to incorporate a gender-andcaste perspective in their work, in recognition of the specific identity and corresponding unique intensity of Dalit women's subordination by gender and caste.

By fulfilling its national and international obligations to protect Dalit women from violence, complemented by adequate focus on improving the socio-economic conditions of Dalit women, the Indian State could contribute to enlarging the choices and agency of Dalit women. Increased Dalit women's agency, in turn, would contribute to social change not only for their families and their communities, but also for the wider Indian society. As the National Federation of Dalit Women has stated in its Declaration of Dalit Women's Rights 2002, Dalit women have the right to life and to freedom from oppression and violence, the right to expression, conscience and autonomy.xiii It is only when support is extended to Dalit women across the country that these women will become empowered and enjoy these fundamental rights on par with the rest of the Indian citizenry.

References

Aloysius Irudayam s.j., *Black Paper: Broken Promises and Dalits Betrayed*, National Campaign on Dalit Human Rights, Bangalore, 1999.

Ambedkar, B.R., "Annihilation of Caste", in Moon, V. (ed), *Dr Ambedkar Writings and Speeches: Volume 1*, Education Department, Government of Maharashtra, 1989,

Chakravarti, U., *Gendering Caste: Through a Feminist Lens*, Stree, Calcutta, 2003 on the use of the term "brahminical patriarchy" to refer to the interlinking of patriarchy and caste structures in India.

Government of India, *National Policy for the Empowerment of Women 2001*, Policy Prescriptions: para.7.1.

National Human Rights Commission, *Report on Prevention of Atrocities against Scheduled Castes: Policy and Performance, Suggested Interventions and Initiatives for NHRC*, New Delhi, 2004, pp.193-4.

9

Dalit and Social Justice

Since Indian independence, significant steps have been taken to provide social justice to Dalits. Various social, religious and political movements rose up in India against the caste system and in support of the human rights of the Dalit community. In 1950, the Constitution of India was adopted, and largely due to the influence of Dr. B.R. Ambedka, it departed from the norms and traditions of the caste system in favor of Justice, Equality, Liberty, and Fraternity, guaranteeing all citizens basic human rights regardless of caste, creed, gender, or ethnicity. The implementation and enforcement of these principles has, unfortunately, been an abysmal failure.

The Government of India passed a number of Acts, which aims to enforce equality, remove disability, stop crimes against Scheduled Castes and Scheduled Tribes and create strategies to counter caste-based discrimination. Many social organizations have encouraged proactive provisions to better the conditions of Dalits through improved education, health and employment. This chapter describes the role of existing laws in the protection and promotion of dalits' social justice.

9.1. Enforcing Equality and Removing Disability

9.1.1. Protection of Civil Rights Act, 1955

The Act deals with enforcement of any disability arising out of untouchability practices with the objective of punishing persons preaching and practising untouchability. Section 3 of the Act prohibits religious disabilities such as preventing persons from entering into a place of public worship, performing any religious service, bathing or using water of any sacred water body. Section 4 prohibits social disabilities like preventing access to shops, restaurants, hotels, public conveyance and places, use of separate utensils, etc. Section 15-A mandates the State to ensure that rights accruing from abolition of untouchability are enjoyed by those who are victims of the practice and provides for a higher punishment if a person resorts to reprisals or revenge for having exercised any right on account of abolition of untouchability. There is also a provision for setting up Vigilance and Monitoring Committees as provided for under Section 16(8). The Protection of Civil Rights Rules were also framed and notified in 1977.

9.1.2. The Structure

Section 15 (2) of the Act directs the state to take specified administrative measures for implementation, such as setting up of Special Courts for trial of offences, appointment of officers for initiating or exercising supervision over prosecutions initiated under the Act, setting up of Committees for monitoring and guidance, etc. It also makes arrangements for legal aid to the victims and preventive measures such as periodic survey on the working of the Act and identification of areas where disabilities arising out of practice of untouchability have been observed with a view to adopting suitable measures for their elimination.

9.1.3. Cases Registered under the Act

With regard to the enforcement of the Act, the following table contains details of the cases registered under the old and amended Acts from 1955 to 2000:

Table 9.1. details of the cases registered under the old and amended Acts from 1955 to 2000

Year	No. of cases Registered
1955	180
1956	693
1957	491
1958	559
1959	481

1960	275
1961	489
1962	389
1963	393
1964	371
1965	366
1966	488
1967	353
1968	214
1969	329
1970	364
1971	526
1972	1515
1973	2456
1974	1908
1975	3528
1976	5108
1977	3425
1978	4729
1979	4911
1980	4303
1981	4085
1982	4087
1983	3949
1984	3925
1985	3332
1991	2944
1992	2900
1993	2531
1994	1731
1995	1528
1996	1417
1997	1216
1998	724
1999	678
2000	666

This statement shows that number of cases registered was very low right from the inception of the Act, but picked up only from the year 1972. There was, however, a substantial increase in the number of cases registered from 1976 when the old Act was comprehensively amended. However, the number of registered cases are showing a progressive decline over the years and their number has gone down considerably since 1998. Ordinarily, these statistical details may lead to the conclusion that the problem of untouchability is gradually disappearing.

But this inference is hardly tenable. The data about the status of prosecution for the year 2000 presented in the 20th Report laid by the Ministry of Social Justice and Empowerment on 23.4.2002 indicates that 62.37% of total number of cases registered have come from A.P. and second in order is Karnataka, which accounts for 11.45%. No cases were registered from such major States as Bihar, Gujarat, Kerala, Punjab, U.P., Uttaranchal, Assam and West Bengal. Can it be said that untouchability practices have ceased to exist? Obviously not. The investigation of cases dealt with by Police shows huge pendency. Of the total number of 2086 cases, 1216 (58.29%) are still pending with police and only 618 have been charge-sheeted (29.63%). The position in respect of pendency in Courts is even worse. 7,366 cases out of 9,949 cases, were pending with Courts. Only 271 (02.72%) cases have ended in conviction while as large as 2312 (23.24%) have ended in acquittal. It is not difficult to see that people have lost faith in the enforcement of law and that is the reason why no registration is taking place. The large number of registered cases in A.P. and, to some extent, in Karnataka may be reflective of the level of enthusiasm in certain areas or the support extended by some NGOs/activist organizations before and after complaints are registered. Some critics have offered another explanation for low registration of cases. Since a more deterrent law, i.e. Scheduled Castes and Scheduled Tribes (Prevention of Atrocities) Act, 1989 has been enacted, it is likely that the prosecution authorities may not be registering cases under the Protection of Civil Rights Act. The vigilant complainants or the organizations backing them may also be preferring the Prevention of Atrocities Act, 1989 for registration. But this has to be established empirically. Prima facie, it does not appear convincing because even in respect of heinous crimes the police machinery in many States has been deliberately avoiding SCs and STs (Prevention of Atrocities) Act, 1989 and registering cases under IPC. In any case, the continuing atrocities on Scheduled Castes are sufficient indication, if one is needed, that caste based discrimination and disabilities still operate and violence is inflicted when they raise their voice against it and claim their constitutional rights to equality. Thus, the declining number of cases under Protection of Civil Rights Act does not represent a marked reduction in the practice of untouchability. Rather, it is a reflection on the ineffectiveness of law – a conclusion which tallies with the view expressed by National Commission for Scheduled Castes/Scheduled Tribes in its Sixth Report.

State Governments have also shown no seriousness in identifying untouchability prone areas and even where this has been done, there is no plan of action to eliminate this practice. There is very little publicity of the provisions of the Act, despite the claim made by most States that this has been done. No periodical surveys are carried out as required. The Administrative arrangements, most notably the setting up of Special Courts and appointment of Special Public Prosecutor for the operation of the Act do not exist in many States. Even if some States did not feel the need for setting up of special courts exclusively for Protection of Civil Rights Act cases, they could have allotted the trial of cases under this Act also to the special courts which are dealing with cases under the Scheduled Castes and Scheduled Tribes (Prevention of Atrocities) Act, 1989. There is virtually no monitoring of the implementation of the Act at any level. Vigilance and Monitoring Committees, as prescribed under the Act, have not been constituted and where such committees exist they hardly function. Meetings of these committees are not held regularly. The quality of prosecution is poor because the functionaries entrusted with the work lack both competence and motivation. Even the reports prepared by the Ministry of Social Justice and Empowerment and placed before Parliament contain merely factual information received from States about registration and disposal of cases; various administrative arrangements made for the function of the Act and funds spent, without any meaningful analysis of the performance of the States which could form the basis for making corrective interventions.

A number of studies have been carried out on the practice of untouchability and atrocities committed against SCs during the last 20 years or so. Four such studies covering States of Karnataka, Andhra Pradesh, Orissa and Gujarat referred to in a paper bring out that the untouchability practices continue in various forms though there is some reduction in respect of some practices. These studies highlight barriers to drawal of water by SCs from public well in rural areas on a substantial scale, though less so in urban areas, widespread restrictions in access to village temples, village tea shops and particularly in relation to essential services such as those of washerman and barber in the village. In public servicc facilities like post offices, health and educational centres, however, the practice had declined. Social mixing and relations across caste barrier continued to be low. In Andhra Pradesh, restrictions were reported in respect of political activities like organizing meetings or taking independent position on political issues or contesting elections. There were no substantial restrictions in access to schools and hospitals. Subtle forms of untouchability were practised in panchayats like separate arrangements of sitting and serving snacks in respect of SC members as reported in Gujarat. The practise of untouchability also declined in buying and selling of commodities in the market. The extent of untouchability has remained in tact in the sphere of house entry. Some States also provide evidence about economic discrimination in occupation, employment, wages and loan, etc. In Andhra Pradesh, the study reports that untouchables were abused and beaten when they wanted to change their traditional occupation. In Karnataka it was revealed that nearly 85% of SC respondents continued with their traditional occupation. Orissa showed that nearly 96% face discrimination in wage payment and some also face discrimination in the share of loan as well as the interest rates charged by the money lender.

The study carried out by National Commission for Scheduled Castes and Scheduled Tribes, in respect of Seven States, corresponds to the findings referred to above in respect of restrictions in access to temples and other places of worship, drinking water, tea stalls and hotels, services of barber and washerman, participation in social ceremonies and sitting arrangement in village Chaupals and Gram Sabhas with variation in intensity in respect of these practices in different States. However, the Commission's study also reports discrimination in educational institutions and public health centres, mainly in Rajasthan and in respect of utensils for use of general public, use of public cremation and burial grounds and in the matter of construction/ acquiring accommodation of residential premises. The report, however, observes that untouchability in its acute form is mainly practised in rural areas and some rural pockets also have shown decline in its intensity due to awareness among SCs. The deep rooted caste system was largely responsible for continuation of these practices.

The Commission has recommended several measures for vigorous enforcement of the Act. These include wide publicity to the provisions of Protection of Civil Rights Act, review by Central Government about the availability of facilities like legal aid to complainants seeking legal action, proper selection of Public Prosecutors and their utilization for initiating and supervising prosecution, setting up of Special Courts, holding of meetings of monitoring committees periodically, reviewing of the enforcement of the Act by State Governments regularly, identification of untouchability prone areas on a time bound basis, preparation of a compendium of guidelines for implementation of the Act and expanding promotional activities like inter-caste marriages, etc. Central Government should also review the work done by NGOs in this field and seek their help and cooperation in enforcement of the Act.

It is surprising in this context that State Governments have also not involved Panchayati Raj institutions in the implementation of this Act. These institutions could play a key role in eliminating untouchability practices and providing necessary social support in the enforcement of the Protection of Civil Rights Act. Even the Central Government has taken no initiative in mobilizing Panchayat Raj Institutions for this work though it has massive leverage which could be effectively used for this purpose. The potential of grass root level democratic institutions remains untapped. National Commission for Scheduled Castes/Scheduled Tribes has also made a mention of it in its recommendations.

9.2. Creating Deterrence against Physical Violence

9.2.1 Scheduled Castes/Scheduled Tribes (Prevention of Atrocities) Act, 1989 –Atrocities against Scheduled Castes – Law, Structure and Implementation

The term 'atrocity' has not been defined in the Act10. Though no conceptual definition has been attempted, S.2(l) (a) mentions that atrocity would mean all those offences which are punishable under S.3.

Thus the definition of 'atrocity' emerges by implication, i.e. actions covering various offences. But as per clarification of the Ministry of Home Affairs the term implies "any offence under the Indian Penal Code committed against members of Scheduled Castes by non-scheduled caste persons.

Similarly, all offences under IPC committed by non-scheduled tribe against members of the Scheduled Tribes are atrocities. Caste consideration as a motive is not necessary to make such an offence in case of atrocity". It is further clarified that the term atrocity signifies "crimes which have ingredients of infliction of suffering in one form or the other should be included for reporting". This is based on the assumption that "where the victims of crime are members of scheduled castes and the offenders do not belong to scheduled caste, caste considerations are really the root cause of the crime, even though caste considerations may not be the vivid and minimum motive for the crime".

The Act has the following main features :

— *Creation of new types of offences:* This Act enlarges the area of criminal liability and includes several acts of omission and commission, which were neither covered under the Indian Penal Code nor Protection of Civil Rights Act, 1955 as amended in 1976.

— *Commission of offences only by specified persons:* The defining paradigm of this Act lies in the caste identification of both the offender and the victim. The offender must be a person other than member of Scheduled Castes/ Scheduled Tribes and the victim should be a member of Scheduled Castes/Scheduled Tribes.

— *Protection from various kinds of atrocities:* The Act provides protection to Scheduled Castes/Scheduled Tribes from various atrocities, affecting social disabilities, property, malicious persecution, political rights and economic exploitation.

— *Administrative measures for enforcement of the Act:* The Act makes arrangements for establishment of Special Courts to try offences under the Act to ensure speedy trial. It also makes provision for appointment of Special Public Prosecutors to conduct trial of offences under the Act in the Special Courts.

- *Special features of the Act:* With a view to giving teeth to the provisions of the Act, Special Courts have been empowered to extern potential offenders from scheduled areas and tribal areas and attachment of moveable or immoveable property or both properties belonging to a person accused of any offence under Section 3 to 6 of the Act in addition to awarding any punishment. The Act prohibits grant of anticipatory bail to the potential accused under the Act and places restrictions on grant of probation to the convict of an offence under the Act. Among the preventive measures are included Rules for cancellation of arms licence of potential accused of an offence under the Act and provision for grant of arms licence to Scheduled Castes/ Scheduled Tribes as a means of self defence.
- *Enhanced punishment for some offences:* The deterrent aspect of the Act, reflected in its most significant feature, is that it provides enhanced punishment for those offences under the IPC which are punishable with imprisonment for a term of 10 years or more.
- *Enhanced minimum punishment for public servants:* A Public Servant as accused under the Act has been made liable to a higher minimum punishment and even neglect of duties has been made liable for punishment.
- *Compensation for victims or their legal heirs:* Provision of minimum relief and compensation to victims of atrocities or their legal heirs has also been made. The norms of compensation are laid down in the Rules made under this Act. This compensation shall be provided in addition to the minimum relief extended to the victim.

9.2.2. The Structure

For the purpose of providing speedy trial, the Act mandates establishment of Special Courts to try the offences under this Act with the concurrence of the Chief Justices of the High Courts. The Act also lays down that the State Government shall specify a Public Prosecutor for conducting the cases in the Court. The Scheduled Castes and Scheduled Tribes (Prevention of Atrocities) Rules, 1995 provide that an offence committed under the Act shall be investigated by a Police Officer, not below the rank of Deputy Superintendent of Police, who shall be so appointed after taking into account his experience and ability to investigate such cases. The Rules also provide that the State Government shall set up Scheduled Castes and Scheduled Tribes Protection Cell at the State Head Quarters under the charge of Director General of Police / Inspector General of Police for supervision in respect of action taken under the Act.

There is provision in the Rules for nomination of a gazetted officer of the level of Secretary to the State Government for coordinating the functioning of District Magistrates and Superintendents of Police or other officers authorized by them for implementing the provisions of the Act. Included in the Rules is also a provision for appointment of a Special Officer, not below the rank of an Additional District Magistrate, at the district level to coordinate with various officers responsible for implementing the provisions of the Act. For enhancing accountability and greater political supervision, the Rules have made arrangement for the constitution of State level Vigilance and Monitoring Committee under the Chairmanship of the Chief Minister. To deliberate on the implementation of the provisions of the Act, relief and rehabilitation facilities provided to the victims, prosecution of the cases under the Act, the role of different officers and agencies and various reports received by the Government. Constitution of similar Vigilance and Monitoring Committees at the district level, has also been incorporated. State Government is required to submit to the Central Government a report every year about the measures taken for implementation of the Act.

9.2.3. Administrative Arrangements

The following statement would indicate the state-wise position regarding the structure and other institutional measures for implementation of the Act and its Rules.

9.2.4. Volume of Cases

The total number of reported criminal cases of atrocities against Scheduled Castes under the IPC, Protection of Civil Rights Act and Scheduled Castes and Scheduled Tribes (Prevention of Atrocities) Act, in the last five years is as under:

Table 9.2. Number of reported criminal cases of atrocities against Scheduled Castes under the IPC

1995	:	32,996
1996	:	31,440
1997	:	27,944
1998	:	25,638
1999	:	25,093
2000	:	—

These figures show a gradual decline in the total number of reported cases of atrocities against scheduled castes.Under-reporting of Atrocities Act cases is a very common phenomenon and therefore the decline in the number of registered cases does not provide a true picture of the incidence of atrocities. One NGO in Gujarat, in a study covered 11 atrocities-prone districts for four years, showed that 36% of atrocities cases were not registered under Atrocities Act and 84.4% of the cases where the Act was applied, the cases were registered under wrong provisions with a view to concealing actual and violent nature of the incidents. The study also documented that 121.2 hours lapsed between registration of murder cases and initiation of police action and for rape cases the gap between the incident and the reported action was 532.9 hours.

The non-registration of cases, apart from reflecting caste bias and corruption, has also been attributed to the pressure on the police to keep reported crime rates low in their jurisdiction. The same NGO reported that according to police record, during the period of four years, the incidents of atrocities increased by 90% due to truthful reporting and yet police reports showed that the general crime rate was down by 1.35%. The increase in crime rate is not viewed favourably in police administration and has negative implication for the police personnel as their superiors feel that they are not doing their job. This can have adverse effect on their career. With a view to presenting lower crime rates in the district, under-reporting of information is done at the district headquarters, which gets further diluted at the State and National level.

9.2.5. Nature of Crimes

With a view to knowing the seriousness of atrocities, it may be relevant to see the incidence of heinous crimes against Scheduled Castes.

The following table gives out the serious cases registered under the three laws. These figures indicate that there has been a marginal decline every year under all heads of crime, except rape which shows a marginal increase.

Table 9.3. heinous crimes against Scheduled Castes

Year	Murder	Hurt	Rape	PCR	SC/ST (Prev)
1995	571	4544	873	1528	13925
1996	543	4585	949	1417	9620
1997	513	3860	1037	1216	8070
1998	516	3809	923	724	7443
1999	506	3241	1000	678	7301

9.2.6. Geographical Distribution of Atrocities

The geographical distribution of atrocities against Scheduled Castes may provide an idea of the areas / locations which are particularly prone to this type of violence. The break-up of crimes committed against Scheduled Castes in major States, as extracted below would provide this information.

The above figures indicate that the largest number of cases have been reported from U.P. every year. This is primarily because U.P. has the largest population of the Scheduled Castes as compared to other States. Besides U.P., Rajasthan, Madhya Pradesh, Gujarat, Andhra Pradesh, Tamil Nadu and Bihar are other States which have contributed substantially to the total crime against Schedules Castes.

9.2.7. Volume of Crime Against Scheduled Castes

Other things being equal, the number of incidents of crime against Scheduled Castes in a particular State would naturally have relevance to the population of Scheduled Castes in that State. Ordinarily, larger the population of the Scheduled Castes in a State, more may be the number of cases of atrocities reported from that State. But this may not necessarily reflect the level of atrocities in the State. Therefore, a more rational way to appreciate the magnitude of atrocities in a particular State is to study the volume of crime i.e. the number of cases reported per unit of population, e.g., one lakh population of Scheduled Castes. These figures are available for the year 1998 which are as under:

These figures indicate that the highest volume of crime against Scheduled Castes is in Rajasthan (73 cases per one lakh population) followed by Gujarat (62 cases per one lakh population) and Madhya Pradesh (42 cases per one lakh of population). Thus, the percentage of SC population in a State does not indicate the extent of atrocities committed against them. The vulnerability of Scheduled Castes to atrocities would depend upon a host of other factors, rigidity of caste based social relations and the relatively weak position of Scheduled Castes in it being the most important.

The Seventh Report of the Ministry of Social Justice and Empowerment for the year 2000 provides information on the number of cases per lakh of population of both SCs and STs for the year 2000 and therefore, it does not seem comparable with the data we have for SCs separately in the Fifth Report of the National Commission. However, Rajasthan with 51.05 number of cases per one lakh of SC & ST population taken together still tops the list.

If Chhattisgarh (40.64) and M.P. (18.01) are taken together, the situation in old M.P. comes second but the figures may bemisleading because population figures quoted in the Report for Chhattisgarh do not include STs. Since Chhattisgarh has substantial tribal population, number of cases per unit of SC/ST population may make difference in interse ranking. On the other hand, number of cases per unit of SC population for Chhattisgarh alone is very high. In any case, in the absence of separate figures for SCs alone, no reliable picture of inter–se ranking can be attempted.

Table 9.4. Volume of Crime Against Scheduled Castes

Year	U.P.	Raj	Madhya Pradesh	Guj	AP	TN	Bihar	N.E. States	UTs	Other States	Total
1995	14205	5197	3979	1724	1764	1293	747	36	32	4019	32996
1996	10963	6623	4075	1764	1629	1812	810	14	24	3726	31440
1997	8500	5624	4269	1831	1880	1403	710	18	43	3666	27944
1998	6511	5586	4051	1884	1605	1562	785	2	21	3631	25638
1999	6122	5623	4667	1781	1749	883	820	22	31	3391	25089

9.2.8. Proneness of States to Specific Crimes

By positioning incidence of specific heinous crimes in major atrocities prone States, the proneness of a State to serious cases of violence, as also to a specific type of atrocity, would be reflected which could then be sociologically investigated to understand the causal connections. The State-wise break-up of heinous crimes against Scheduled Castes is provided in the following tables:

Table 9.5.State-wise break-up of heinous crimes against Scheduled Castes

S.No	State/UT	SC Population (Census 1991) in lakhs	Cases of atrocity 1998	Cases per lakh of SC population per year	Rank
1.	Andhra Pradesh	105.92	1813	17.12	VI
2.	Bihar 1	25.72	785	6.24	XIII
3.	Gujarat	30.6	1884	61.57	II
4.	Haryana	32.51	159	4.9	XIV
5.	Himachal Prad.	13.50	59	4.4	XV
6.	J & K	6.41	17	2.65	XVI
7.	Karnataka	73.69	1148	15.58	VII
8.	Kerala	28.86	786	27.23	IV
9.	Madhya Pradesh	96.27	4051	42.08	III
10.	Maharashtra	87.58	683	7.8	XI
11.	Orissa	51.29	703	13.71	IX
12.	Punjab	57.43	23	0.4	XVIII
13.	Rajasthan	76.08	5585	73.4	I I
14.	Sikkim	0.24	2	8.3	X
15.	Tamilnadu	107.35	1562	14.58	VIII
16.	UP	292.76	6511	22.24	V
17.	Delhi	17.95	11	0.61	XVII
18.	Pondicherry	1.37	10	7.30	XII

Even for heinous crimes, UP is the highest contributor, followed by Madhya Pradesh, Rajasthan, Andhra Pradesh, Tamilnadu and Gujarat.But the data presented above also brings out the interesting point that the number of atrocities cases in a State in absolute terms may not reflect the level of vulnerability of Scheduled Castes. Rajasthan and M.P. emerge as more atrocityprone than U.P. and therefore SCs are more vulnerable there as compared to U.P.

Table 9.6. Murder

Year	U.P.	Raj	Madhya Pradesh	Guj	AP	TN	Bihar	N.E. States	UTs	Other States	Total
1995	296	35	86	27	25	29	18	02	00	53	571
1996	330	47	50	22	21	15	19	01	01	38	543
1997	261	53	66	18	33	11	33	00	00	38	513
1998	259	49	67	21	35	30	12	00	00	43	516
1999	279	49	55	26	26	20	05	01	00	44	506

Table 9. 7. Hurt

Year	U.P.	Raj	Madhya Pradesh	Guj	AP	TN	Bihar	N.E. States	UTs	Other States	Total
1995	1067	303	681	216	516	858	226	06	00	671	4544
1996	1060	184	687	206	318	1361	276	04	00	489	4585
1997	706	197	635	215	303	983	225	08	00	588	3860
1998	782	218	680	243	364	650	253	01	00	618	3809
1999	672	154	751	363	437	165	230	08	00	458	3241

The following statements give state-wise incidence of crime committed against Scheduled Castes during 1999 and 2000, which may throw light on the proneness of State to a particular type of atrocity:

The two statements indicate the following:

— In murder cases, U.P. tops the list, while rape cases are very high in M.P., Rajasthan and U.P.

— Karnataka has registered the second largest number of cases under the Scheduled Castes and Scheduled Tribes (Prevention of Atrocities) Act, 1989. But the serious offences in Karnataka are few which may perhaps reflect the seriousness with which cases under the Act are registered.

— Only AP, Karnataka, Maharashtra and Tamilnadu have shown seriousness in registering cases under Protection of Civil Rights Act 1955.

The abstract of data relating to number of cases (category-wise) of atrocities against Scheduled Castes registered during 1999 and 2000 along with their percentage in the context of total volume of crime against them (in brackets) is given below, which shows increase in number of rape cases:

Table 9.8. Rape Cases

Year	U.P.	Raj	Madhya Pradesh	Guj	AP	TN	Bihar	N.E. States	UTs	Other States	Total
1995	321	94	224	15	64	06	13	01	00	135	873
1996	324	----	----	15	50	19	27	01	00	116	949
1997	302	158	315	21	59	09	20	02	00	1151	1037
1998	238	138	269	20	46	04	23	01	00	184	923
1999	276	146	305	28	61	12	22	03	00	147	1000

Table 9.9. Atrocities Committed on Scheduled Castes

S.No.	Nature of Crime	Number of Cases of crimes during 1999	2000
1.	Murder	506 (2.01%)	486 (2.05%)
2.	Grievous Hurt	3241 (12.92%)	3298 (13.89%)
3.	Rape	1000 (3.98%)	1034 (4.36%)
4.	Arson	337 (1.35%)	260 (1.09%)
5.	Other Offences	20,009 (79.79%)	18,664 (78.61%)
	Total	25,093 (100.00%)	23,742 (100.00%)

The National Commission for Scheduled Castes and Scheduled Tribes has also compared the data of crime against Scheduled Castes with the figures of crime against Scheduled Tribes and has come to the conclusion that the incidence of crime and atrocities against Scheduled Castes is about 6 to 7 times more than the incidence of crime against Scheduled Tribes, though the population of Scheduled Castes is only twice that of Scheduled Tribes. As per experience of the Commission, Punjab ranks as the worst in this regard, because the superior hierarchy of the organization tends to be extremely protective of its members and even the interventions by National Commission for SCs and STs in extremely serious cases have failed to get any positive response.

9.2.9. Disposal of Cases

Number of chargesheeted cases was 53.04% of the total no. of cases while 22.54% of cases were closed after investigation and number of cases pending with police at the end of the year constituted 24.42%. Only 7.83% of the total cases were disposed of during the year and only 11.04% of the disposed of cases ended up in conviction. 88.96% of cases ended in acquittal and 92.17% of cases were pending with courts. Number of cases pending before the courts in most of the major States is alarming. Ministry of Social Justice and Empowerment has expressed concern over low rates of conviction.

The position in respect of Rajasthan is very critical because the number of cases closed after investigation is the largest in that State and also highest as a percentage of total number of cases registered. This is true for the year 1999 as well as 2000. The pendency of cases with Police relative to the number of cases registered is very large in States of Bihar, Andhra Pradesh and Kerala. West Bengal and Assam have not registered any cases at all. Does it imply that no crime is being committed against Scheduled Castes in these States? Obviously, the enforcement of this Act is not taken seriously. Perhaps the cases are not being registered under the Act at all but are being booked under Indian Penal Code. This is certainly true of West Bengal where State Government takes a view that caste based violence does not occur in their State in view of their leftist political ideology. Thus as a matter of policy the provisions of the Act are not applied to the incidents and therefore not enforced. Reasons for not registering cases under the Act in Assam are not known. It may be just apathy or bias. A large number of cases of atrocities go unregistered, mainly because of reluctance on the part of police officials to entertain complaints and also because of lack of awareness among the members of SCs about the provisions of the SCs and STs (Protection of Civil Rights) Act, 1989 (as also the Protection of Civil Rights Act, 1955). In addition, there are delays in investigation, collusion with offenders and manipulation of witnesses and evidence all of which contribute to reduce the effectiveness of legislation on atrocities. In almost all the States the meetings of the Monitoring and Vigilance Committees at State level, which is an important mechanism for ensuring proper implementation of these laws, are not held regularly.

States have not taken much interest in identifying atrocities prone areas even though they have access to district based crime figures against the Scheduled Castes, in addition to various reports which their own field machinery generates. While the Ministry of

Social Justice and Empowerment may continue to pursue with States the need to expeditiously complete this exercise, it is learnt that National Commission for SCs and STs have already identified such areas evidently on the basis of information they have received from States and statistics brought out by the National Crime Records Bureau.

In this context, a study has been carried out by some researchers in respect of crime against women with a view to identifying regions (Districts) which are prone to such crimes. The Research Wing of the Commission may undertake a similar task of studying the district based crime figures and map out atrocities prone areas (for SCs and STs separately) which could then be discussed with States and finalised. Interestingly, the study carried out in respect of crime against women has brought out that the crimes are roughly centred at Madhya Pradesh and spread in different directions with M.P. as the center and neighbouring districts of Maharashtra and Rajasthan adjoining it. This region accounts for 56% of all 'high crimes against women' districts. Rest of the Districts outside this belt, but have 'high crime rates against women, are scattered in Jammu & Kashmir, Himachal Pradesh in north, Andhra Pradesh, Tamilnadu and Kerala in South and Sikkim and Mizoram in the East. Apart from these latter districts, there are strips of districts constituting crime belt, which also account for large incidence of crime against women-one is the stretch of contiguous districts of Maharashtra from Gadchiroli to Aurangabad and the other contiguous strip is from Banswara (Rajasthan) to Narasinhapur (M.P). Virtually all districts of M.P. have been identified into high rate rape group and several neighbouring districts in Rajasthan and Maharashtra also belong to this club. Together they constitute over half of the high rape rate districts in India. If similar exercises were to be carried out in respect of crimes against scheduled castes, overall and major crime-wise, it is likely that broadly similar spatial concentration may emerge. It should, therefore, be possible to identify the regions where atrocities seem to get frequented so that, among other measures specific to the area, a regional strategy of curbing violence against scheduled castes could be worked out on the basis of sociological analysis of the factors giving rise to these atrocities.

It needs to be specially mentioned that in the case of *Gangula Ashok and others v/s State of Andhra Pradesh*, the Supreme Court has observed that "No Special Court, being Court of Sessions, can obviate the interdict contained in Section 193 of the Code of Criminal Procedure (henceforth Code) as there is no provision in the Scheduled Castes and Scheduled Tribes (Prevention of Atrocities) Act 1989 empowering the Special Courts to take cognizance of such offences as a Court of original jurisdiction. It can take cognizance of the offence when the case is committed to it by the Magistrate in accordance with the provisions of the Act. A complaint or a charge sheet cannot straight away be lodged before the Special Court under the Act.

Provisions of the Act of Criminal Procedure should be applicable to the extent, in the absence of any contrary provisions in the Special Act or any special provision including the jurisdiction or applicability of the Court". (Judgement dated January 28, 2000 in Criminal No. 94 of {arising out of SLP [Criminal] No. 3828}). With this judgement, the objective of the Act stands defeated because the time taken in commitment proceedings would slow down the pace of disposal of the case and would strike a deadly blow on the morale of the victims, which would unquestionably affect the outcome of the proceedings. It would therefore not be unreasonable to infer that with this ruling the deterrence aspect of the Act would get further eroded and perpetrators of atrocities may get emboldened in their designs. The affected members of Scheduled Castes are likely to feel more frustrated than ever before. The Commission has therefore suggested an immediate amendment to the SCs and STs (Prevention of Atrocities) Act, 1989 to remove the lacunae that has arisen as a result of the Supreme Court judgement.

A large number of documents and reports prepared by various Human Rights organisations, inquiry commissions, open hearings, research bodies and investigative teams have highlighted acts of omissions and commissions of law enforcement agencies in respect of cases of atrocities and how SC (and ST) victims of atrocities have failed to get any justice. It is extremely sad that despite availability of this well researched material no initiative has been taken to pursue the matter with the concerned State, or the Central agencies, as the case may be, about action taken by them in the light of the findings of these bodies. To the best of our knowledge, National Commission for SCs and STs have also not done so.

National Human Rights Commission is debarred from looking into such cases by virtue of Section 36(2) of the Protection of Human Rights Act, 1993, which lays down that "The Commission shall not enquire into any matter after the expiry of one year from the date on which alleged human rights violation has been committed". Most of the case reports become older than one year by the time attention of National bodies is drawn. It is extremely sad that enormous pains taken by Human Rights organisations and other bodies in producing investigative material has not produced any result in terms of action against the guilty officials or brought any relief to the victims. This has shaken the faith of the victims in the whole process of law. Many cases in this list of atrocities are those where excesses have been committed by members of law enforcement machinery themselves. If the faith of SCs in the fairness and impartiality of the system has to be restored and their sense of alienation has to be removed, it is necessary that some mechanism is evolved under which investigative and researched material brought out by non official agencies in respect of cases of atrocities is taken note of, pursued with concerned State/Central Agencies and taken to its logical conclusion of,

— fixing responsibility for omissions and commissions and following it up by initiating appropriate punitive action on that basis,
— providing compensation to victims of atrocities,
— issuing directions regarding corrective measures to be taken so that such occurrences are not repeated. There is no such mechanism in prevalence today.

9.2.10. Central Government's Role in the Enforcement of the Act

Central Government has the same role in the implementation of the SCs and STs (Prevention of Atrocities) Act, 1989 which has been outlined in the case of Protection of Civil Rights Act 1955. Ministry of Social Justice and Empowerment is the nodal Ministry for discharging the role under the Central Government. As per provisions of the Act, it is required to place every year a report on the implementation of the Act before the Parliament. This apparently has not happened as the Seventh Report covering the year 2000 has not been placed before the Parliament. Thus the mandatory provision of submission of yearly report is not being adhered to. State Governments also share the blame in this regard for not supplying the required information in time to the Central Ministry for preparation of the report.

9.2.11. Assistance for Implementation of the Central Acts

A centrally sponsored scheme was introduced initially for implementation of the provision of Protection of Civil Rights Act, 1955 in the year 1974-75. The scheme was later extended to cover Scheduled Castes and Scheduled Tribes (Prevention of Atrocities) Act, 1989 as well, in the year 1990-91. Under this scheme 50% financial assistance is provided to the State Governments and 100% to Union Territory administrations. The Scheme provides assistance for strengthening the enforcement machinery and judicial administration, publicity and relief and rehabilitation of affected persons. The amount of central assistance released to the State Govts. and UTs during the 9th Five Year Plan is as follows:

Table 9.10. Central assistance released to the State Govts

1997-1998	:	Rs. 16.47 crores
1998-1999	:	Rs. 15.50 crores
1999-2000	:	Rs. 24.94 crores
2000-2001	:	Rs. 27.08 crores
2001-2002	:	Rs. 29.06 crores (as on 16.1.2002)

There has been substantial increase in provision of financial assistance, particularly during the last three years of the Plan. The following statement indicates the funds released to State Govts. under the Scheme.

Table 9.11. Funds released to State Govts

S.No.	State/UTs	1997-98	1998-99	1999-2000	000-01	2001-02 (As on 17.2.2002)
1.	A P	18.00	294.68	361.33	208.60	165.01
2.	Assam		–	–	2.00	--
3.	Bihar	9.50	50.00	–	34.03	--
4.	Goa	0.70	0.575	–	–	--

5.	Gujarat	156.24	50.00	270.93	325.79	178.20
6.	Haryana	–	21.70	7.83	11.53	13.781
7.	H P	1.00	1.81	–	4.88	--
8.	Karnataka	15.50	136.68	170.70	150.44	174.585
9.	Kerala	2.50	2.00	10.00	41.95	44.15
10.	M P	500.85	682.06	732.96	977.24	812.86
11.	Maharashtra	23.00	50.00	100.00	190.44	--
12.	Orissa	–	3.60	4.00	0.57	0.97
13.	Punjab	10.70	20.64	25.00	18.38	33.10
14.	Rajasthan	16.00	50.00	50.00	150.00	317.38
15.	Sikkim	–	0.25	1.00	–	--
16.	Tamilnadu	14.550	100.00	50.00	89.08	409.96
17.	UP	844.51	50.00	636.24	448.19	700.00
18.	West Bengal	–	–	–	–	
19.	A & N. Islands	–	0.0929	–	–	
20.	Delhi	–	1.40	–	–	
21.	Dadra & N. Haveli	15.88	15.90	30.99	27.00	25.00
22.	Pondicherry	18.28	18.60	34.16	28.63	31.50
23.	Daman & Diu	–	–	9.01	–	
	Total	1647.00	1550.00	2494.16	2708.75	2906.50

The distribution of financial assistance to states brings out that:

— The funds released to states bear no correspondence to volume of atrocity cases therein.

— The drawal of assistance by some States is extremely low despite the sizeable percentage of SC population and also high incidence of cases of violence against SCs. The States in this category include Bihar, Orissa, Punjab, West Bengal, Assam, Himachal Pradesh, etc. The case of West Bengal is particularly striking because it has the second largest SC population in the country. Perhaps nonregistration of cases under the Act may be the reason why the State is not claiming adequate assistance. This obviously points towards indifference in the implementation of the Act.

— There is uneven distribution of assistance across years in various States, except for some States like Madhya Pradesh, Karnataka, Gujarat. This may be due to unsatisfactory utilization of the assistance already provided in certain years. If this is so it would further reflect the laxity in the implementation of the Acts.

— Some States are drawing disproportionately large amounts in certain years, such as UP, Tamilnadu, Rajasthan - reasons for which are not very clear. This, however, does show uneven implementation of the Acts across States and within the same State during different years. Madhya Pradesh is the only State which has been consistently asking for large amounts.

— The lower level of demand from States which have high percentage of SC population as well as high incidence of cases of atrocities can only be explained by lack of interest in implementation of the Act.

It is necessary that the ground level position in respect of implementation of the scheme State-wise with reference to the level of atrocities is examined in depth by the Ministry of Social Justice and Empowerment and the problems arising in its implementation in different States are clearly brought out in the Annual Report submitted to the Parliament.

Being a centrally sponsored scheme, it is governed by the condition that 50% of the entitlement under it has to be contributed by the State Government, except for UTs which receive 100% central funds, over and above the committed liability to be borne by the State/UT Governments for various measures taken. The inability of some States to contribute this amount and match the share of Central Government may have stood in the way of receiving central share. Thus effective implementation of the Act becomes a hostage to budgetary constraints of the concerned State Governments, which may, in turn, also reflect the level of commitment towards dealing with this problem at the highest level. It has been mentioned in the report of National Commission of Scheduled Castes and Scheduled Tribes that the Government of Orissa does not provide economic relief to victims of atrocities as per scale laid down in Rule 4 of the SCs & STs (Prevention of Atrocities) Act, 1989. This may also be true in some other States, since the funds spent in the State under the Scheme on this item bear no relationship to the number of atrocities taking place in that State, which entitle the victims to a certain level of compensation. It has been seen that West Bengal does not register any cases under the Act, as a matter of policy, since it refuses to acknowledge that atrocities on Scheduled Castes are committed due to caste factor. Some other States have also not been registering cases under the Act, though no such official grounds are advanced. Assam appears to be one such case. In these States the SC victims do not receive any help despite the provisions of law. But victims of atrocities are deprived of their entitled compensation for other reasons also. For example, Punjab has refused to pay any compensation to the victims of atrocities on account of financial crisis.

In some States the deprivation of this benefit is on account of enormous delay in deciding about payment of compensation which defeats the very purpose of the provision. As per experience of the Commission, Madhya Pradesh is one such State in this regard. The Commission has also information that in some States, compensation is cornered by officials and intermediaries through misuse of their power. This, therefore, emerges as a very important area of intervention by the Central Government and the National Commissions which play a watchdog role.

Should the victims of atrocities across the country be treated differently just because either the State, due to its ideological inclination or the State agencies out of apathy or bias do not register cases under the Act? It is extremely important that the National Human Rights Commission and National Commission for SCs and STs should jointly evolve an understanding that irrespective of whether cases are registered under the SCs and STs (Prevention of Atrocities) Act, 1989 or not, if the atrocities are committed on Scheduled Castes the compensation entitlement, as per the Act and rules framed thereunder, should be provided to them. In case there are any legal obstacles in doing so, the matter may be taken up by the Ministry of Social Justice and Empowerment and a decision of the Government arrived at in this regard most expeditiously. It should not be left to the State to decide whether compensation to the victims of atrocities be paid or not. Being a central law, it is the duty of Central Government to ensure that States are not allowed to defeat it's objectives. The corrupt practices in disbursement of compensation should be eliminated in consultation with the States, so that entitled compensation is delivered to the victims.

It would thus be evident that even in respect of such a non-contentious matter as payment of compensation to the SC victims according to their entitlement, the subtle bias/ lack of sensitivity operates even at the highest level, both bureaucratic and political. Not only this, most States also do not provide other assistance/entitlements such as travelling allowance, maintenance expenses, daily allowance and reimbursement of medical expenditure to victims and witnesses, which is also required to be met from the funds under the Scheme. Overall, therefore, the legal framework of protection against atrocities is neither able to ensure punishment to the offenders nor payment of cash compensation and other relief to victims.

References

Francine R. and M.S.A. Rao (eds.). *Dominance and State Power in Modern India,* Vol. II, Delhi, OUP. 1990.

Frankel Francine R. and M.S.A. Rao (eds.) *Dominance and State Power in Modern India,* Vol. I, Delhi, OUP. 1989.

Ghurye, G. S. *Caste, Class and Occupation.* Popular Book Depot, Bombay. 1961.

Gupta, S.K. *The Scheduled Castes in Modern Indian Politics: Their Emergence as a Political Power.* New Delhi. Munshiram Manoharlal Publishers Pvt. Ltd. 1985.

Jenkins Rob. Where the BJP Survived : Rajasthan Assembly Election, 1993, *Economic and Political Weekly,* March 12. 1994.

Karve Iravati and V.M. Dandekar. *Anthropometric Measures of Maharashtra,* Poona, Deccan College. 1951.

Bibliography

Aloysius Irudayam s.j., *Black Paper: Broken Promises and Dalits Betrayed,* National Campaign on Dalit Human Rights, Bangalore, 1999.

Ambedkar, B. R. "Castes in India." In *Dr. Babasaheb Ambedkar, Writings and Speeches,* edited by Vasant Moon, vol. 1. Bombay: Education Department, Government of Maharashtra, 1979.

--------., "Annihilation of Caste", in Moon, V. (ed), *Dr Ambedkar Writings and Speeches: Volume 1*, Education Department, Government of Maharashtra, 1989,

--------. *Pakistan or the Partition of India.* Thackers Publishers.

Anandan, T.R. "The Failure of Anti-Caste Movements." The Hindu, 24 July, 2001. Reg. ed.: OB-1.

Ansari, Ghaus. *Muslim Caste in Uttar Pradesh: A Study of Culture Contact.* Lucknow, 1960.

Ashok Kumar, E.N. Caste metamorphosis: the Korachas of Dharmapura. pp 187-211, in Simon R. Charsley & G.K. Karanth eds *Challenging Untouchability. Dalit initiative and experience from Karnataka.* New Delhi: Sage Publications Publications. 1998.

Bakshi S.R., Ambedkar B.R., "Statesman and Constitutionalist", *Indian Freedom Fighters Series*, 1992.

Barbara R. Joshi, *Untouchable!: Voices of the Dalit Liberation Movement*, Zed Books, 1986.

Bayly, Susan. *Caste, Society and Politics in India from the Eighteenth Century to the Modern Age.* Cambridge University Press. 1999.

Bikshu Sangharakshita, *Ambedkar and Buddhism*, Windhorse Publications, Mar 1989.

Bikshu Sangharakshita, *Ambedkar and Buddhism*, Windhorse Publications, Mar 1989.

Broken People: Caste Violence against India's Untouchables. New York: Human Rights Watch, 1999.

Brouwer, Jan. *The Makers of the World. Caste, craft and mind of South Asian artisans.* New Delhi: Oxford University Press. 1995.

Chakravarti, U., *Gendering Caste: Through a Feminist Lens*, Stree, Calcutta, 2003 on the use of the term "brahminical patriarchy" to refer to the interlinking of patriarchy and caste structures in India.

Chanchreek K.L., *Dr. B.R Ambedkar: A Rebel Dalit Leader*, New Delhi, Shree Pub., 2006.

Charsley, Simon R. Caste, cultural resources and social mobility. In *Challenging Untouchability. Dalit initiative and experience from Karnataka*, ed. Simon R. Charsley & G.K. Karanth. New Delhi: Sage Publications. 1998.

Chokhamela. *On the Threshold: Songs of Chokhamela.* Translated by Rohini Mokashi-Punekar. Delhi: Book Review Literary Trust, 2002.

Christophe Jaffrelot, *Dr. Ambedkar and Untouchability: Analyzing and Fighting Caste*, 2005.

Das, Ashol. "Untouchability not an issue in Telengana." Hindustan Times 9 July, 2001 Reg. ed.: 9.

David Pandyan K., *Dr. B.R. Ambedkar and the Dynamics of Neo-Buddhism*, 1996.

Deliège, Robert. Replication and consensus: Untouchability, caste and ideology in India, *Man* (n.s.) 27, pp 155-73. 1992.

--------. *The Untouchables of India.* Trans. Nora Scott. Berg, 1999.

Dhananjay Keer, *Dr. Ambedkar: Life and Mission*, published by Popular Prakashan, Bombay, India.

Dumont, Louis. *Homo Hierarchicus: The Caste System and Its Implications.* Translated by Mark Sainsbury, Louis Dumont, and Basia Gulati. Rev. ed. Chicago: University of Chicago Press, 1980.

Eleanor Zilliot, *From Untouchable to Dalit - Essays on the Ambedkar Movement*, Manohar, 2005.

Forster, E.M. *A Passage To India.* San Diego, A Harvest Book/Harcourt, 1924.

Francine R. and M.S.A. Rao (eds.). *Dominance and State Power in Modern India*, Vol. II, Delhi, OUP. 1990.

Frankel Francine R. and M.S.A. Rao (eds.) *Dominance and State Power in Modern India*, Vol. I, Delhi, OUP. 1989.

Gail Omvedt. *Dalits and the Democratic Revolution - Dr. Ambedkar and the Dalit Movement in Colonial India*, Sage Publications. 1994.

Gautam C., *Life of Babasaheb Ambedkar*, Ambedkar Memorial Trust, London, Milan House, 8 Kingsland Road, London E2 8DA Second Edition, May 2000.

Ghurye, G. S. *Caste, Class and Occupation.* Popular Book Depot, Bombay. 1961.

Gore M. S., *The Social Context of an Ideology: Ambedkar's Political and Social Thought,* 1993.

Government of India, *National Policy for the Empowerment of Women 2001*, Policy Prescriptions: para.7.1.

Gupta, S.K. *The Scheduled Castes in Modern Indian Politics: Their Emergence as a Political Power.* New Delhi. Munshiram Manoharlal Publishers Pvt. Ltd. 1985.

Hazari. *Untouchable: The Autobiography of The Indian Outcaste*. New York: Fredrick A. Praeger, 1951.

Human Rights Watch, *Broken People: Caste Violence Against India's "Untouchables"*. New York: Human Rights Watch. 1999.

Jaffrelot, Christophe, *Dr. Ambedkar and Untouchability: Fighting the Indian Caste System*, New York: Columbia University Press, 2005.

Jenkins Rob. Where the BJP Survived : Rajasthan Assembly Election, 1993, *Economic and Political Weekly,* March 12. 1994.

Jha, Vivekananda. "Stages in the History of Untouchables." *Indian Historical Review* 2 (1975):

Johannes Beltz, *Mahar, Buddhist. Religious Conversion and Socio-Political Emancipation*, New Delhi, Manohar, 2005.

Jondhale, Surendra, and Johannes Beltz. *Reconstructing the World: B.R. Ambedkar and Buddhism in India*. New Delhi: Oxford University Press. 2004.

Justice V.R. Krishna Iyer, *Ambedkar Centenary: Social Justice and the Undone Vast*, 1992.

Kadam K.N. (Editor), "Dr. B.R. Ambedkar: The Emancipator of the Oppressed", *A Centenary Commemoration Volume*, 1993.

Karve Iravati and V.M. Dandekar. *Anthropometric Measures of Maharashtra,* Poona, Deccan College. 1951.

Keer, Dhananjay, Dr. *Ambedkar Life and Mission*, Bombay, Popular Prakashan, 1995.

Khairmode, C.B., *Dr. Bhimrao Ramji Ambedkar Charitra*, Vol. II, Bauddha Jan Panchayat, Parel, Bombay, Kshirsagar, 1958.

Kothari, Rajni. *Caste in Indian Politics*. Orient Longman.2004.

Kuber W.N., *Dr. Ambedkar: A Critical Study*, People's Publishing House, New Delhi, India.

Kusum Sharma, *Ambedkar and Indian Constitution*, 1992.

Mendelsohn, Oliver, and Marika Vicziany. *The Untouchables: Subordination, Poverty and State in Modern India*. Cambridge University Press, 1998.

Michael, S.M., (ed.) *Untouchable: Dalits in Modern India*. Boulder. Lynne Rienner Publishers. 1999.

Moon, Vasant. *Growing Up Untouchable in India: A Dalit Autobiography*. Roman and Littlefield, 2000.

Mulk Raj Anand. *An Anthology Of Dalit Literature*, by 1992, Gyan Books.

Narula, Smita. Broken People: Caste Violence Against India's "Untouchables." *Human Rights Watch*, 1999.

National Human Rights Commission, *Report on Prevention of Atrocities against Scheduled Castes: Policy and Performance, Suggested Interventions and Initiatives for NHRC*, New Delhi, 2004, pp.193-4.

Omvedt, Gail, *Dalits and the Democratic Revolution. Dr. Ambedkar and the Dalit Movement in Colonial India*, 1993.

Pandey B.N., ed., *The Leadership of Babasaheb Ambedkar*, Leadership in South Asia, University of London symposium, New Delhi: Vikas, 1977.

Pauline Kolenda. *Caste in Contemporary India: Beyond Organic Solidarity* Menlo Park. Benjamin/Cumming Publishing Co. 1978.

Pradeep K. Sharma, *Dalit Politics and Literature*, Shipra Publications, 2006.

Rajshekhar. V.T. *Dalit - The Black Untouchables of India*, Clarity Press, Inc., 2003.

Ranabira Samaddara, Ghanshyam Shah, *Dalit Identity and Politics*, Sage Publications, 2001.

Robert Pen, *Evaluating Ambedkar's Social Philosophy in the Context of Casteism in India, SDB*. 63-70, 1995.

Rodrigues, Valerian, ed. *The Essential Writings of B. R. Ambedkar*. Oxford University Press, 2002.

Sangharakshita. *Ambedkar and Buddhism*. Glasgow: Windhorse Publications. 1986.

Shah, Ghanshyam, ed. *Dalit Identity and Politics*. Sage Publications, 2001.

Sharma, Kusum. *Ambedkar and Indian Constitution*. New Delhi: Ashish Pub. House. 1992.

Sidney, Bashiruddin Ahmed, and Anil Bhatt. *Caste, Race, and Politics: A Comparative Study of India And The United States*. Beverly Hills: Sage Publications, Inc., 1971.

Srinivas, M. N. *Religion and Society among the Coorgs of South India*. Oxford, 1952.

Index